D1034667

X-MEN PHOENIX ENDSONG

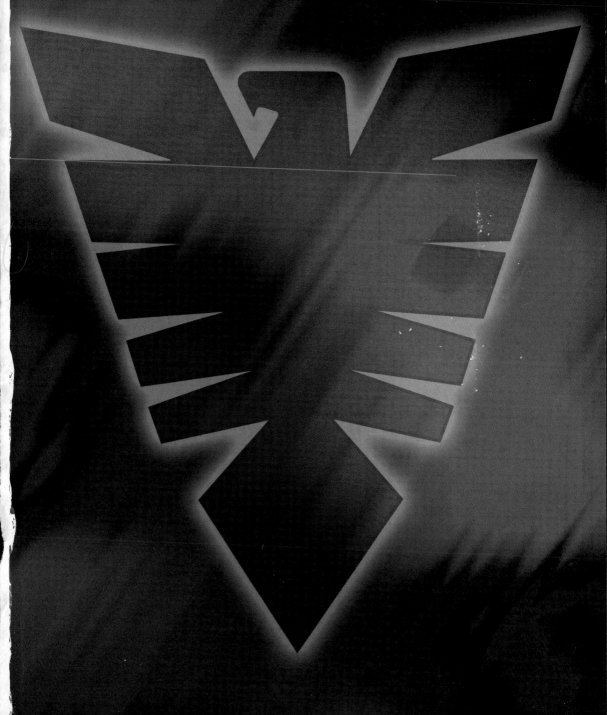

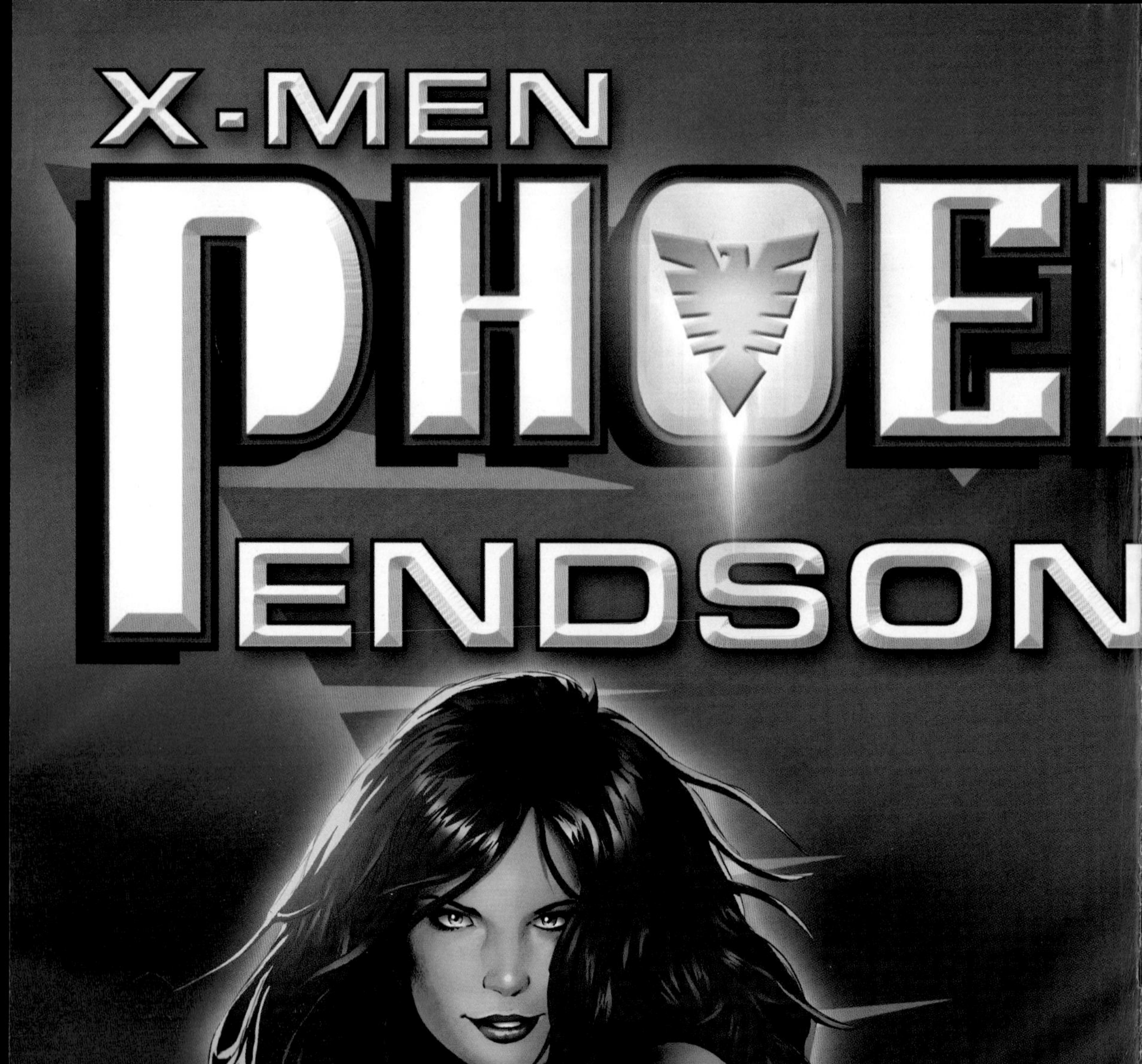

X-MEN
PHOE
ENDSON

X-MEN: PHOENIX - ENDSONG. Contains material originally published in magazine form as X-MEN: PHOENIX - ENDSONG #1-5. First printing 2005. ISBN# 0-7851-1641-9. Published by MARVEL COMICS, a division of MARVEL ENTERTAINMENT GROUP, INC. OFFICE OF PUBLICATION: 10 East 40th Street, New York, NY 10016. Copyright © 2005 Marvel Characters, Inc. All rights reserved. $13.99 per copy in the U.S. and $22.50 in Canada (GST #R127032852); Canadian Agreement #40668537. All characters featured in this issue and the distinctive names and likenesses thereof, and all related indicia are trademarks of Marvel Characters, Inc. No similarity between any of the names, characters, persons, and/or institutions in this magazine with those of any living or dead person or institution is intended, and any such similarity which may exist is purely coincidental. **Printed in the U.S.A.** AVI ARAD, Chief Creative Officer; ALAN FINE, President & CEO of Toy Biz and Marvel Publishing; DAN CARR, Director of Production; ELAINE CALLENDER, Director of Manufacturing; DAVID BOGART, Managing Editor; STAN LEE, Chairman Emeritus. For information regarding advertising in Marvel Comics or on Marvel.com, please contact Joe Maimone, Advertising Director, at jmaimone@marvel.com or 212-576-8534.

10 9 8 7 6 5 4 3 2 1

Writer: Greg Pak
Penciler: Greg Land
Inker: Matt Ryan
Colorist: Justin Ponsor

Letterer: Clem Robins
Assistant Editors: Stephanie Moore & Sean Ryan
Associate Editor: Nick Lowe
Editor: Mike Marts

Senior Editor, Special Projects: Jeff Youngquist
Collection Editor: Jennifer Grünwald
Director of Sales: David Gabriel
Production: Loretta Krol
Book Designer: Jeof Vita
Creative Director: Tom Marvelli

Editor in Chief: Joe Quesada
Publisher: Dan Buckley

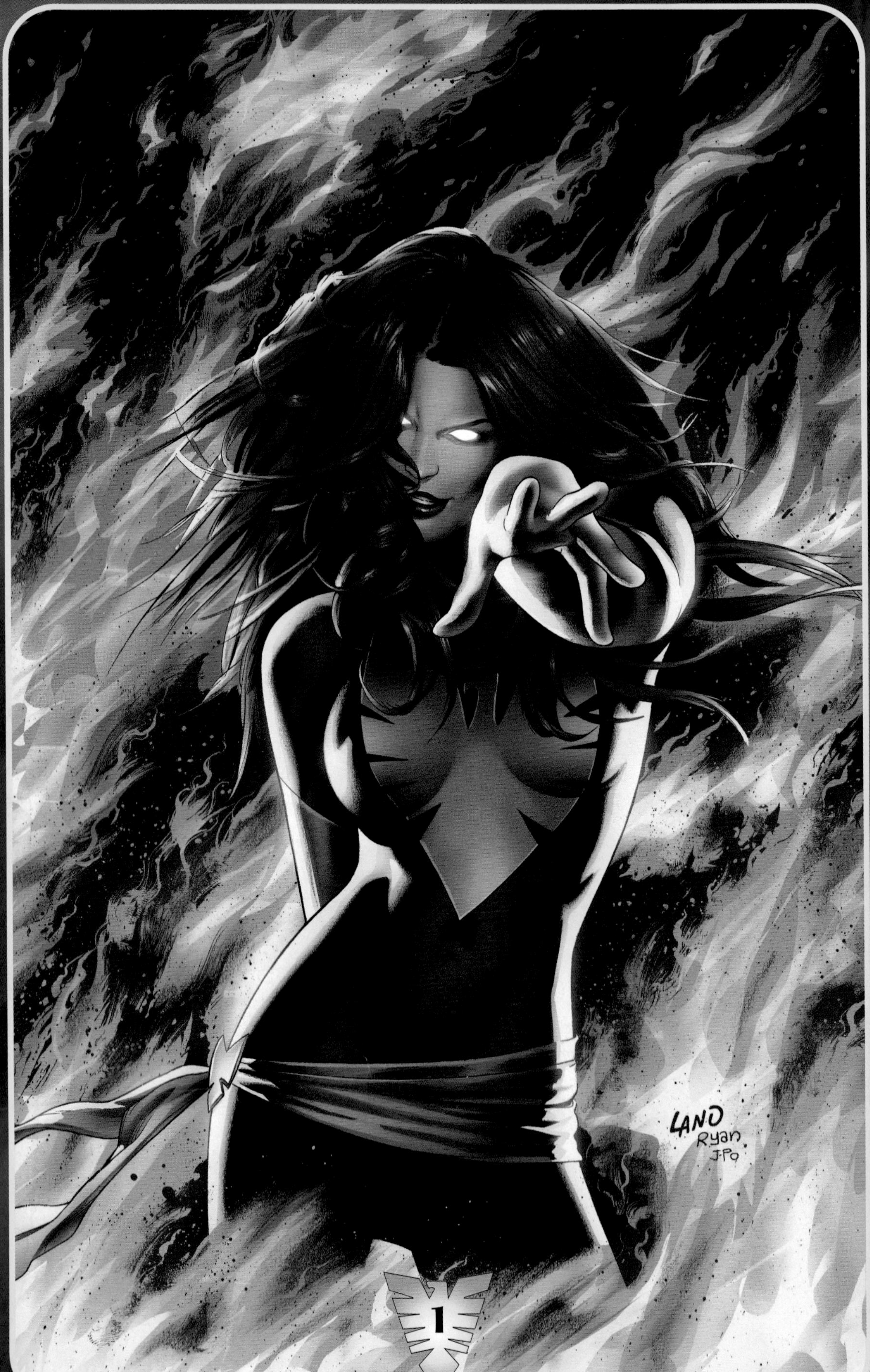
LAND
Ryan
J-Po
1

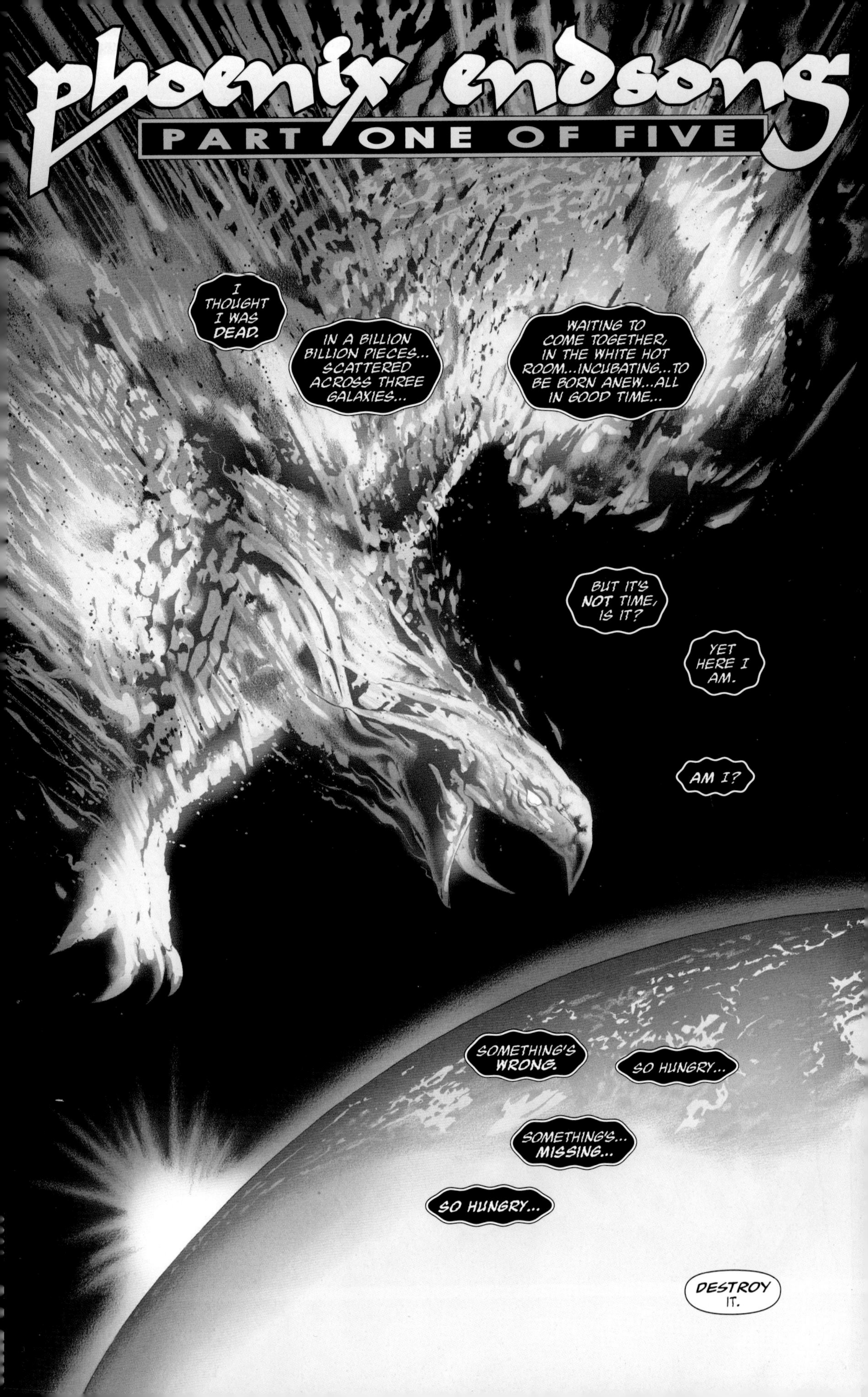
phoenix endsong
PART ONE OF FIVE
I THOUGHT I WAS DEAD.
IN A BILLION BILLION PIECES... SCATTERED ACROSS THREE GALAXIES...
WAITING TO COME TOGETHER, IN THE WHITE HOT ROOM...INCUBATING...TO BE BORN ANEW...ALL IN GOOD TIME...
BUT IT'S NOT TIME, IS IT?
YET HERE I AM.
AM I?
SOMETHING'S WRONG.
SO HUNGRY...
SOMETHING'S... MISSING...
SO HUNGRY...
DESTROY IT.

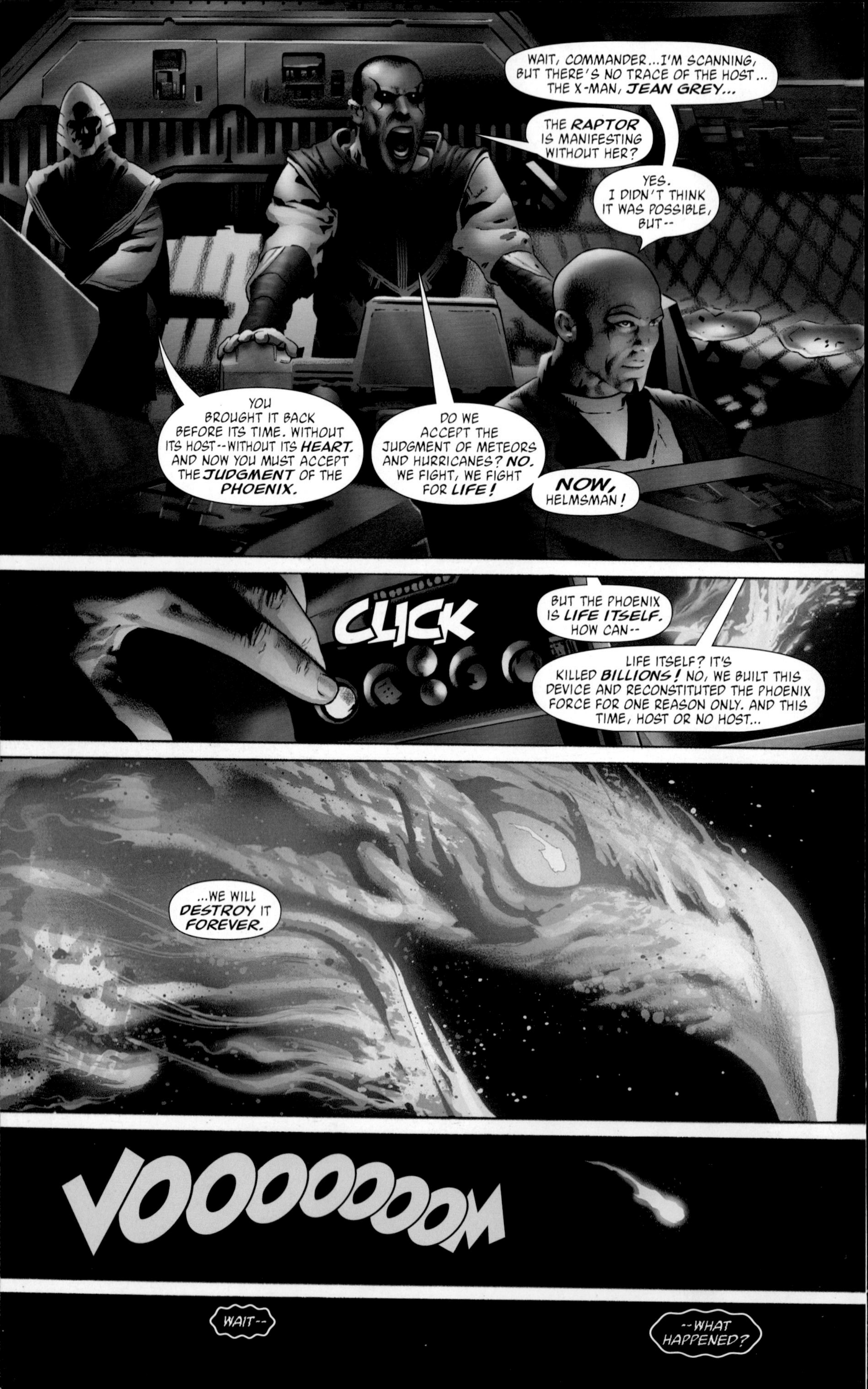
WAIT, COMMANDER...I'M SCANNING, BUT THERE'S NO TRACE OF THE HOST... THE X-MAN, JEAN GREY...
THE RAPTOR IS MANIFESTING WITHOUT HER?
YES. I DIDN'T THINK IT WAS POSSIBLE, BUT--
YOU BROUGHT IT BACK BEFORE ITS TIME. WITHOUT ITS HOST--WITHOUT ITS HEART. AND NOW YOU MUST ACCEPT THE JUDGMENT OF THE PHOENIX.
DO WE ACCEPT THE JUDGMENT OF METEORS AND HURRICANES? NO. WE FIGHT, WE FIGHT FOR LIFE!
NOW, HELMSMAN!
CLICK
BUT THE PHOENIX IS LIFE ITSELF. HOW CAN--
LIFE ITSELF? IT'S KILLED BILLIONS! NO, WE BUILT THIS DEVICE AND RECONSTITUTED THE PHOENIX FORCE FOR ONE REASON ONLY. AND THIS TIME, HOST OR NO HOST...
...WE WILL DESTROY IT FOREVER.
VOOOOOOOM
WAIT--
--WHAT HAPPENED?

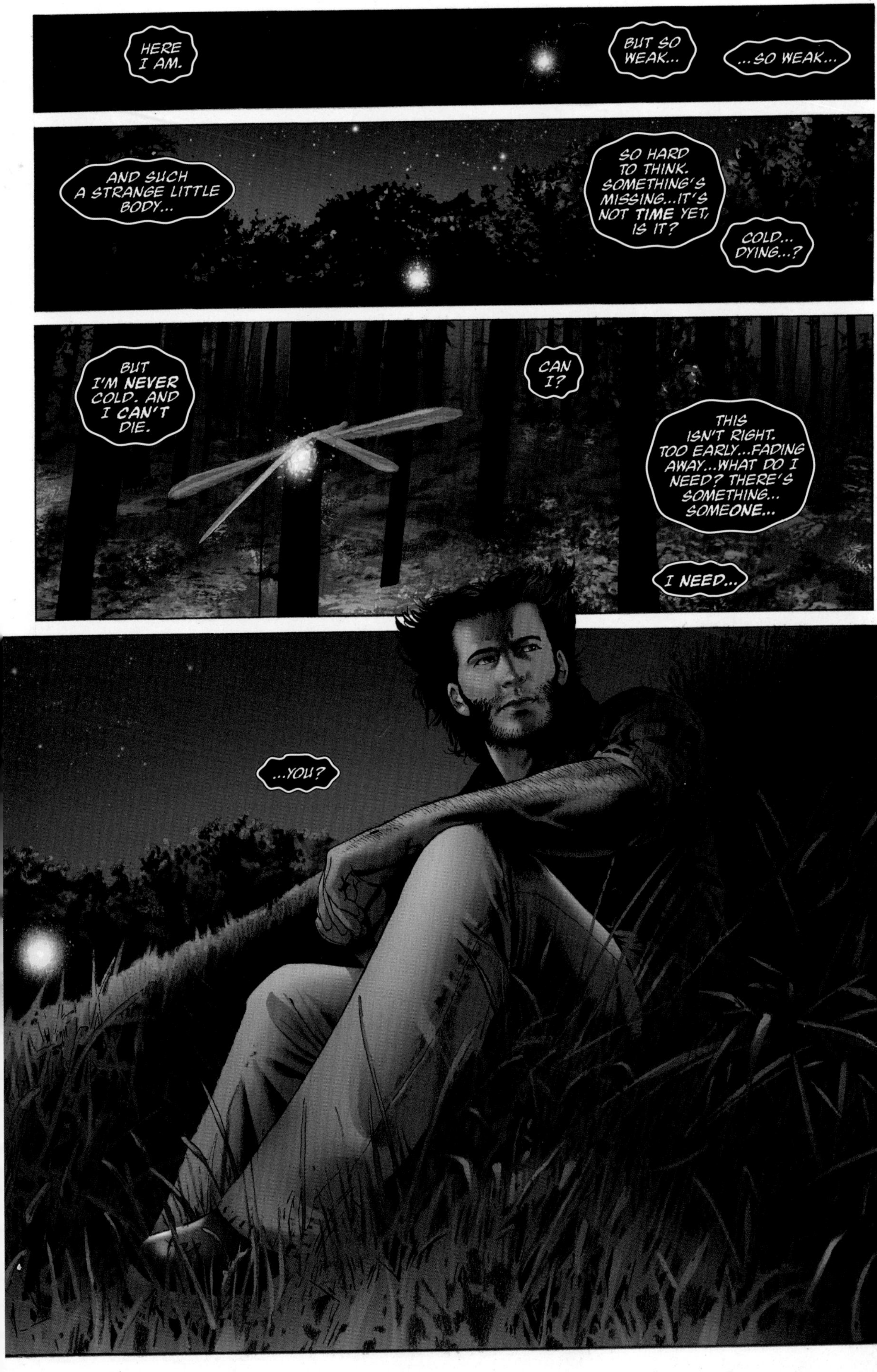
HERE I AM.
BUT SO WEAK...
...SO WEAK...
AND SUCH A STRANGE LITTLE BODY...
SO HARD TO THINK. SOMETHING'S MISSING...IT'S NOT TIME YET, IS IT?
COLD... DYING...?
BUT I'M NEVER COLD. AND I CAN'T DIE.
CAN I?
THIS ISN'T RIGHT. TOO EARLY...FADING AWAY...WHAT DO I NEED? THERE'S SOMETHING... SOMEONE...
I NEED...
...YOU?

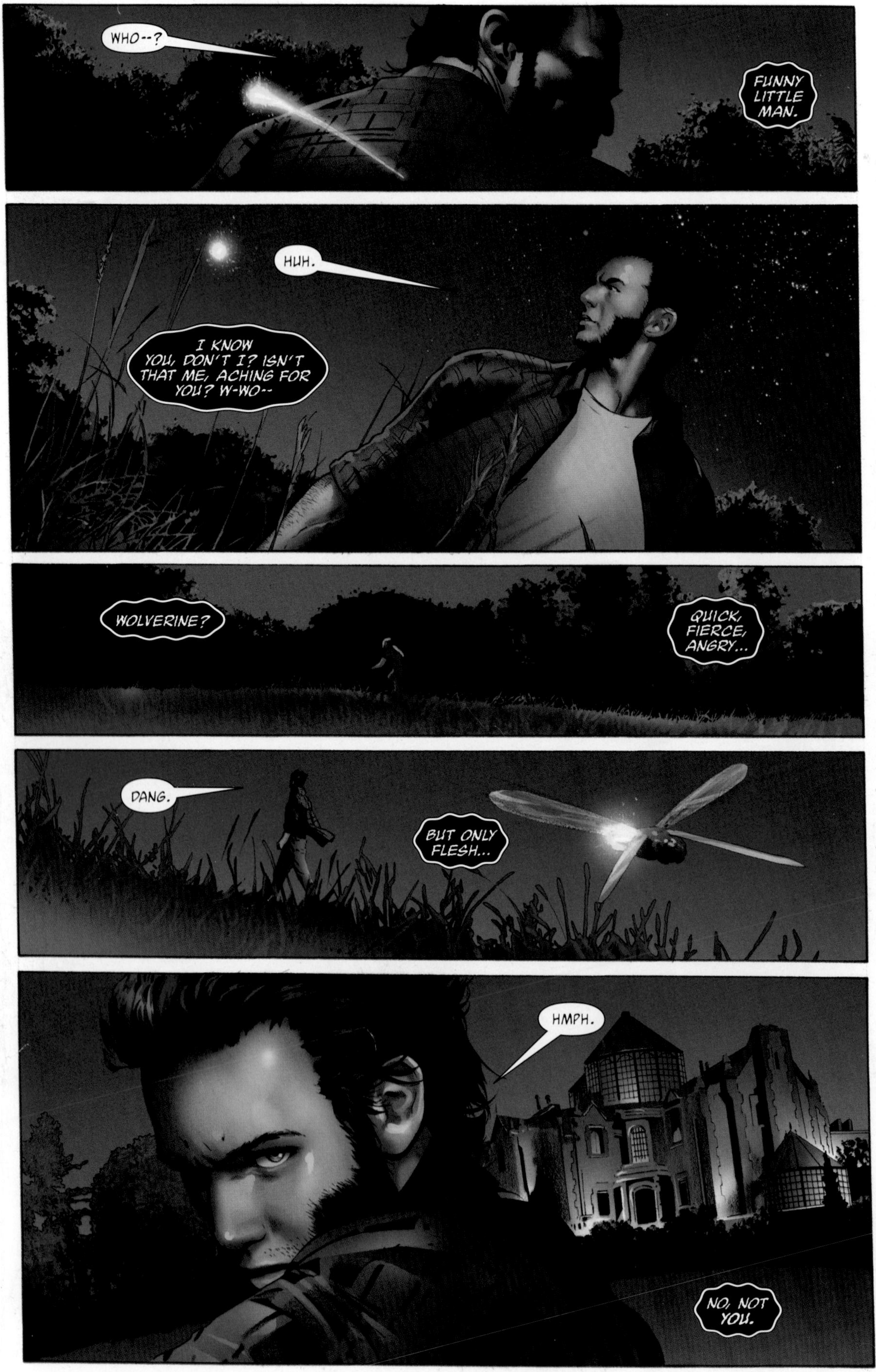
WHO--?
FUNNY LITTLE MAN.
HUH.
I KNOW YOU, DON'T I? ISN'T THAT ME, ACHING FOR YOU? W-WO--
WOLVERINE?
QUICK, FIERCE, ANGRY...
DANG.
BUT ONLY FLESH...
HMPH.
NO, NOT YOU.

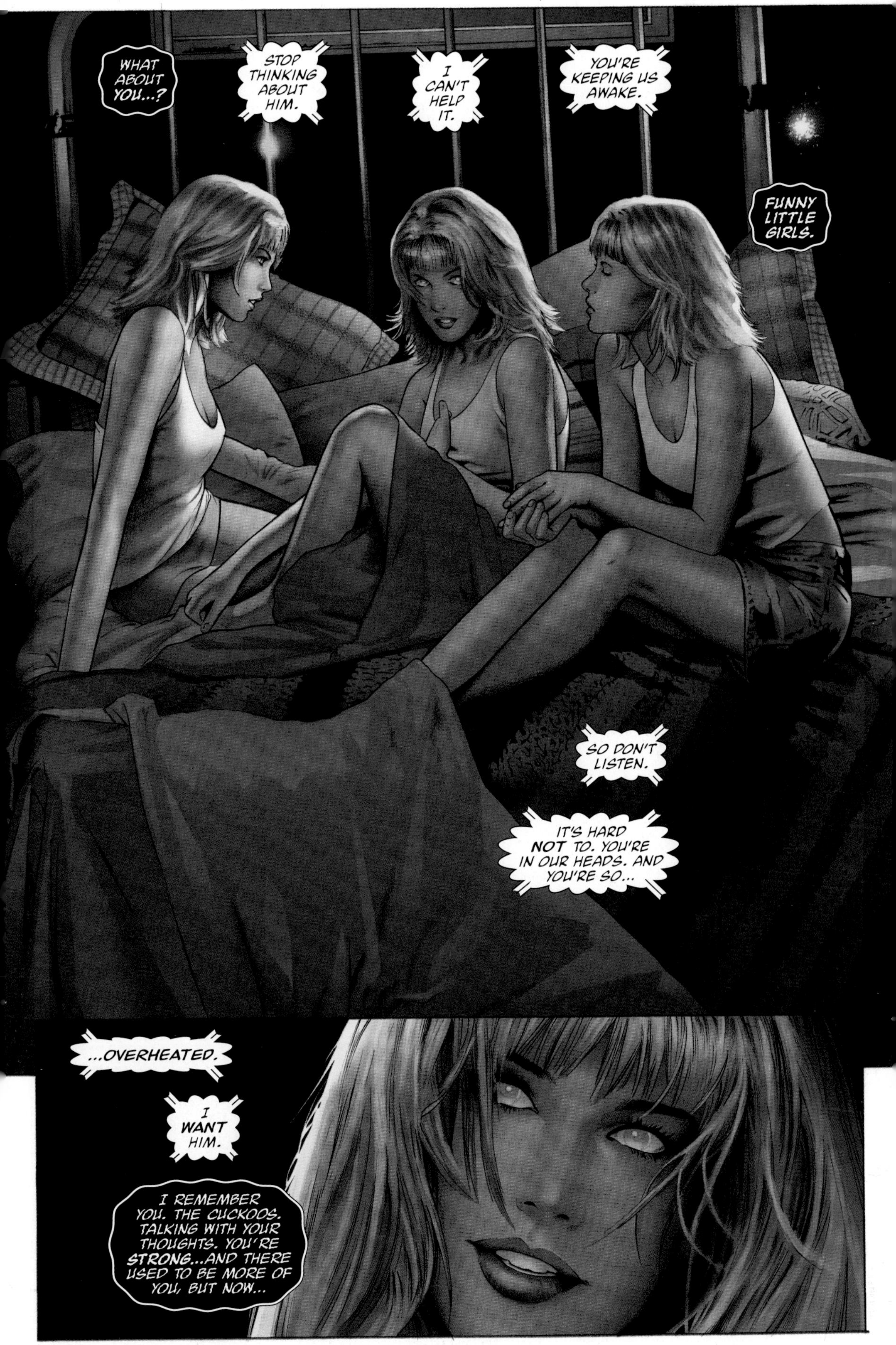
WHAT ABOUT YOU...?
STOP THINKING ABOUT HIM.
I CAN'T HELP IT.
YOU'RE KEEPING US AWAKE.
FUNNY LITTLE GIRLS.
SO DON'T LISTEN.
IT'S HARD NOT TO. YOU'RE IN OUR HEADS. AND YOU'RE SO...
...OVERHEATED.
I WANT HIM.
I REMEMBER YOU. THE CUCKOOS. TALKING WITH YOUR THOUGHTS. YOU'RE STRONG...AND THERE USED TO BE MORE OF YOU, BUT NOW...

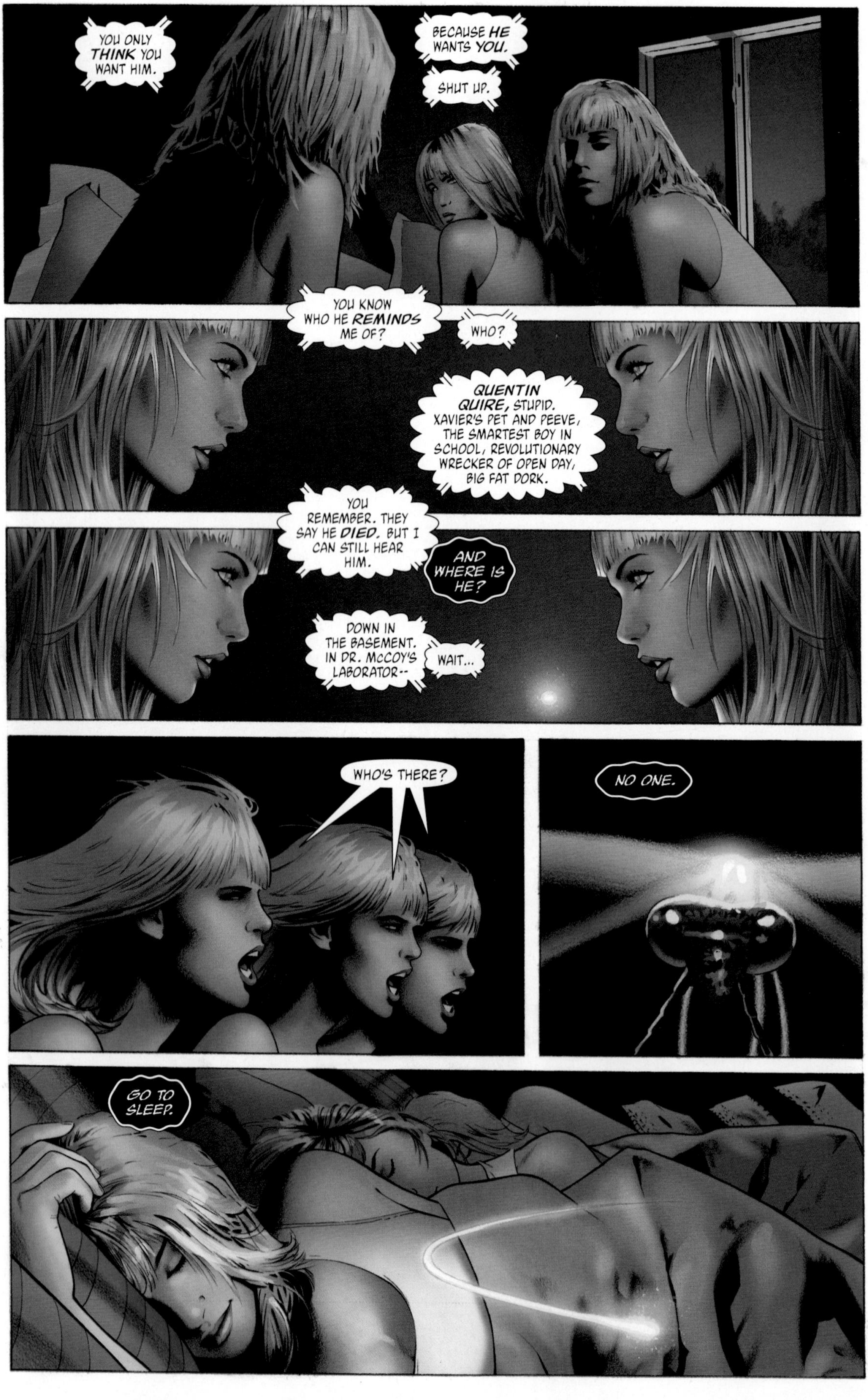
YOU ONLY THINK YOU WANT HIM.
BECAUSE HE WANTS YOU.
SHUT UP.
YOU KNOW WHO HE REMINDS ME OF?
WHO?
QUENTIN QUIRE, STUPID. XAVIER'S PET AND PEEVE, THE SMARTEST BOY IN SCHOOL, REVOLUTIONARY WRECKER OF OPEN DAY, BIG FAT DORK.
YOU REMEMBER. THEY SAY HE DIED. BUT I CAN STILL HEAR HIM.
AND WHERE IS HE?
DOWN IN THE BASEMENT. IN DR. McCOY'S LABORATOR--
WAIT...
WHO'S THERE?
NO ONE.
GO TO SLEEP.

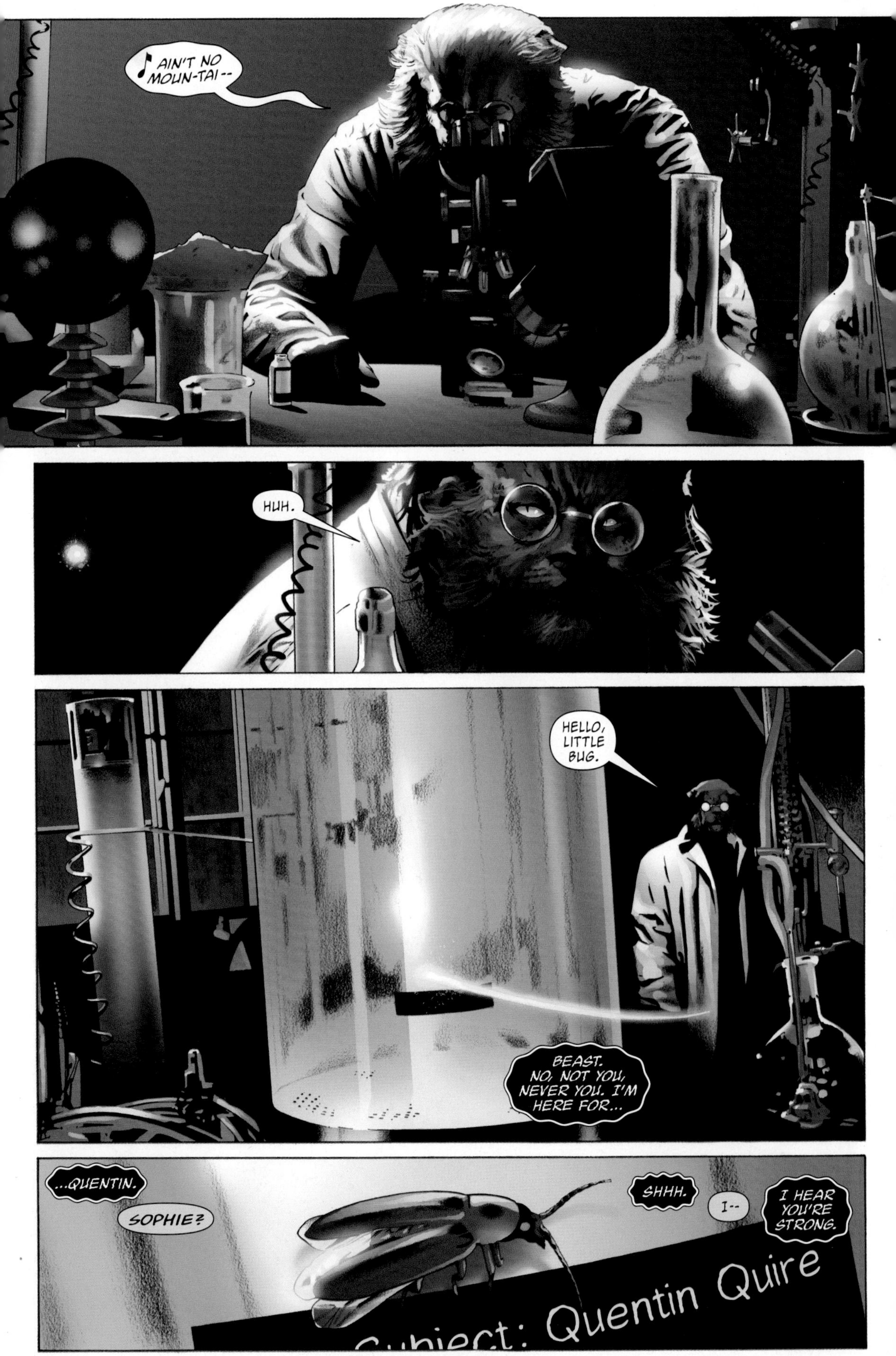
♪ AIN'T NO MOUN-TAI--
HUH.
HELLO, LITTLE BUG.
BEAST. NO, NOT YOU, NEVER YOU. I'M HERE FOR...
...QUENTIN.
SOPHIE?
SHHH.
I--
I HEAR YOU'RE STRONG.
Subject: Quentin Quire

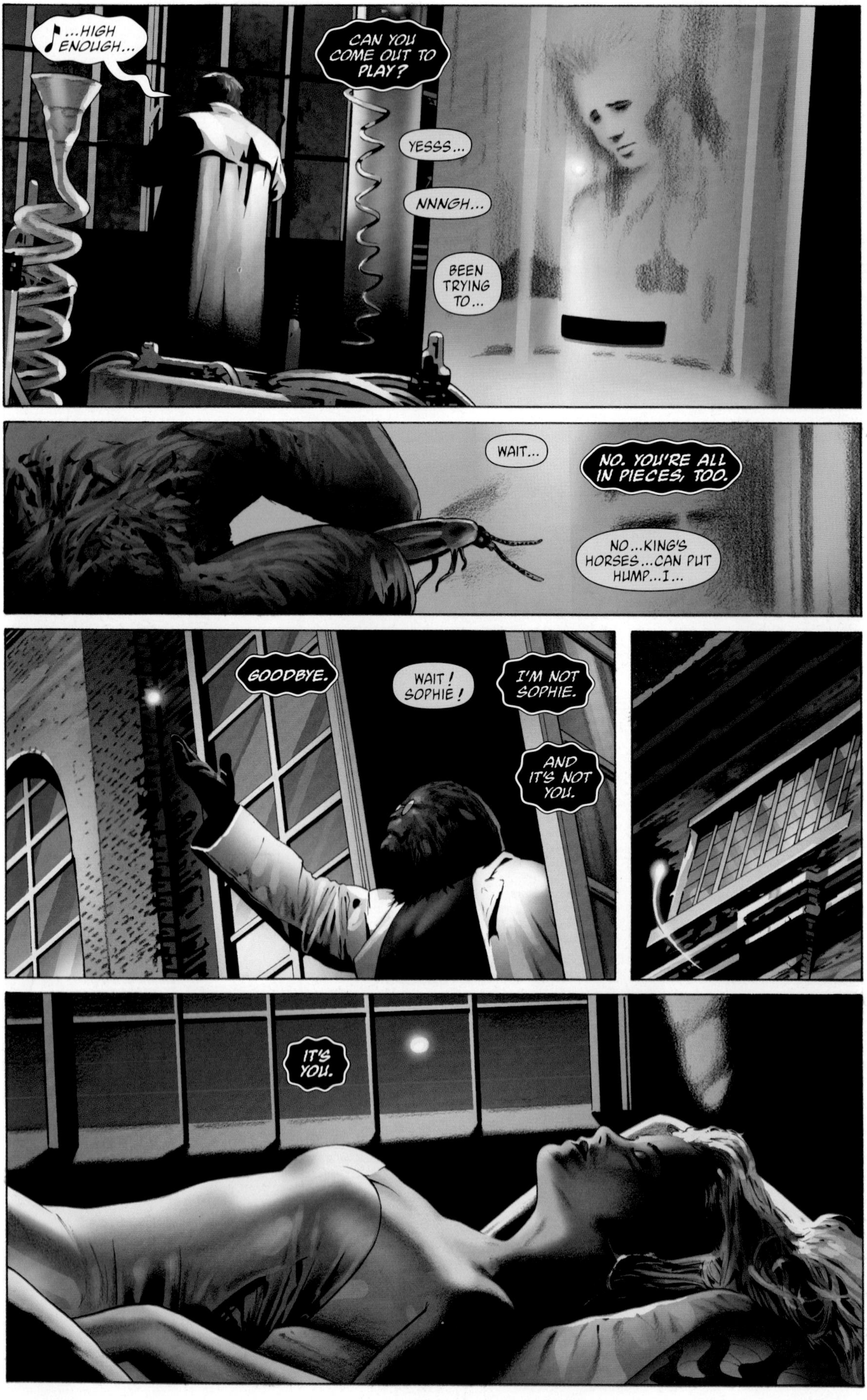
♪ ...HIGH ENOUGH...
CAN YOU COME OUT TO PLAY?
YESSS...
NNNGH...
BEEN TRYING TO...
WAIT...
NO. YOU'RE ALL IN PIECES, TOO.
NO...KING'S HORSES...CAN PUT HUMP...I...
GOODBYE.
WAIT! SOPHIE!
I'M NOT SOPHIE.
AND IT'S NOT YOU.
IT'S YOU.

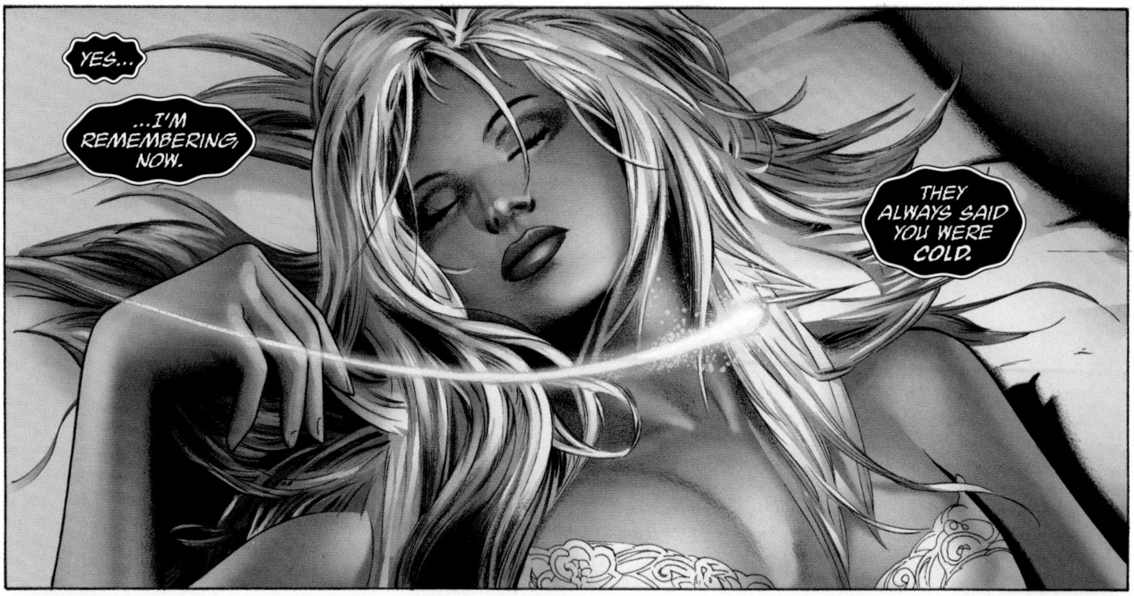
YES...
...I'M REMEMBERING, NOW.
THEY ALWAYS SAID YOU WERE COLD.

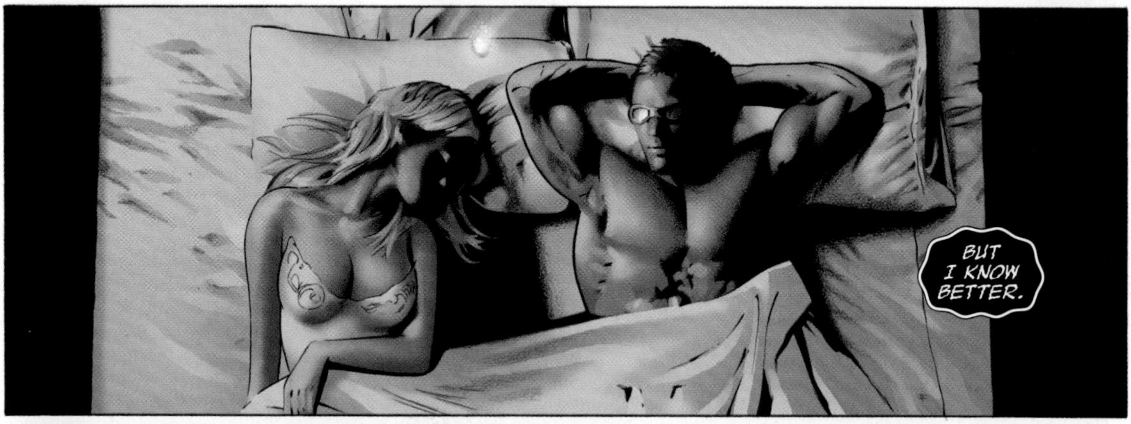
BUT I KNOW BETTER.

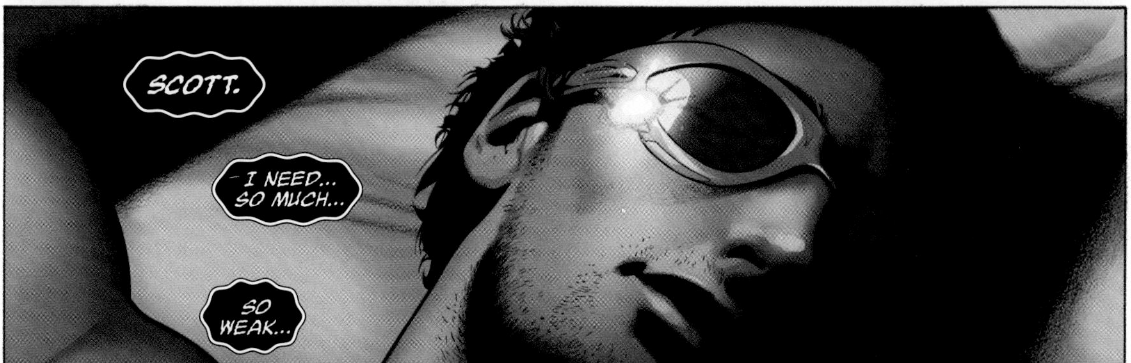
SCOTT.
I NEED... SO MUCH...
SO WEAK...
CAN I EVEN...?

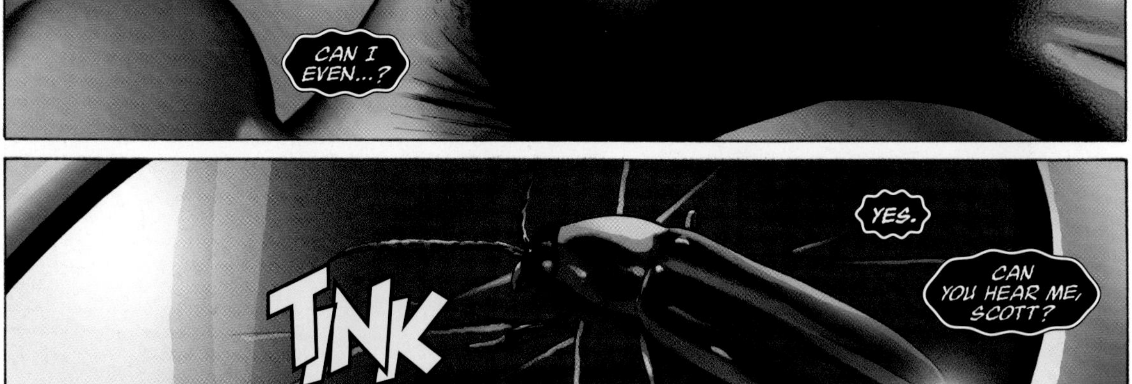
YES.
CAN YOU HEAR ME, SCOTT?
TINK

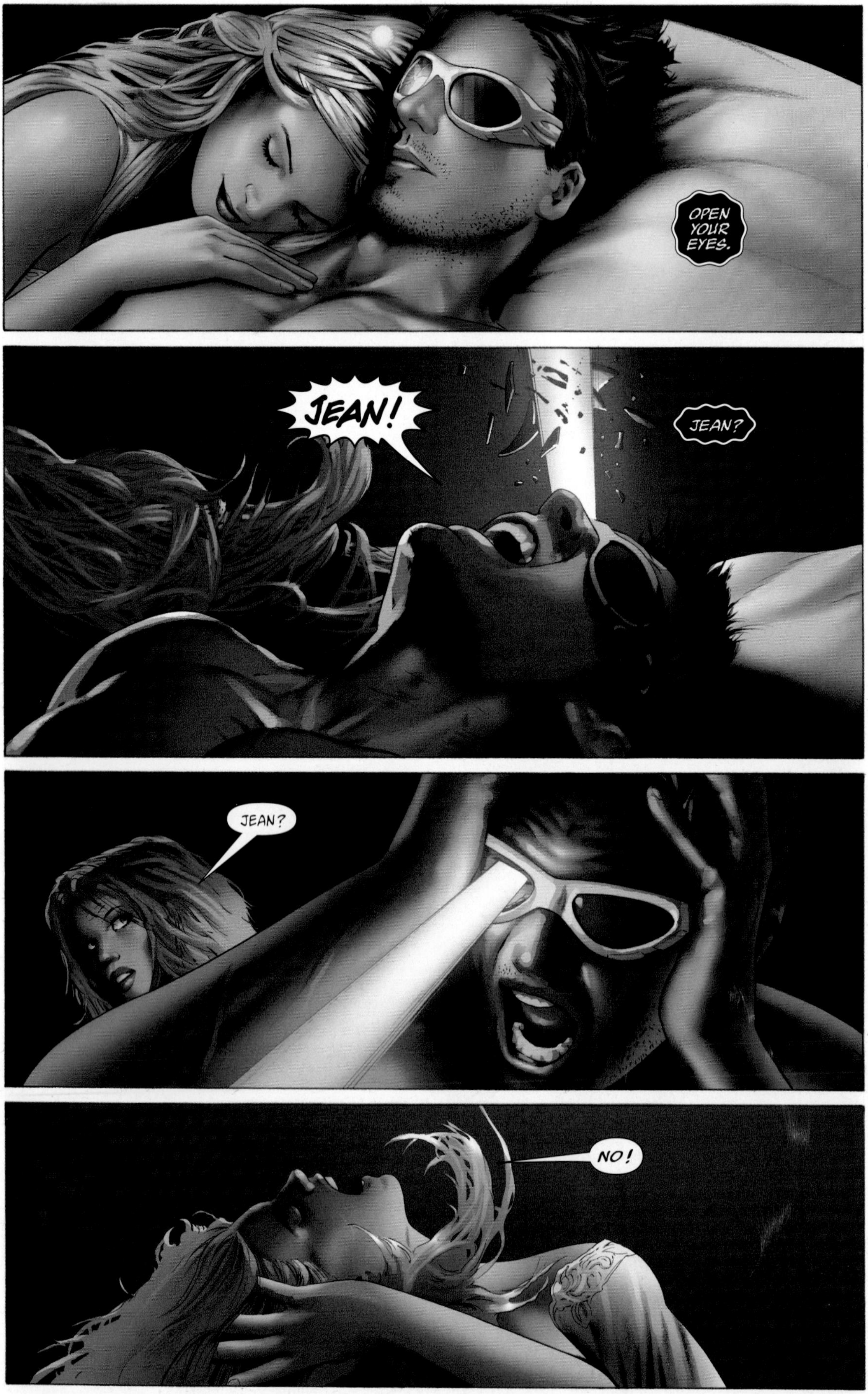

OPEN YOUR EYES.
JEAN!
JEAN?
JEAN?
NO!

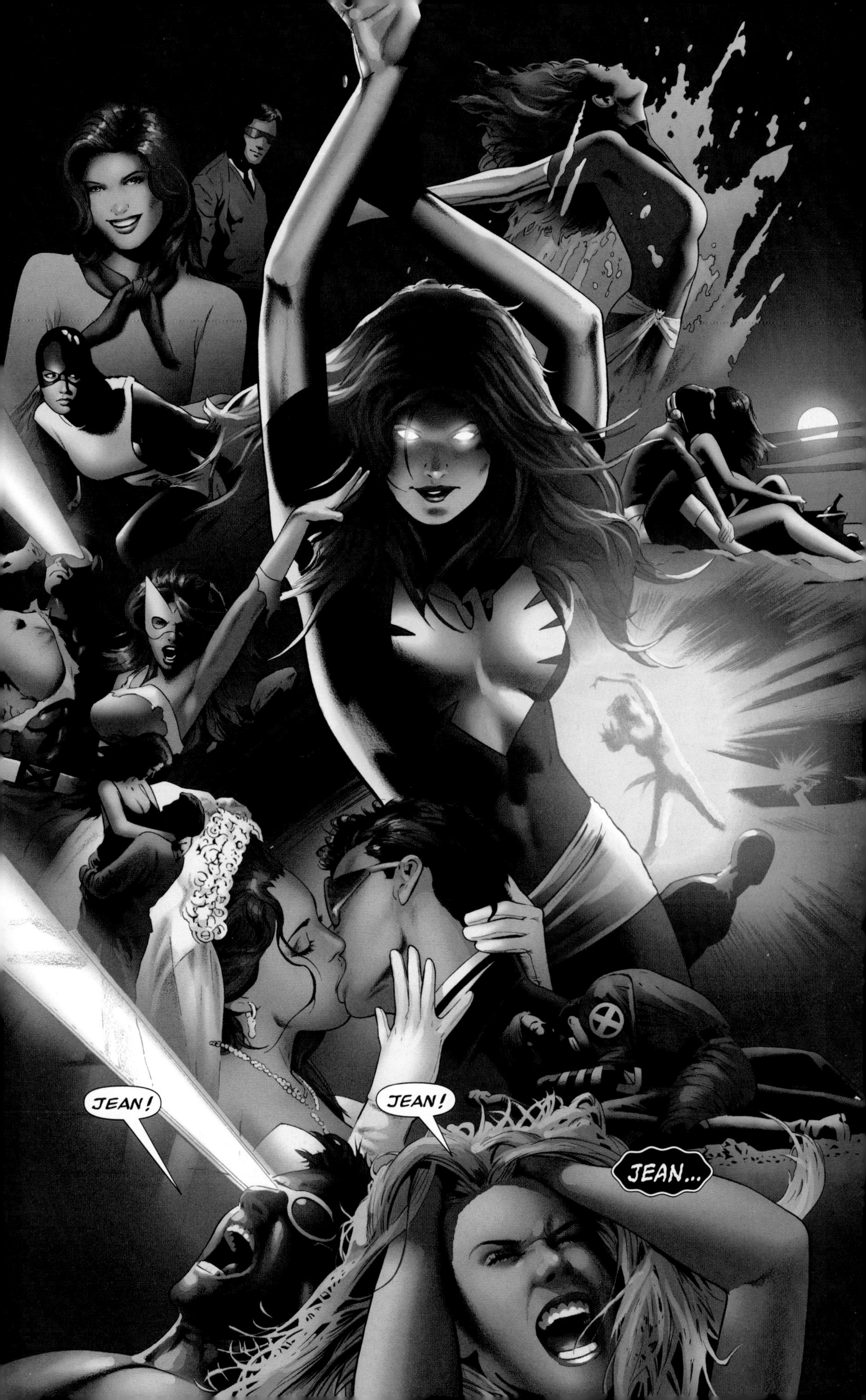
JEAN!
JEAN!
JEAN...

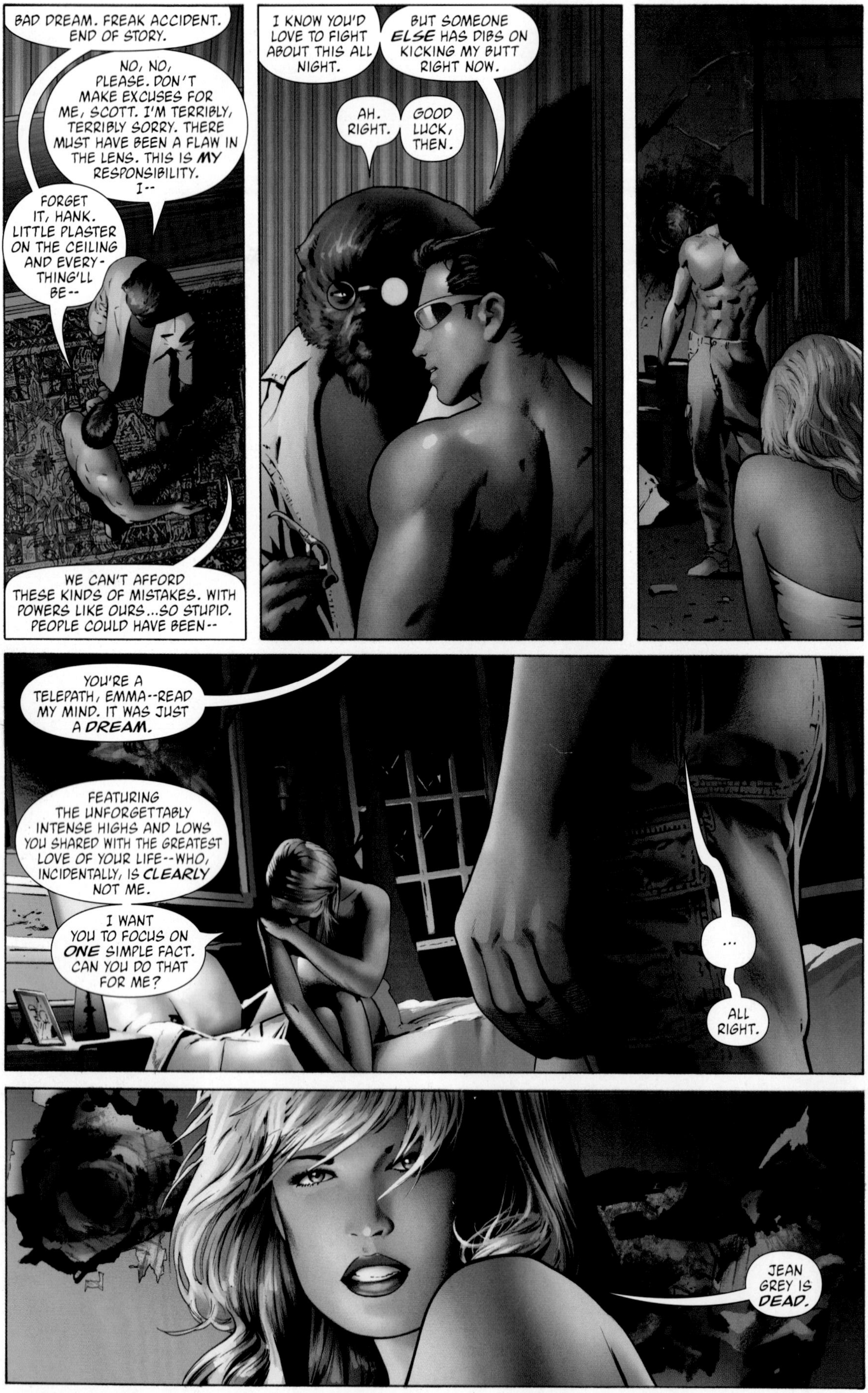

BAD DREAM. FREAK ACCIDENT. END OF STORY.
NO, NO, PLEASE. DON'T MAKE EXCUSES FOR ME, SCOTT. I'M TERRIBLY, TERRIBLY SORRY. THERE MUST HAVE BEEN A FLAW IN THE LENS. THIS IS *MY* RESPONSIBILITY. I--
FORGET IT, HANK. LITTLE PLASTER ON THE CEILING AND EVERY-THING'LL BE--
WE CAN'T AFFORD THESE KINDS OF MISTAKES. WITH POWERS LIKE OURS...SO STUPID. PEOPLE COULD HAVE BEEN--
I KNOW YOU'D LOVE TO FIGHT ABOUT THIS ALL NIGHT.
BUT SOMEONE *ELSE* HAS DIBS ON KICKING MY BUTT RIGHT NOW.
AH. RIGHT.
GOOD LUCK, THEN.
YOU'RE A TELEPATH, EMMA--READ MY MIND. IT WAS JUST A ***DREAM.***
FEATURING THE UNFORGETTABLY INTENSE HIGHS AND LOWS YOU SHARED WITH THE GREATEST LOVE OF YOUR LIFE--WHO, INCIDENTALLY, IS ***CLEARLY*** NOT ME.
I WANT YOU TO FOCUS ON ***ONE*** SIMPLE FACT. CAN YOU DO THAT FOR ME?
...
ALL RIGHT.
JEAN GREY IS ***DEAD.***

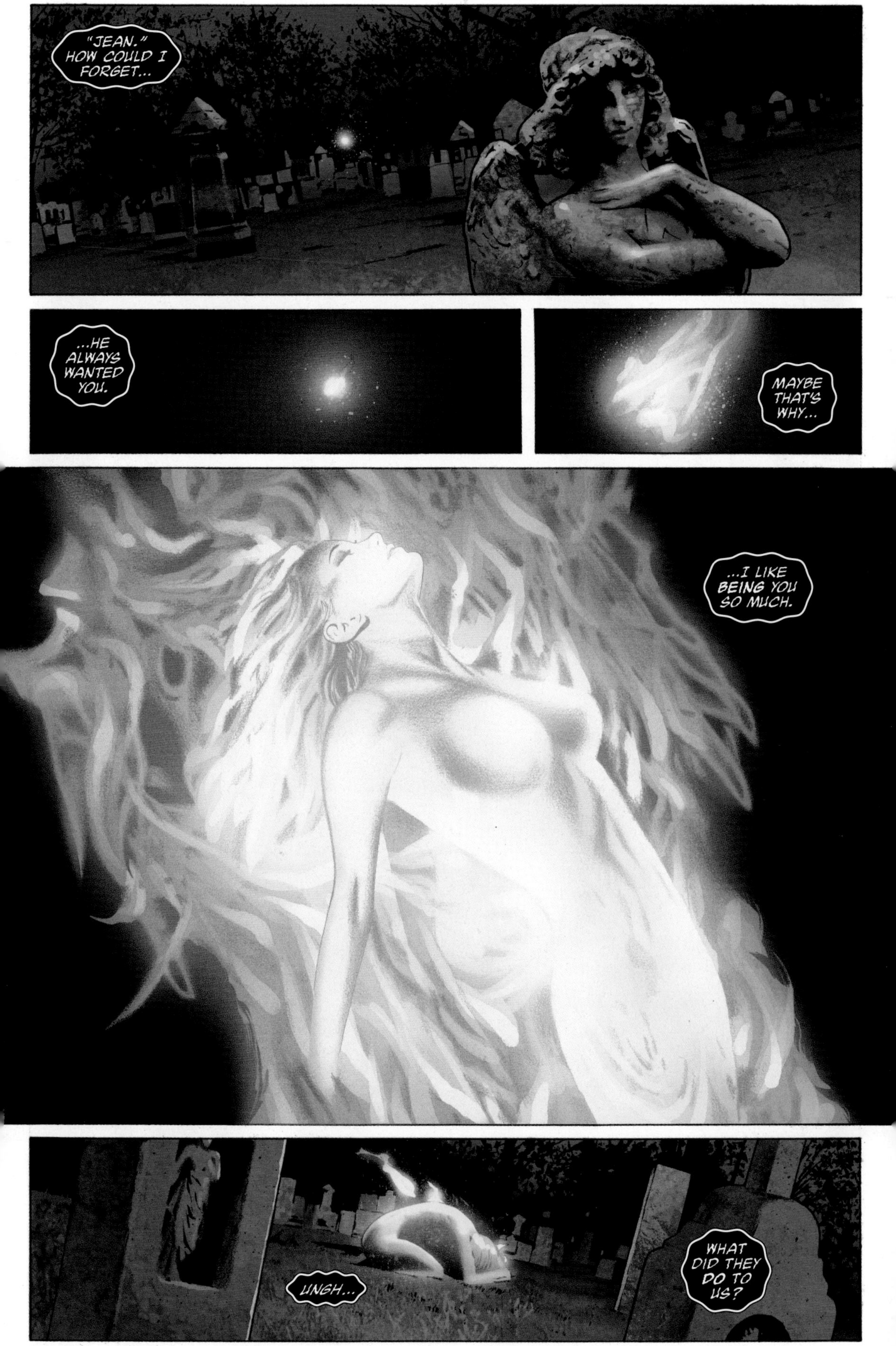
"JEAN."
HOW COULD I FORGET...
...HE ALWAYS WANTED YOU.
MAYBE THAT'S WHY...
...I LIKE BEING YOU SO MUCH.
UNGH...
WHAT DID THEY DO TO US?

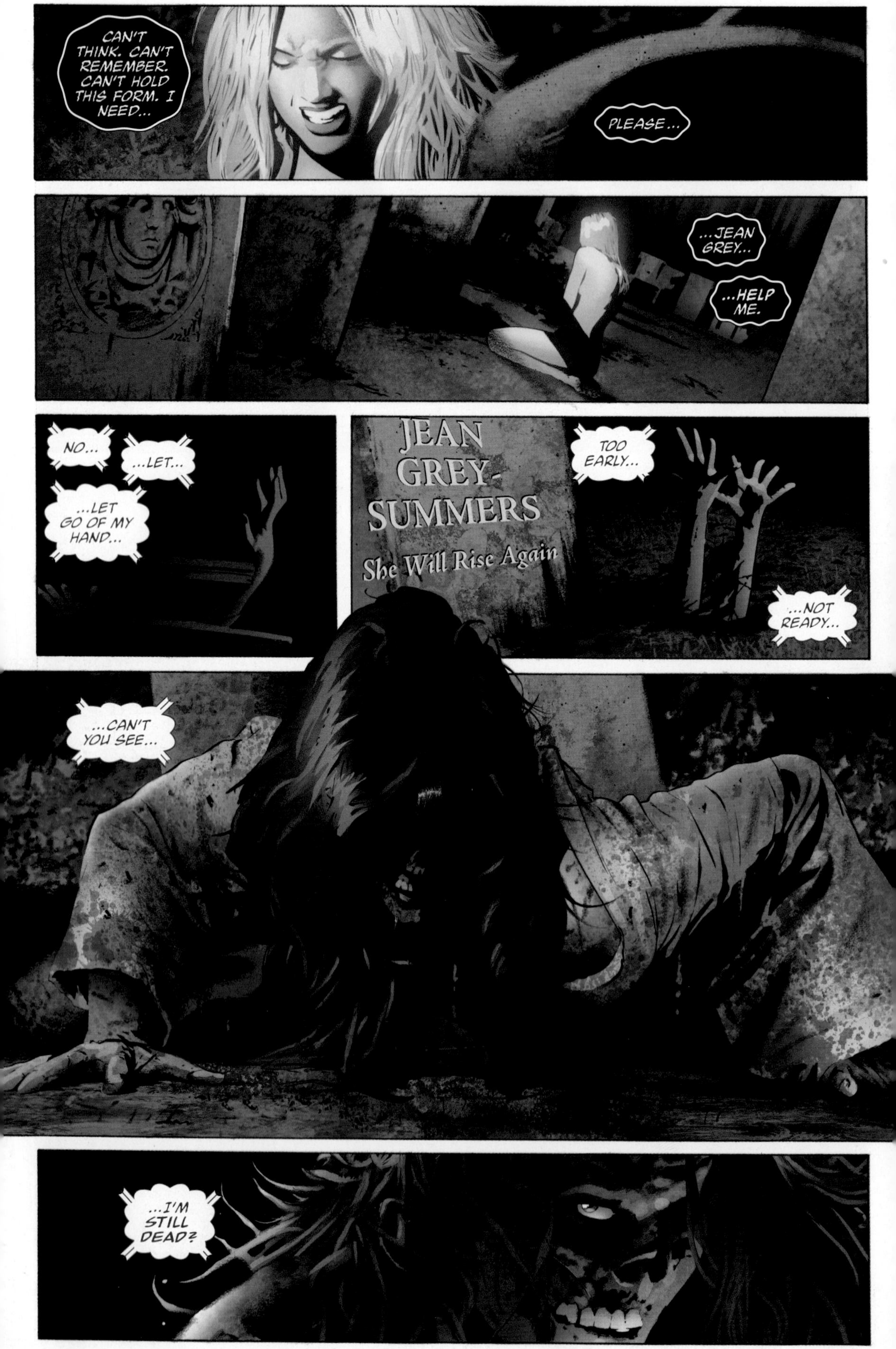
CAN'T THINK. CAN'T REMEMBER. CAN'T HOLD THIS FORM. I NEED...
PLEASE...
...JEAN GREY...
...HELP ME.
NO...
...LET...
...LET GO OF MY HAND...
JEAN GREY-SUMMERS
She Will Rise Again
TOO EARLY...
...NOT READY...
...CAN'T YOU SEE...
...I'M STILL DEAD?

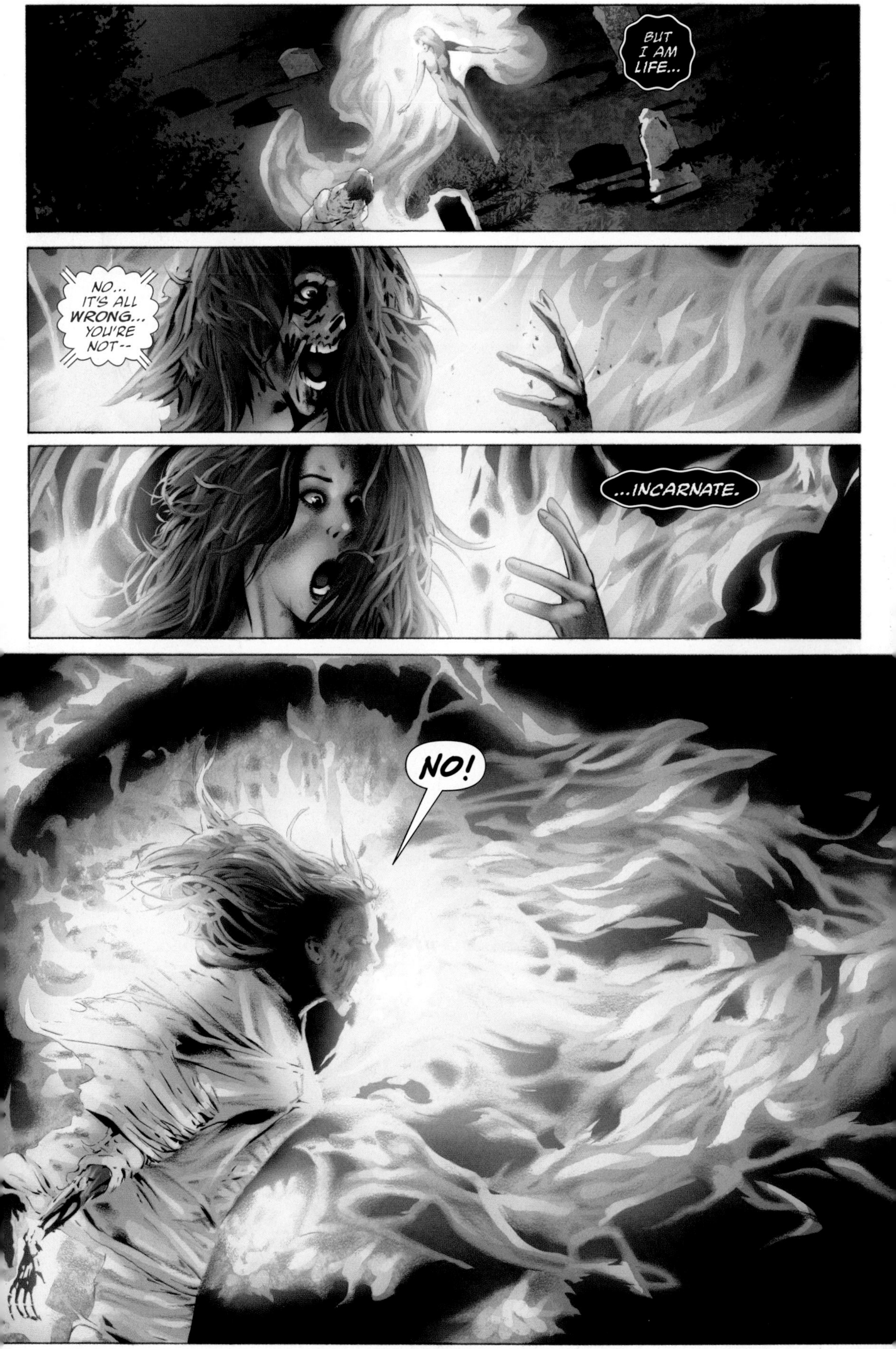
BUT I AM LIFE...
NO... IT'S ALL WRONG... YOU'RE NOT--
...INCARNATE.
NO!

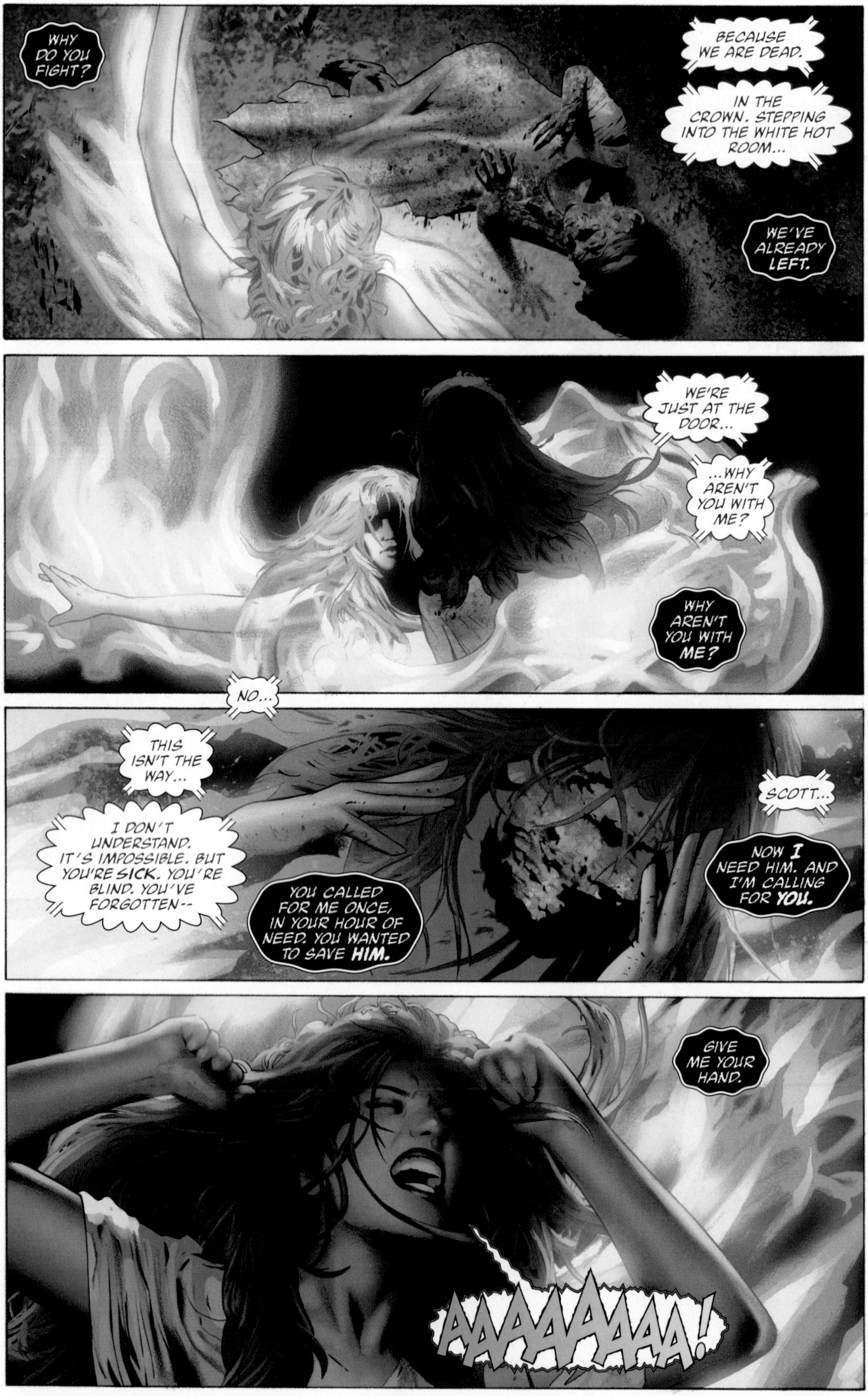
WHY DO YOU FIGHT?
BECAUSE WE ARE DEAD.
IN THE CROWN. STEPPING INTO THE WHITE HOT ROOM...
WE'VE ALREADY LEFT.
WE'RE JUST AT THE DOOR...
...WHY AREN'T YOU WITH ME?
WHY AREN'T YOU WITH ME?
NO...
THIS ISN'T THE WAY...
I DON'T UNDERSTAND. IT'S IMPOSSIBLE. BUT YOU'RE SICK. YOU'RE BLIND. YOU'VE FORGOTTEN--
YOU CALLED FOR ME ONCE, IN YOUR HOUR OF NEED. YOU WANTED TO SAVE HIM.
SCOTT...
NOW I NEED HIM. AND I'M CALLING FOR YOU.
GIVE ME YOUR HAND.
AAAAAAAA!

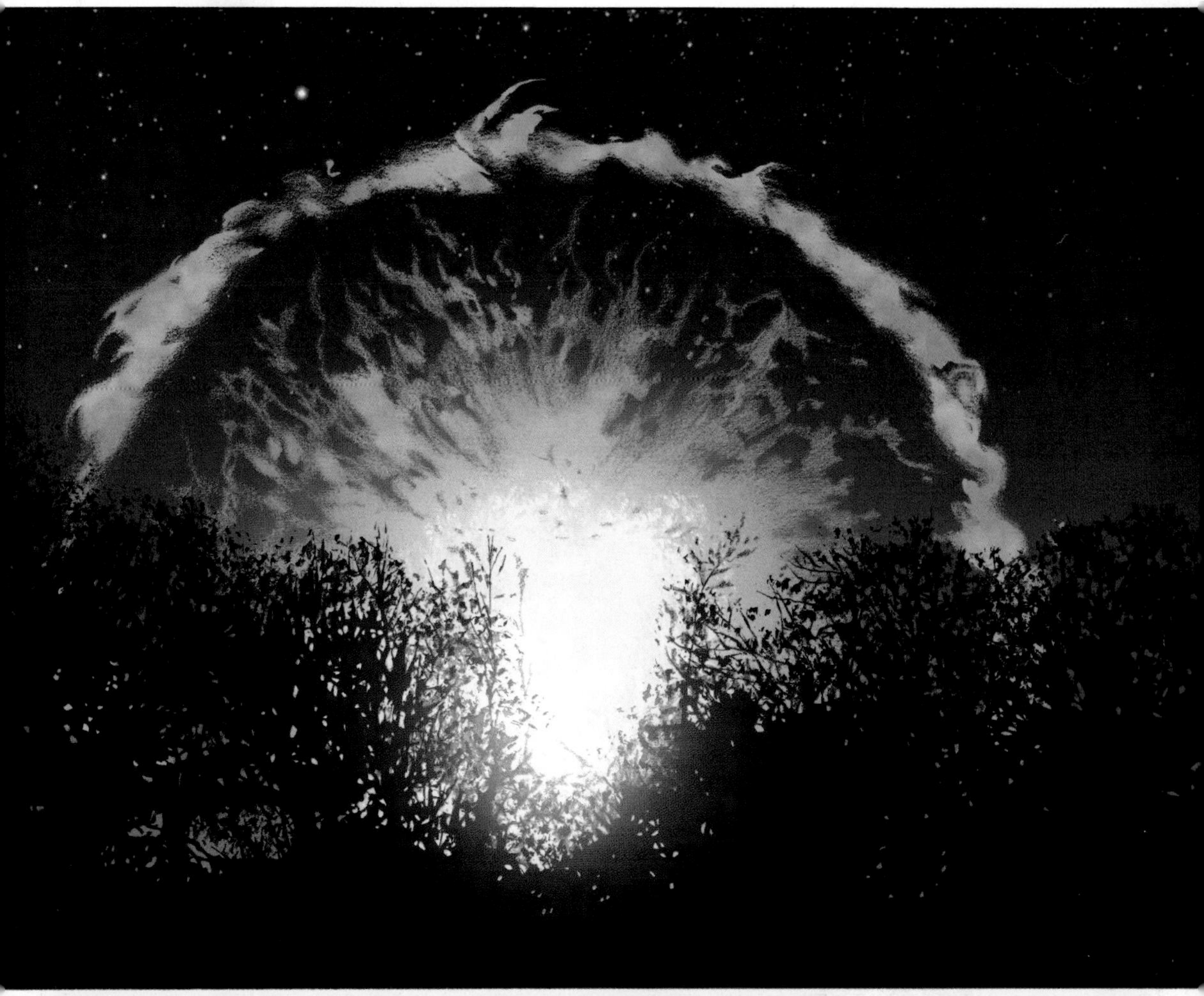

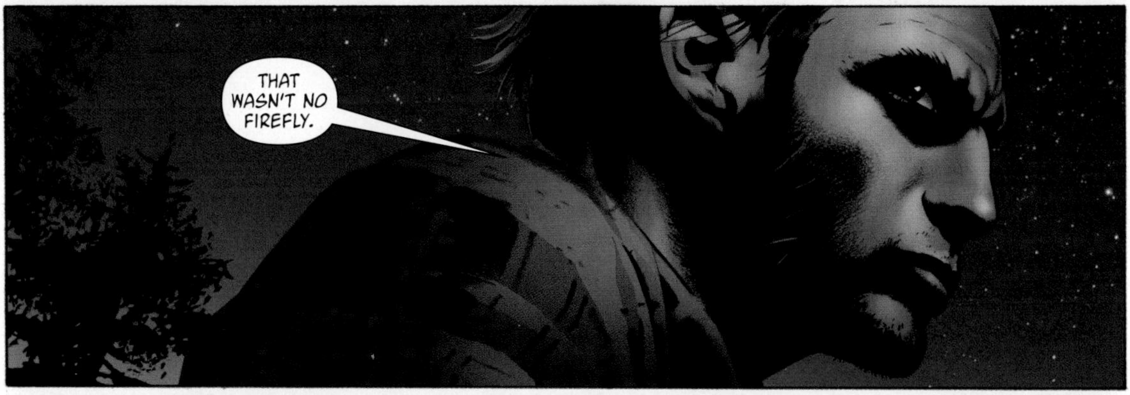
THAT WASN'T NO FIREFLY.

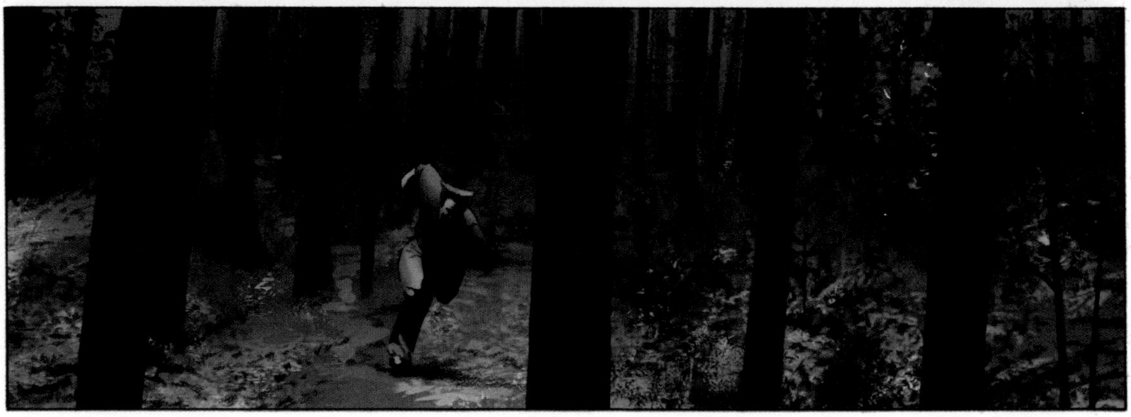

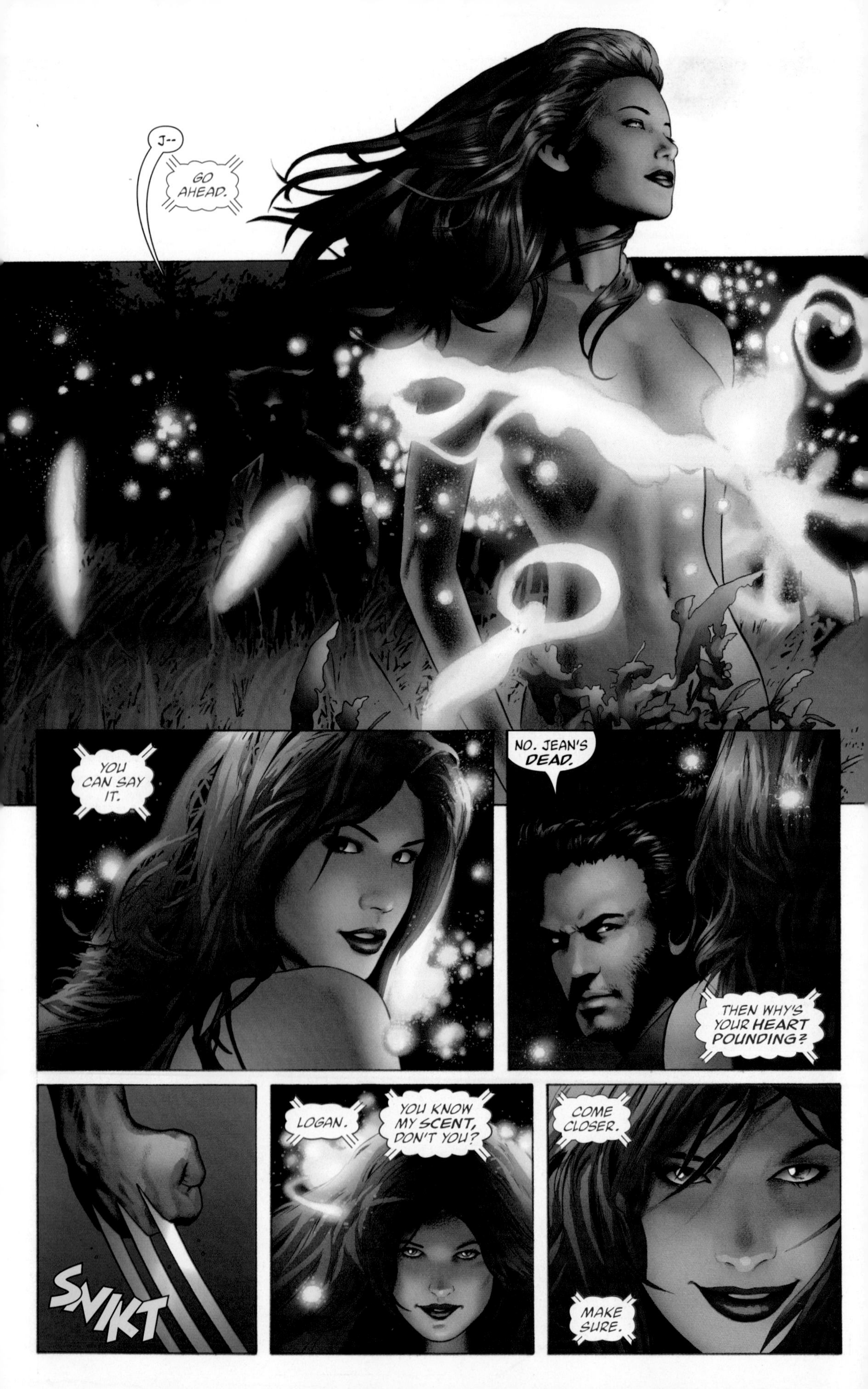
J--
GO AHEAD.
YOU CAN SAY IT.
NO. JEAN'S DEAD.
THEN WHY'S YOUR HEART POUNDING?
SNIKT
LOGAN.
YOU KNOW MY SCENT, DON'T YOU?
COME CLOSER.
MAKE SURE.

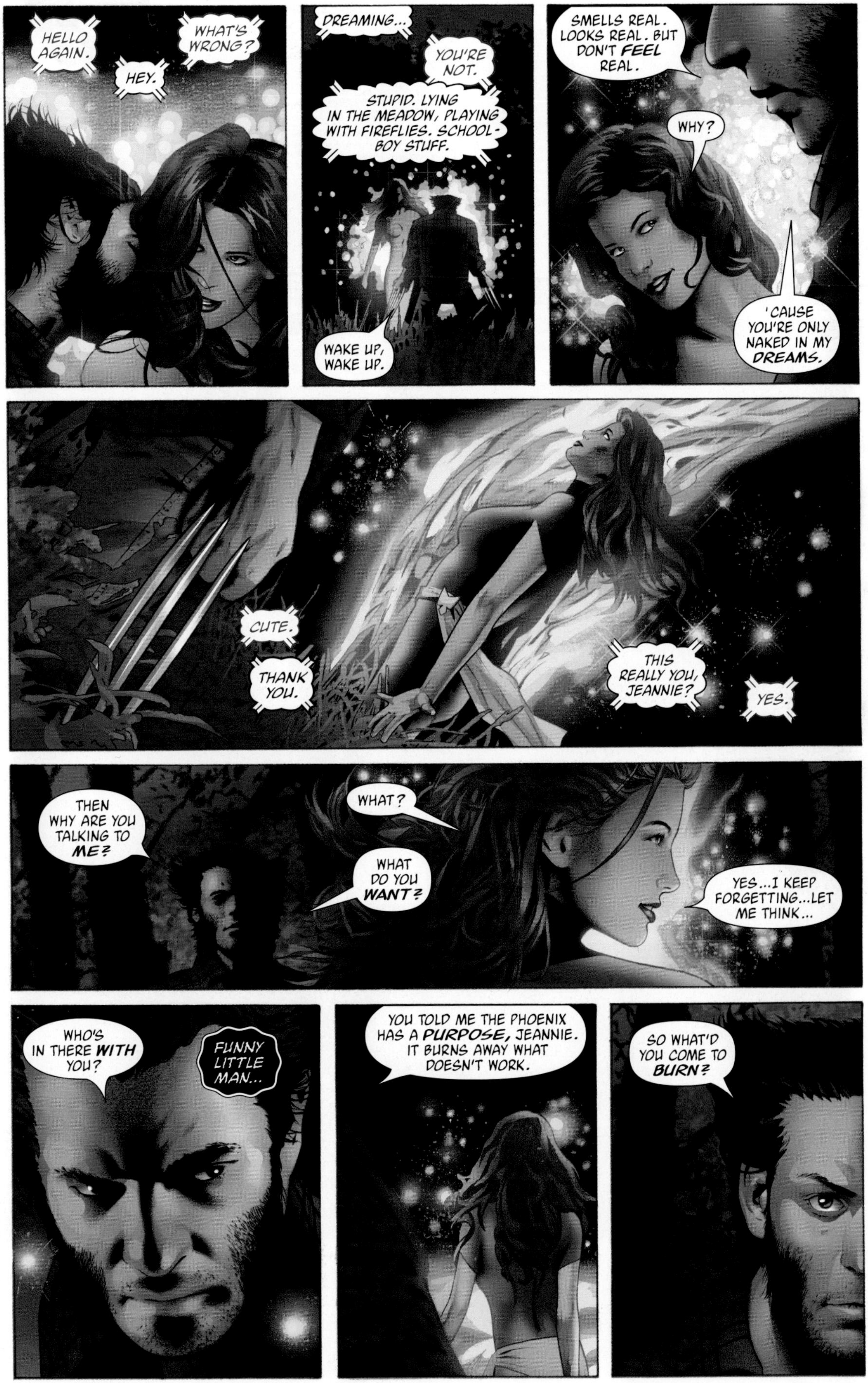
HELLO AGAIN.
HEY.
WHAT'S WRONG?
DREAMING...
YOU'RE NOT.
STUPID. LYING IN THE MEADOW, PLAYING WITH FIREFLIES. SCHOOL-BOY STUFF.
WAKE UP, WAKE UP.
SMELLS REAL. LOOKS REAL. BUT DON'T FEEL REAL.
WHY?
'CAUSE YOU'RE ONLY NAKED IN MY DREAMS.
CUTE.
THANK YOU.
THIS REALLY YOU, JEANNIE?
YES.
THEN WHY ARE YOU TALKING TO ME?
WHAT?
WHAT DO YOU WANT?
YES...I KEEP FORGETTING...LET ME THINK...
WHO'S IN THERE WITH YOU?
FUNNY LITTLE MAN...
YOU TOLD ME THE PHOENIX HAS A PURPOSE, JEANNIE. IT BURNS AWAY WHAT DOESN'T WORK.
SO WHAT'D YOU COME TO BURN?

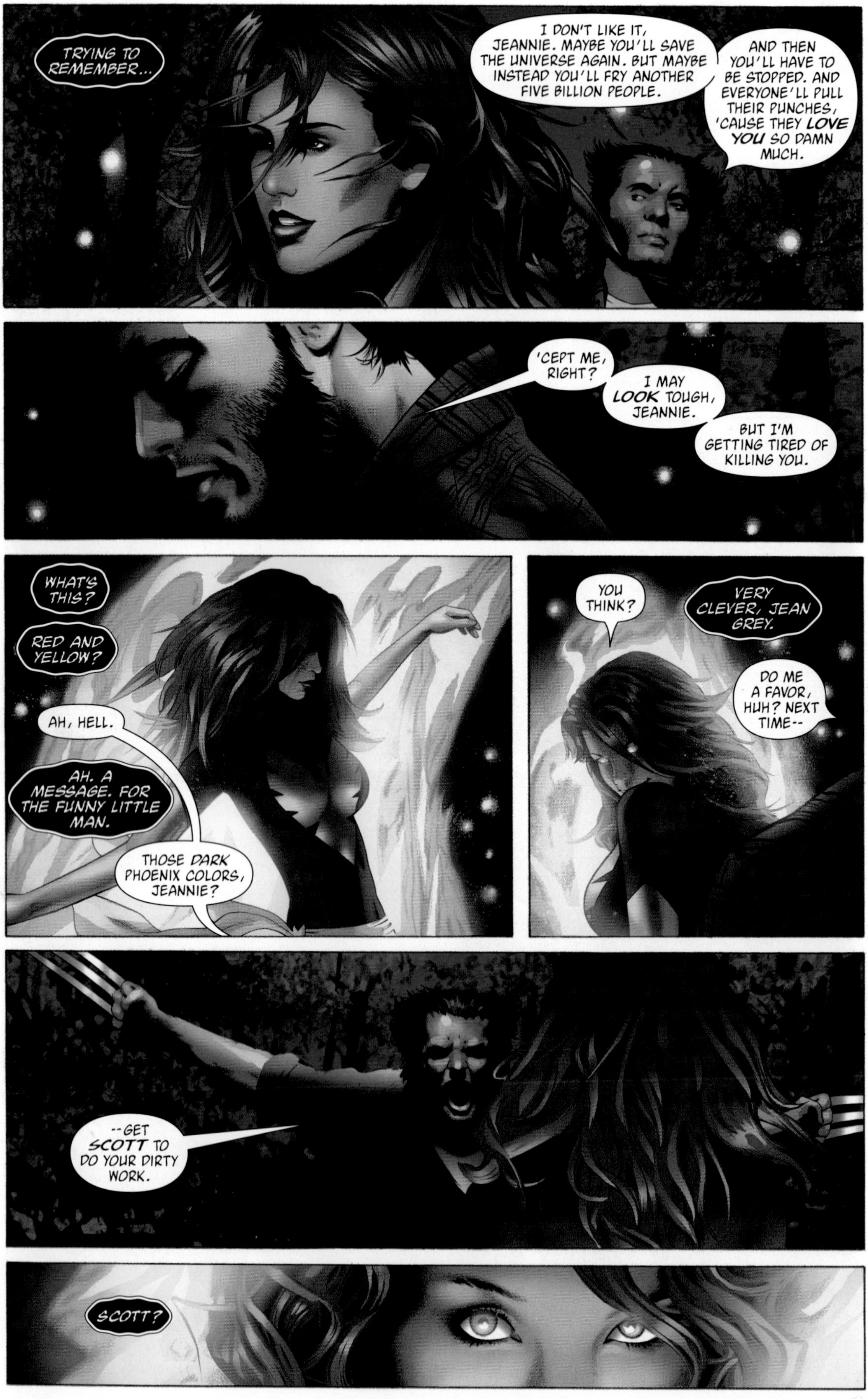

TRYING TO REMEMBER...
I DON'T LIKE IT, JEANNIE. MAYBE YOU'LL SAVE THE UNIVERSE AGAIN. BUT MAYBE INSTEAD YOU'LL FRY ANOTHER FIVE BILLION PEOPLE.
AND THEN YOU'LL HAVE TO BE STOPPED. AND EVERYONE'LL PULL THEIR PUNCHES, 'CAUSE THEY LOVE YOU SO DAMN MUCH.
'CEPT ME, RIGHT?
I MAY LOOK TOUGH, JEANNIE.
BUT I'M GETTING TIRED OF KILLING YOU.
WHAT'S THIS?
RED AND YELLOW?
AH, HELL.
AH. A MESSAGE. FOR THE FUNNY LITTLE MAN.
THOSE DARK PHOENIX COLORS, JEANNIE?
YOU THINK?
VERY CLEVER, JEAN GREY.
DO ME A FAVOR, HUH? NEXT TIME--
--GET SCOTT TO DO YOUR DIRTY WORK.
SCOTT?

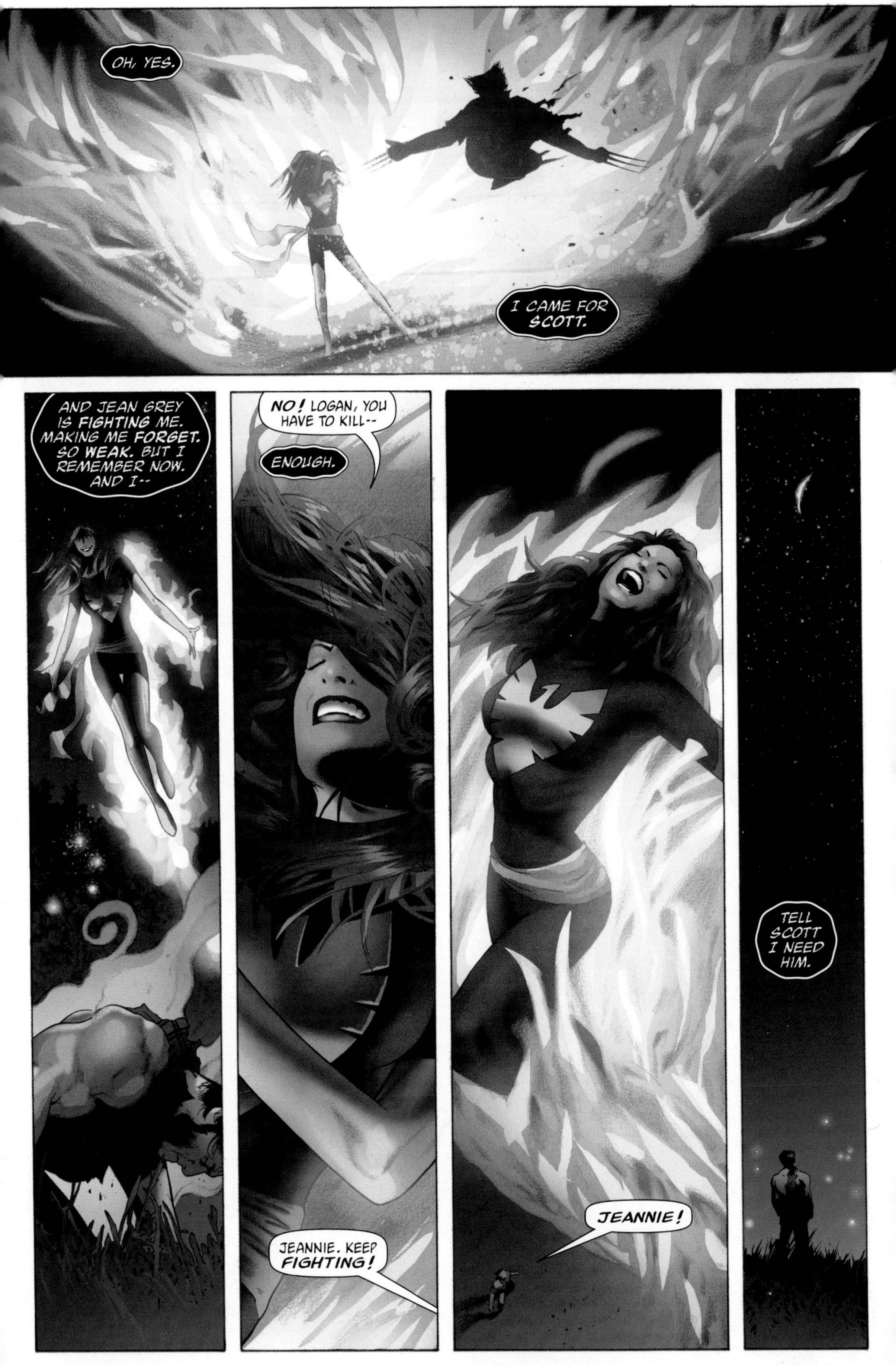
OH, YES.
I CAME FOR SCOTT.
AND JEAN GREY IS FIGHTING ME. MAKING ME FORGET. SO WEAK. BUT I REMEMBER NOW. AND I--
NO! LOGAN, YOU HAVE TO KILL--
ENOUGH.
JEANNIE. KEEP FIGHTING!
JEANNIE!
TELL SCOTT I NEED HIM.

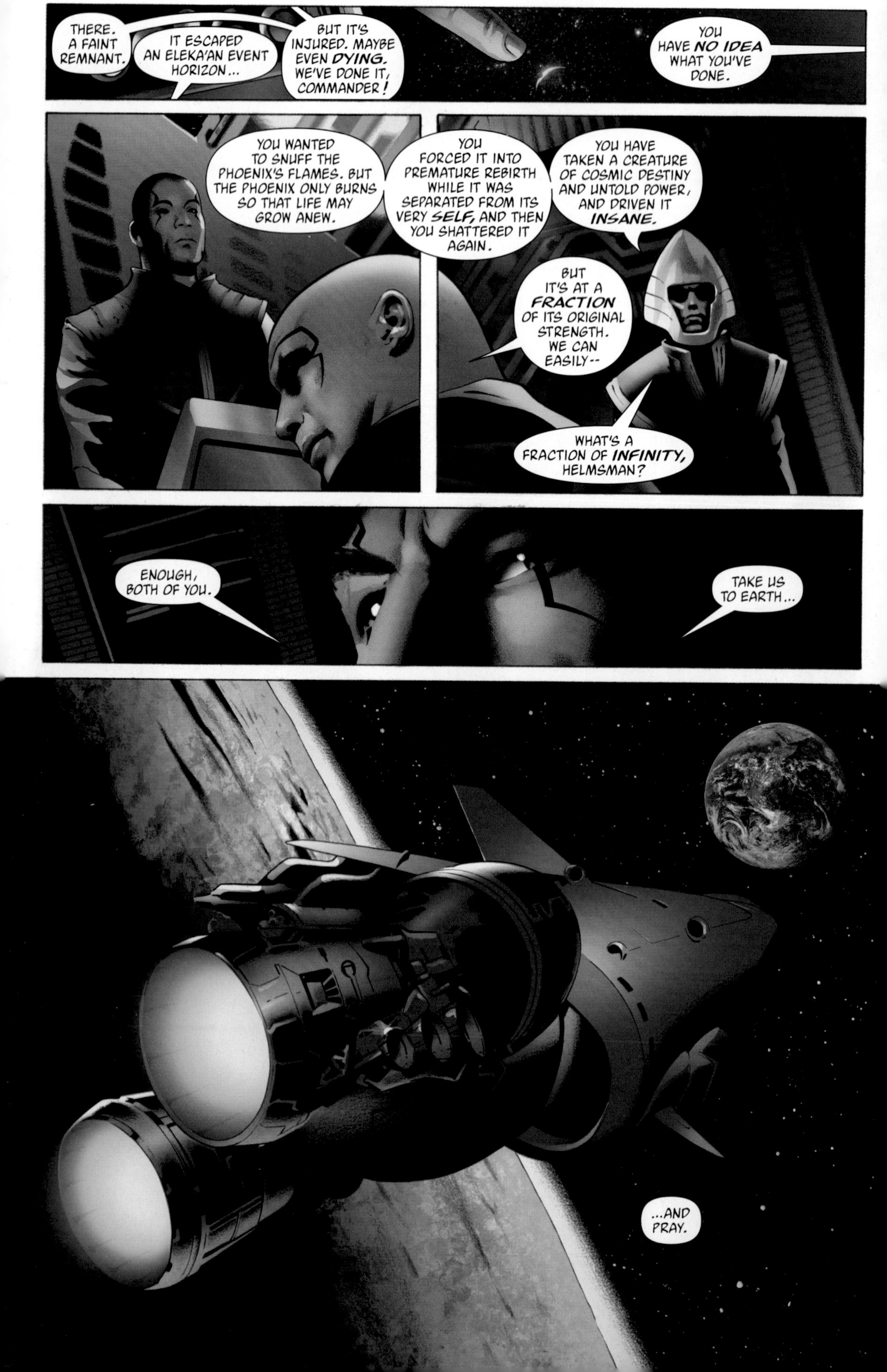
THERE. A FAINT REMNANT.
IT ESCAPED AN ELEKA'AN EVENT HORIZON...
BUT IT'S INJURED. MAYBE EVEN DYING. WE'VE DONE IT, COMMANDER!
YOU HAVE NO IDEA WHAT YOU'VE DONE.
YOU WANTED TO SNUFF THE PHOENIX'S FLAMES. BUT THE PHOENIX ONLY BURNS SO THAT LIFE MAY GROW ANEW.
YOU FORCED IT INTO PREMATURE REBIRTH WHILE IT WAS SEPARATED FROM ITS VERY SELF, AND THEN YOU SHATTERED IT AGAIN.
YOU HAVE TAKEN A CREATURE OF COSMIC DESTINY AND UNTOLD POWER, AND DRIVEN IT INSANE.
BUT IT'S AT A FRACTION OF ITS ORIGINAL STRENGTH. WE CAN EASILY--
WHAT'S A FRACTION OF INFINITY, HELMSMAN?
ENOUGH, BOTH OF YOU.
TAKE US TO EARTH...
...AND PRAY.

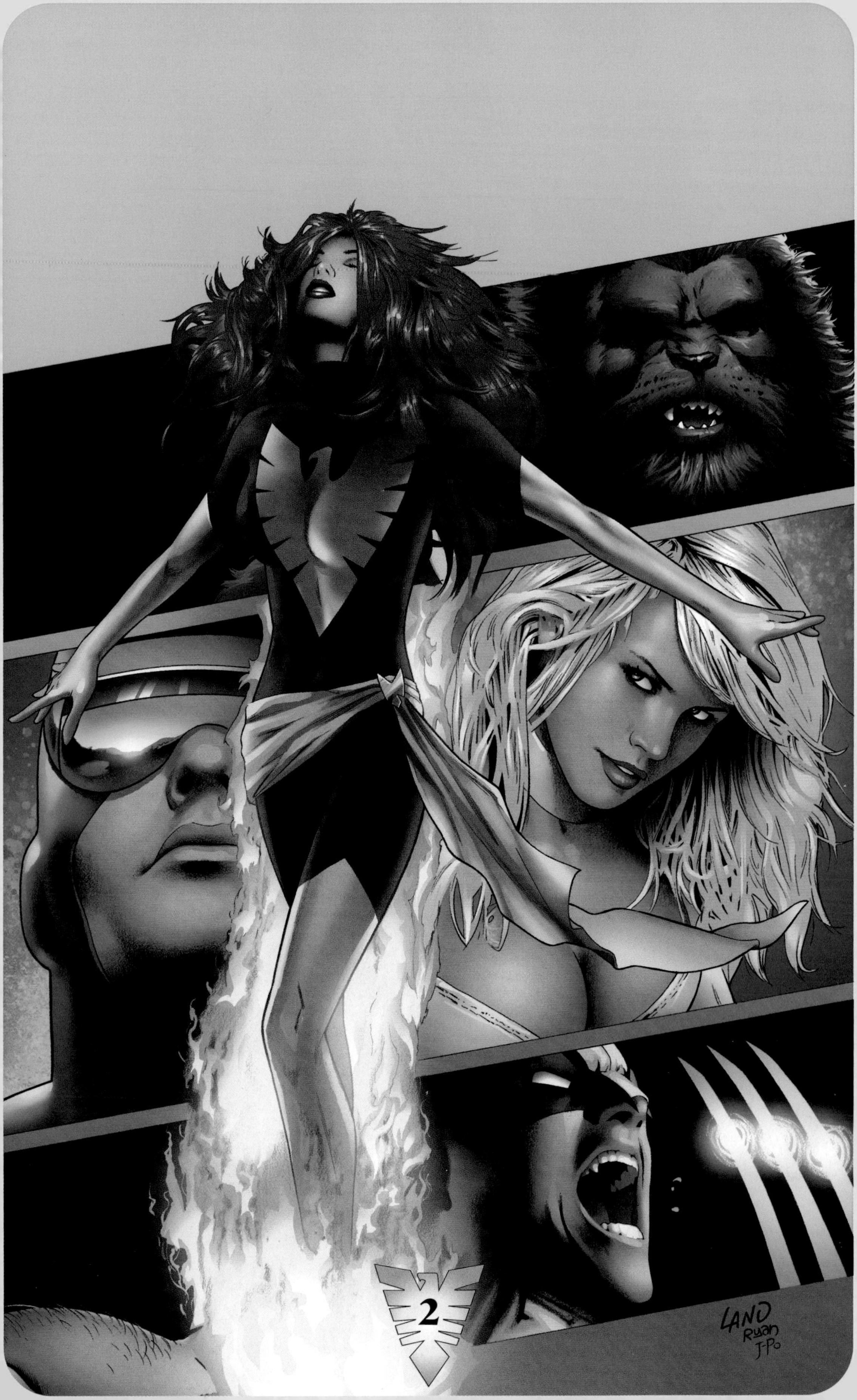
2
LAND
Ryan
J-Po

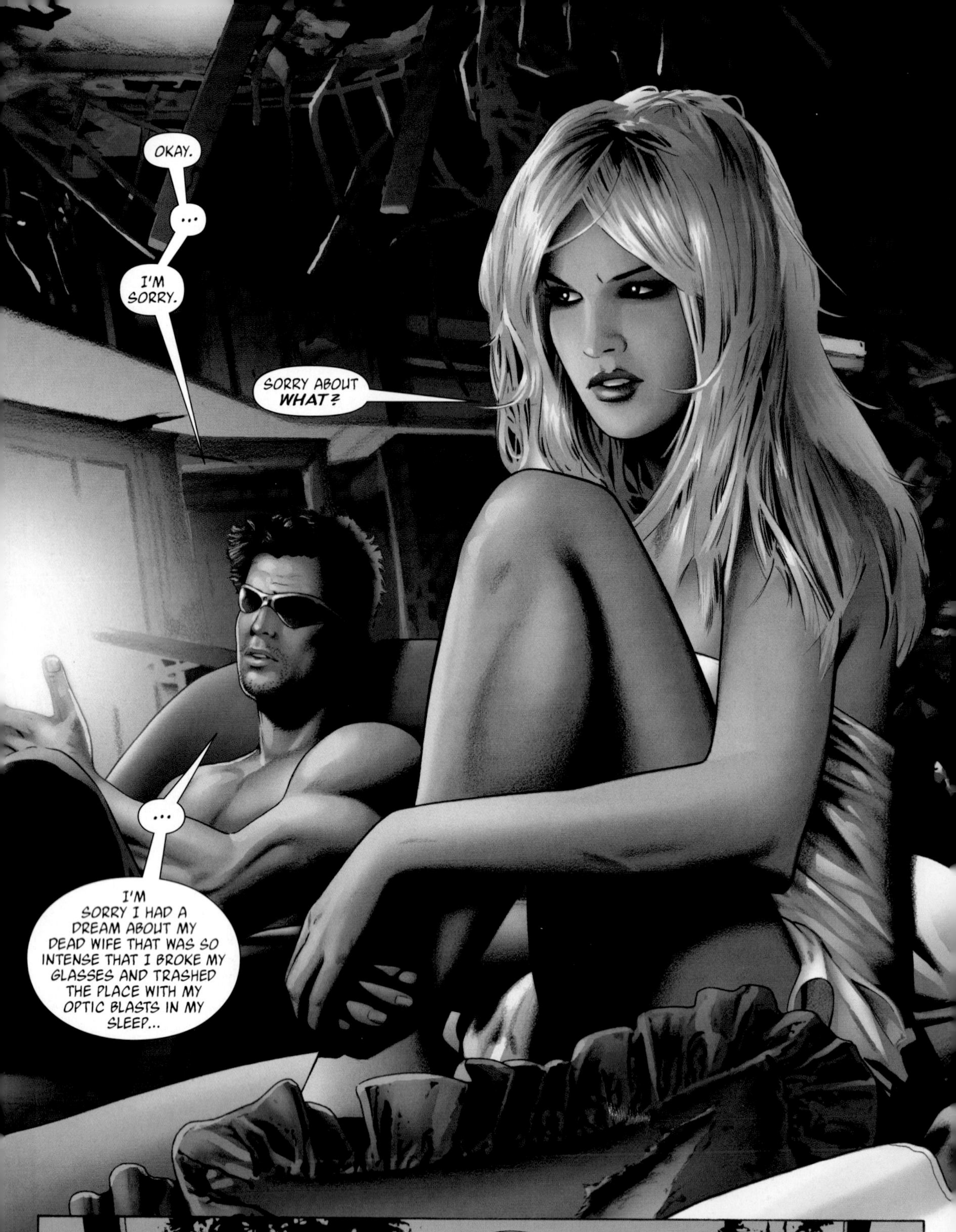
OKAY.
...
I'M SORRY.
SORRY ABOUT WHAT?
...
I'M SORRY I HAD A DREAM ABOUT MY DEAD WIFE THAT WAS SO INTENSE THAT I BROKE MY GLASSES AND TRASHED THE PLACE WITH MY OPTIC BLASTS IN MY SLEEP...

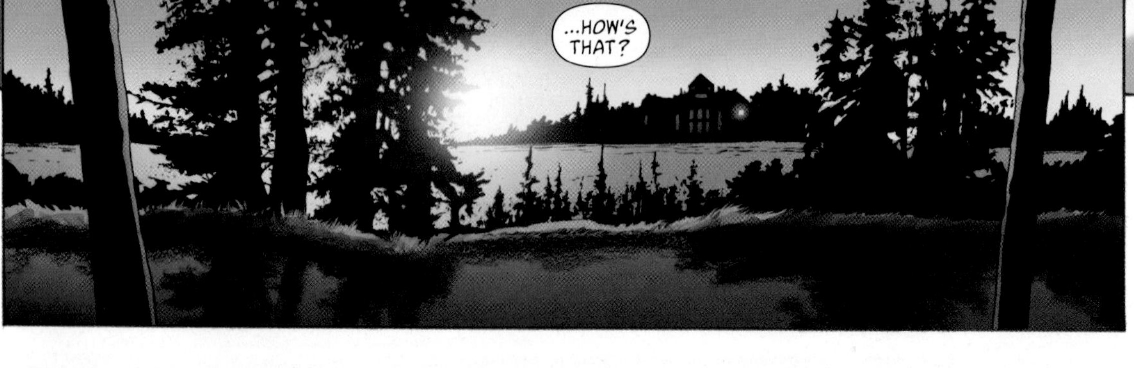
...HOW'S THAT?

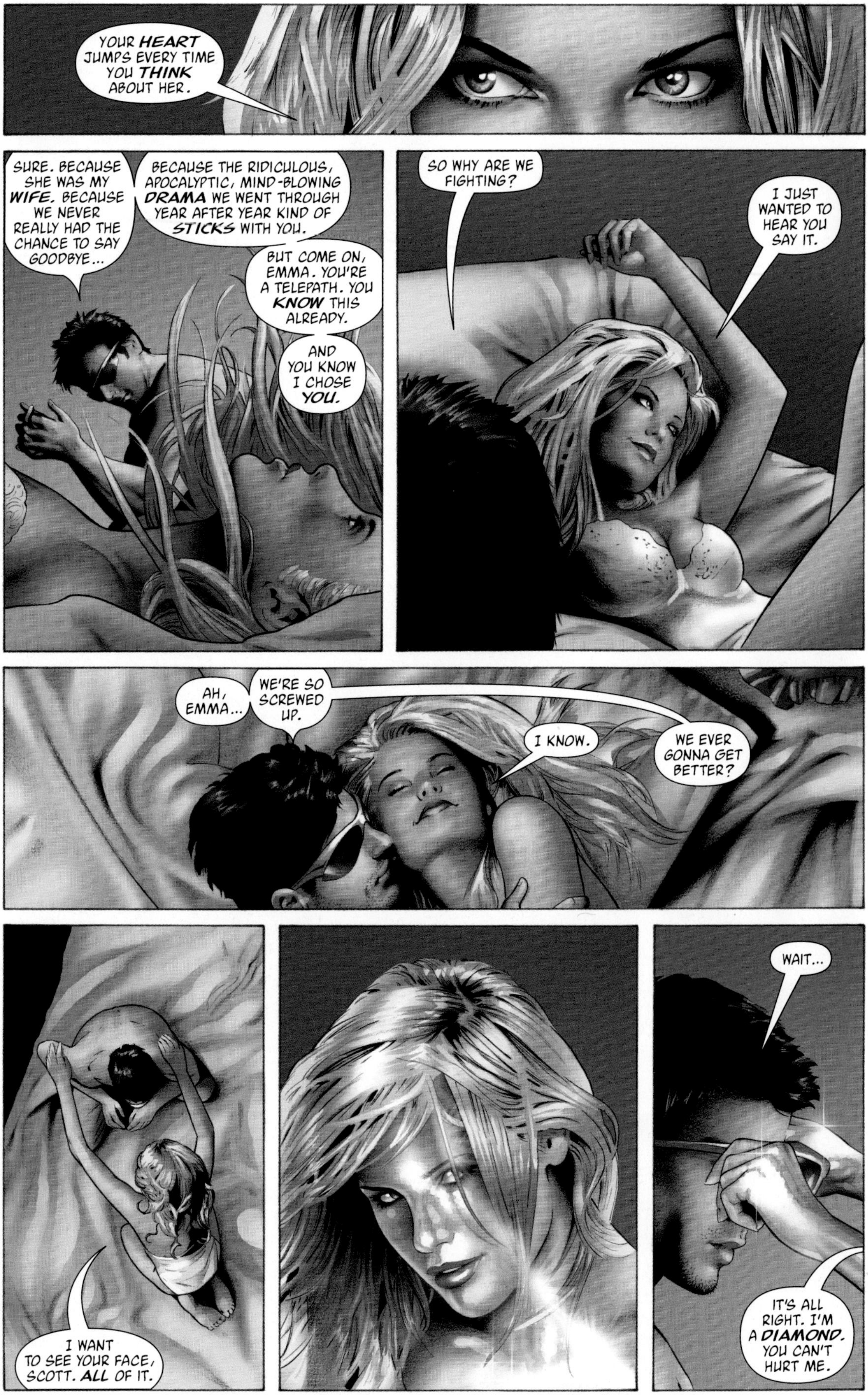
YOUR **HEART** JUMPS EVERY TIME YOU **THINK** ABOUT HER.
SURE. BECAUSE SHE WAS MY **WIFE.** BECAUSE WE NEVER REALLY HAD THE CHANCE TO SAY GOODBYE...
BECAUSE THE RIDICULOUS, APOCALYPTIC, MIND-BLOWING **DRAMA** WE WENT THROUGH YEAR AFTER YEAR KIND OF **STICKS** WITH YOU.
BUT COME ON, EMMA. YOU'RE A TELEPATH. YOU **KNOW** THIS ALREADY.
AND YOU KNOW I CHOSE **YOU.**
SO WHY ARE WE FIGHTING?
I JUST WANTED TO HEAR YOU SAY IT.
AH, EMMA...
WE'RE SO SCREWED UP.
I KNOW.
WE EVER GONNA GET BETTER?
I WANT TO SEE YOUR FACE, SCOTT. **ALL** OF IT.
WAIT...
IT'S ALL RIGHT. I'M A **DIAMOND.** YOU CAN'T HURT ME.

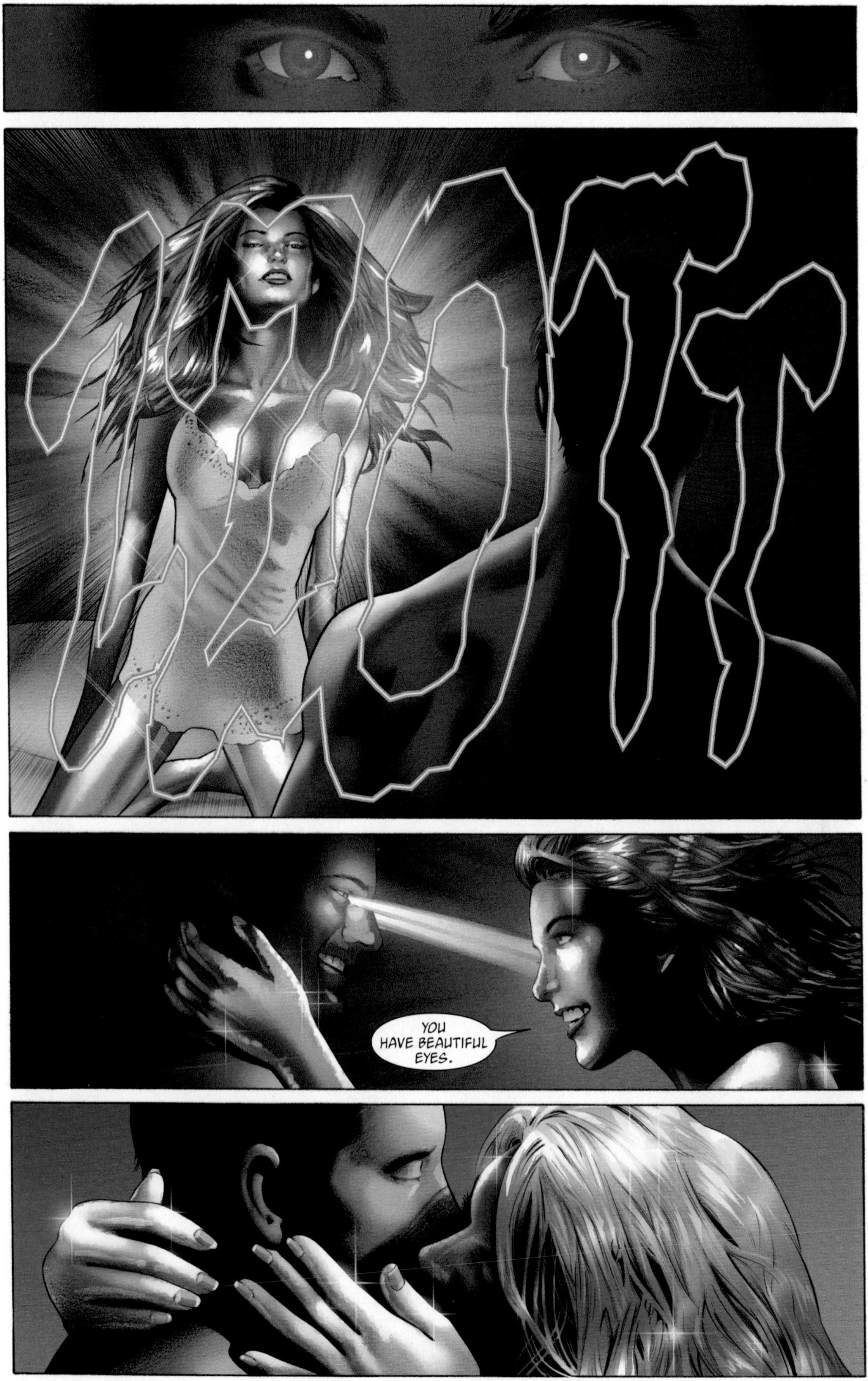
YOU HAVE BEAUTIFUL EYES.

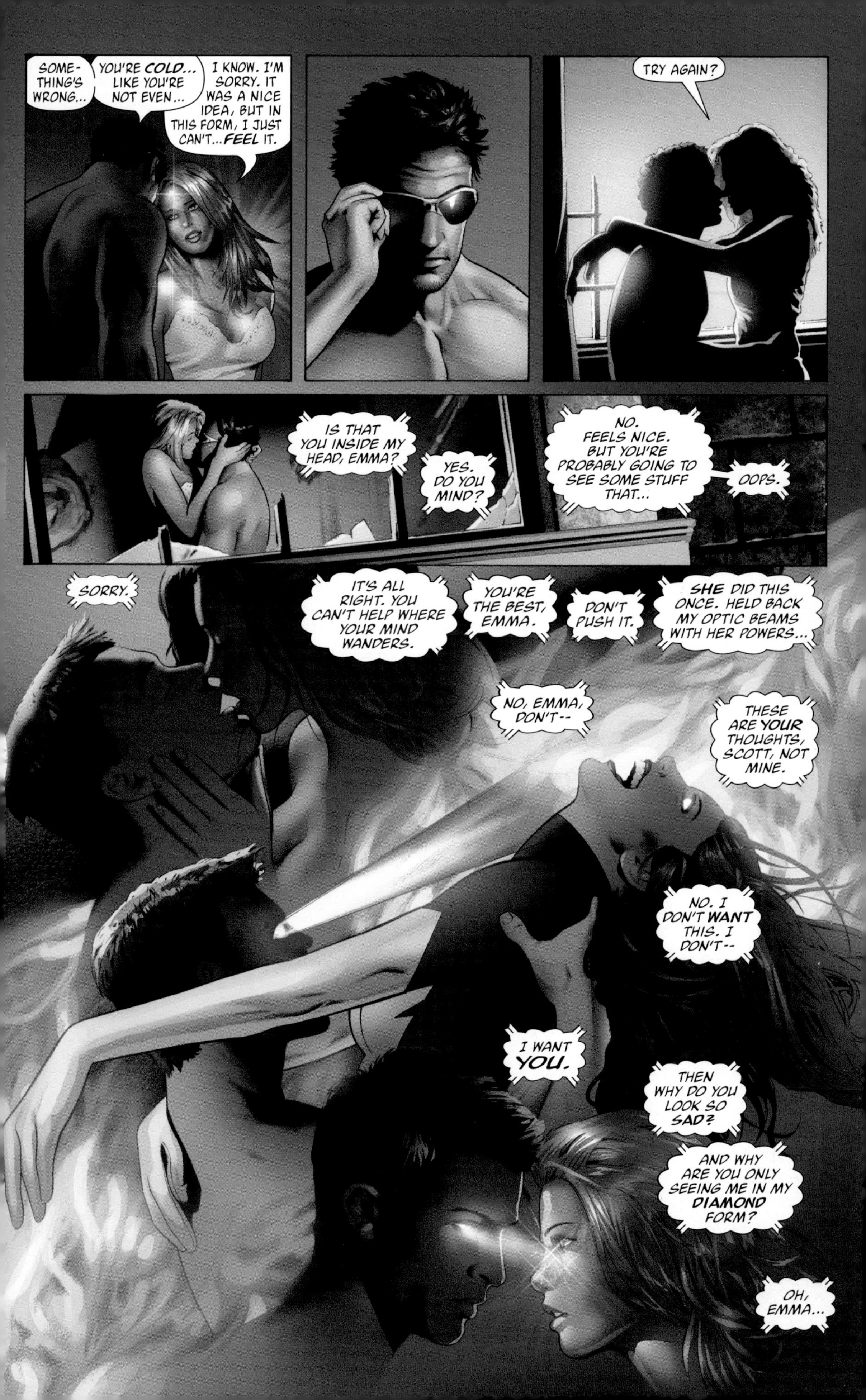
SOMETHING'S WRONG...
YOU'RE COLD... LIKE YOU'RE NOT EVEN...
I KNOW. I'M SORRY. IT WAS A NICE IDEA, BUT IN THIS FORM, I JUST CAN'T... FEEL IT.
TRY AGAIN?
IS THAT YOU INSIDE MY HEAD, EMMA?
YES. DO YOU MIND?
NO. FEELS NICE. BUT YOU'RE PROBABLY GOING TO SEE SOME STUFF THAT...
OOPS.
SORRY.
IT'S ALL RIGHT. YOU CAN'T HELP WHERE YOUR MIND WANDERS.
YOU'RE THE BEST, EMMA.
DON'T PUSH IT.
SHE DID THIS ONCE. HELD BACK MY OPTIC BEAMS WITH HER POWERS...
NO, EMMA, DON'T--
THESE ARE YOUR THOUGHTS, SCOTT, NOT MINE.
NO. I DON'T WANT THIS. I DON'T--
I WANT YOU.
THEN WHY DO YOU LOOK SO SAD?
AND WHY ARE YOU ONLY SEEING ME IN MY DIAMOND FORM?
OH, EMMA...

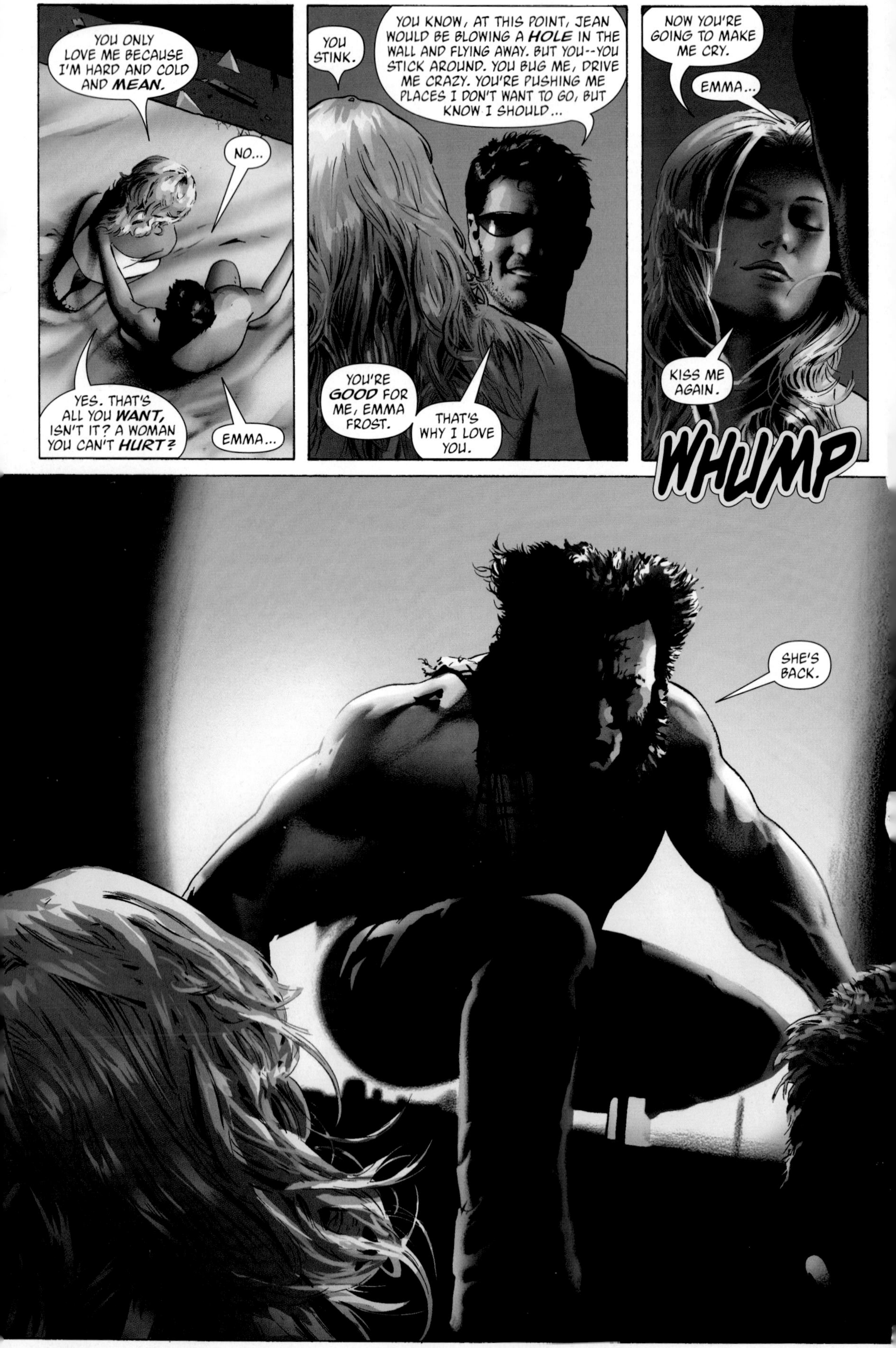
YOU ONLY LOVE ME BECAUSE I'M HARD AND COLD AND MEAN.
NO...
YES. THAT'S ALL YOU WANT, ISN'T IT? A WOMAN YOU CAN'T HURT?
EMMA...
YOU STINK.
YOU KNOW, AT THIS POINT, JEAN WOULD BE BLOWING A HOLE IN THE WALL AND FLYING AWAY. BUT YOU--YOU STICK AROUND. YOU BUG ME, DRIVE ME CRAZY. YOU'RE PUSHING ME PLACES I DON'T WANT TO GO, BUT KNOW I SHOULD...
YOU'RE GOOD FOR ME, EMMA FROST.
THAT'S WHY I LOVE YOU.
NOW YOU'RE GOING TO MAKE ME CRY.
EMMA...
KISS ME AGAIN.
WHUMP
SHE'S BACK.

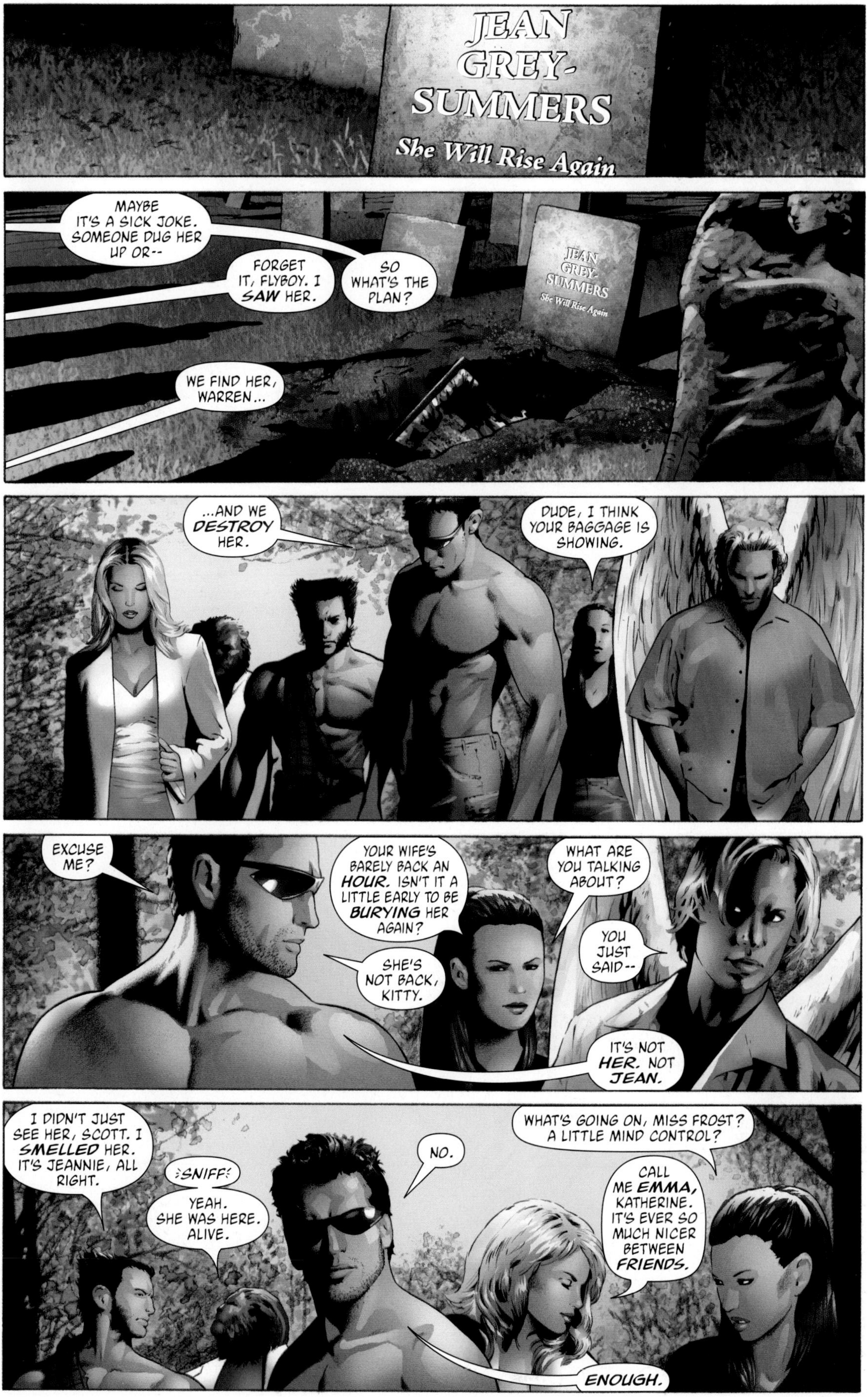
JEAN GREY-SUMMERS
She Will Rise Again
MAYBE IT'S A SICK JOKE. SOMEONE DUG HER UP OR--
FORGET IT, FLYBOY. I SAW HER.
SO WHAT'S THE PLAN?
JEAN GREY-SUMMERS
She Will Rise Again
WE FIND HER, WARREN...
...AND WE DESTROY HER.
DUDE, I THINK YOUR BAGGAGE IS SHOWING.
EXCUSE ME?
YOUR WIFE'S BARELY BACK AN HOUR. ISN'T IT A LITTLE EARLY TO BE BURYING HER AGAIN?
WHAT ARE YOU TALKING ABOUT?
YOU JUST SAID--
SHE'S NOT BACK, KITTY.
IT'S NOT HER. NOT JEAN.
I DIDN'T JUST SEE HER, SCOTT. I SMELLED HER. IT'S JEANNIE, ALL RIGHT.
SNIFF
YEAH. SHE WAS HERE. ALIVE.
NO.
WHAT'S GOING ON, MISS FROST? A LITTLE MIND CONTROL?
CALL ME EMMA, KATHERINE. IT'S EVER SO MUCH NICER BETWEEN FRIENDS.
ENOUGH.

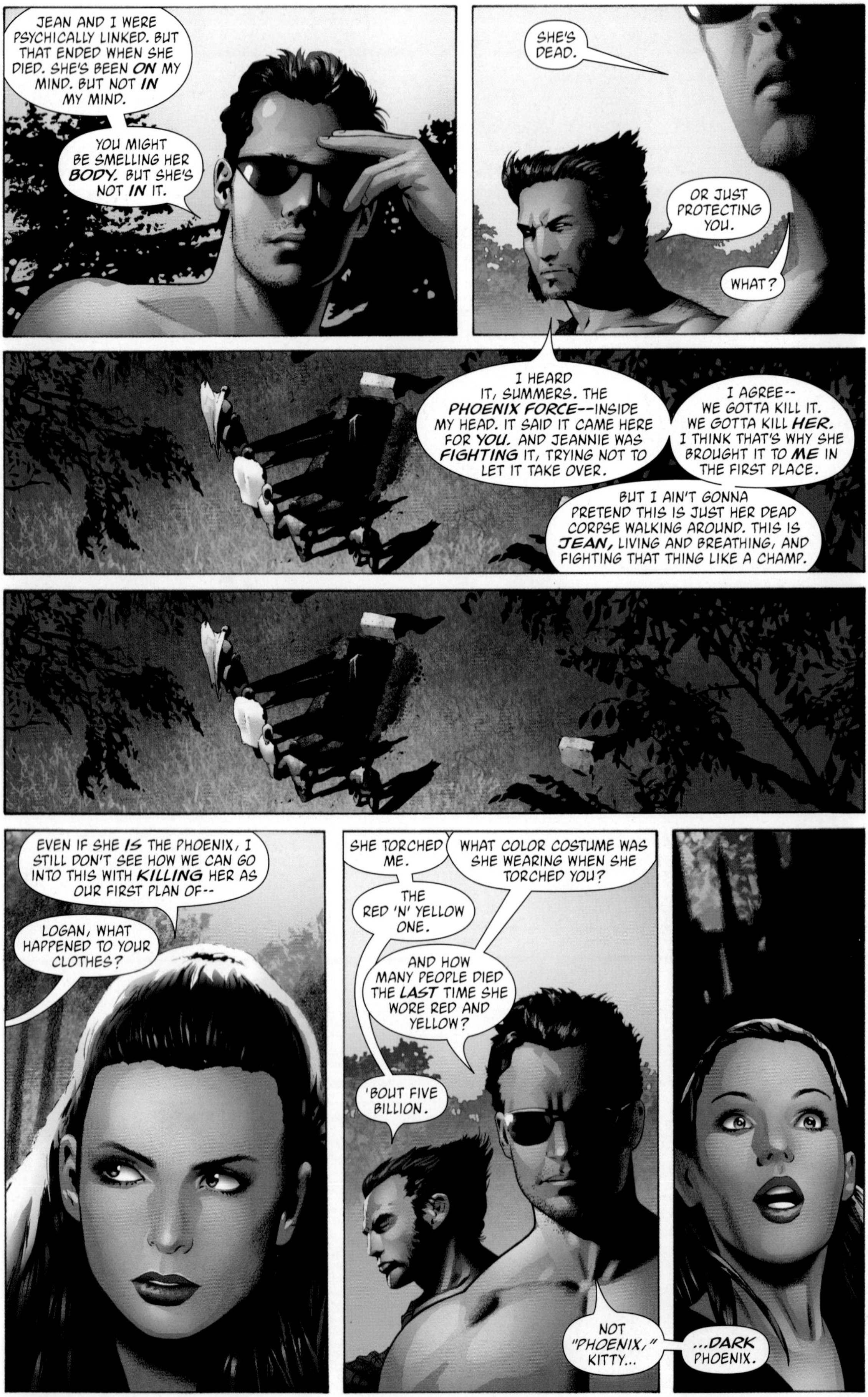
JEAN AND I WERE PSYCHICALLY LINKED. BUT THAT ENDED WHEN SHE DIED. SHE'S BEEN ON MY MIND. BUT NOT IN MY MIND.
YOU MIGHT BE SMELLING HER BODY. BUT SHE'S NOT IN IT.
SHE'S DEAD.
OR JUST PROTECTING YOU.
WHAT?
I HEARD IT, SUMMERS. THE PHOENIX FORCE--INSIDE MY HEAD. IT SAID IT CAME HERE FOR YOU. AND JEANNIE WAS FIGHTING IT, TRYING NOT TO LET IT TAKE OVER.
I AGREE--WE GOTTA KILL IT. WE GOTTA KILL HER. I THINK THAT'S WHY SHE BROUGHT IT TO ME IN THE FIRST PLACE.
BUT I AIN'T GONNA PRETEND THIS IS JUST HER DEAD CORPSE WALKING AROUND. THIS IS JEAN, LIVING AND BREATHING, AND FIGHTING THAT THING LIKE A CHAMP.
EVEN IF SHE IS THE PHOENIX, I STILL DON'T SEE HOW WE CAN GO INTO THIS WITH KILLING HER AS OUR FIRST PLAN OF--
LOGAN, WHAT HAPPENED TO YOUR CLOTHES?
SHE TORCHED ME.
WHAT COLOR COSTUME WAS SHE WEARING WHEN SHE TORCHED YOU?
THE RED 'N' YELLOW ONE.
AND HOW MANY PEOPLE DIED THE LAST TIME SHE WORE RED AND YELLOW?
'BOUT FIVE BILLION.
NOT "PHOENIX," KITTY...
...DARK PHOENIX.

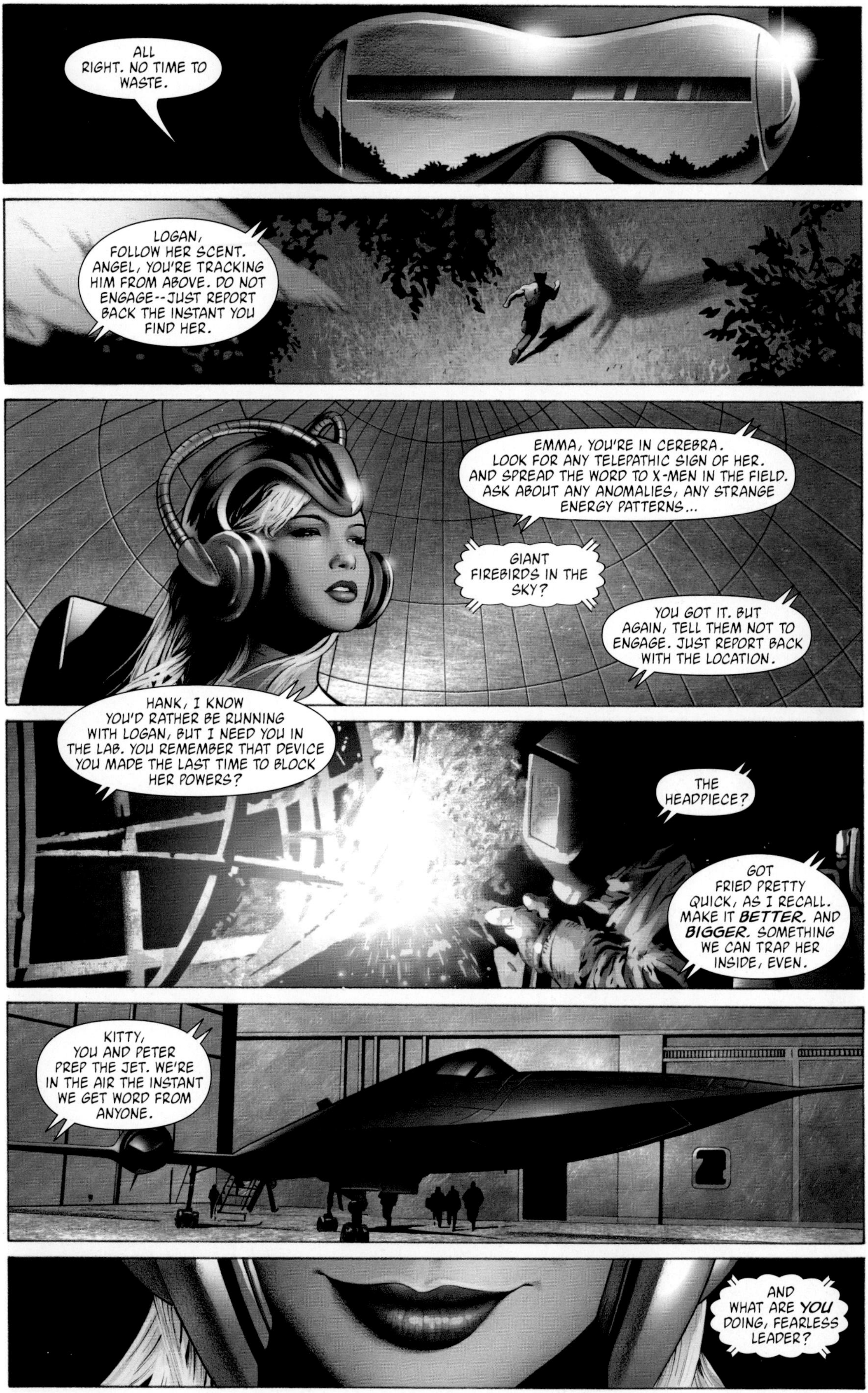
ALL RIGHT. NO TIME TO WASTE.
LOGAN, FOLLOW HER SCENT. ANGEL, YOU'RE TRACKING HIM FROM ABOVE. DO NOT ENGAGE--JUST REPORT BACK THE INSTANT YOU FIND HER.
EMMA, YOU'RE IN CEREBRA. LOOK FOR ANY TELEPATHIC SIGN OF HER. AND SPREAD THE WORD TO X-MEN IN THE FIELD. ASK ABOUT ANY ANOMALIES, ANY STRANGE ENERGY PATTERNS...
GIANT FIREBIRDS IN THE SKY?
YOU GOT IT. BUT AGAIN, TELL THEM NOT TO ENGAGE. JUST REPORT BACK WITH THE LOCATION.
HANK, I KNOW YOU'D RATHER BE RUNNING WITH LOGAN, BUT I NEED YOU IN THE LAB. YOU REMEMBER THAT DEVICE YOU MADE THE LAST TIME TO BLOCK HER POWERS?
THE HEADPIECE?
GOT FRIED PRETTY QUICK, AS I RECALL. MAKE IT BETTER. AND BIGGER. SOMETHING WE CAN TRAP HER INSIDE, EVEN.
KITTY, YOU AND PETER PREP THE JET. WE'RE IN THE AIR THE INSTANT WE GET WORD FROM ANYONE.
AND WHAT ARE YOU DOING, FEARLESS LEADER?

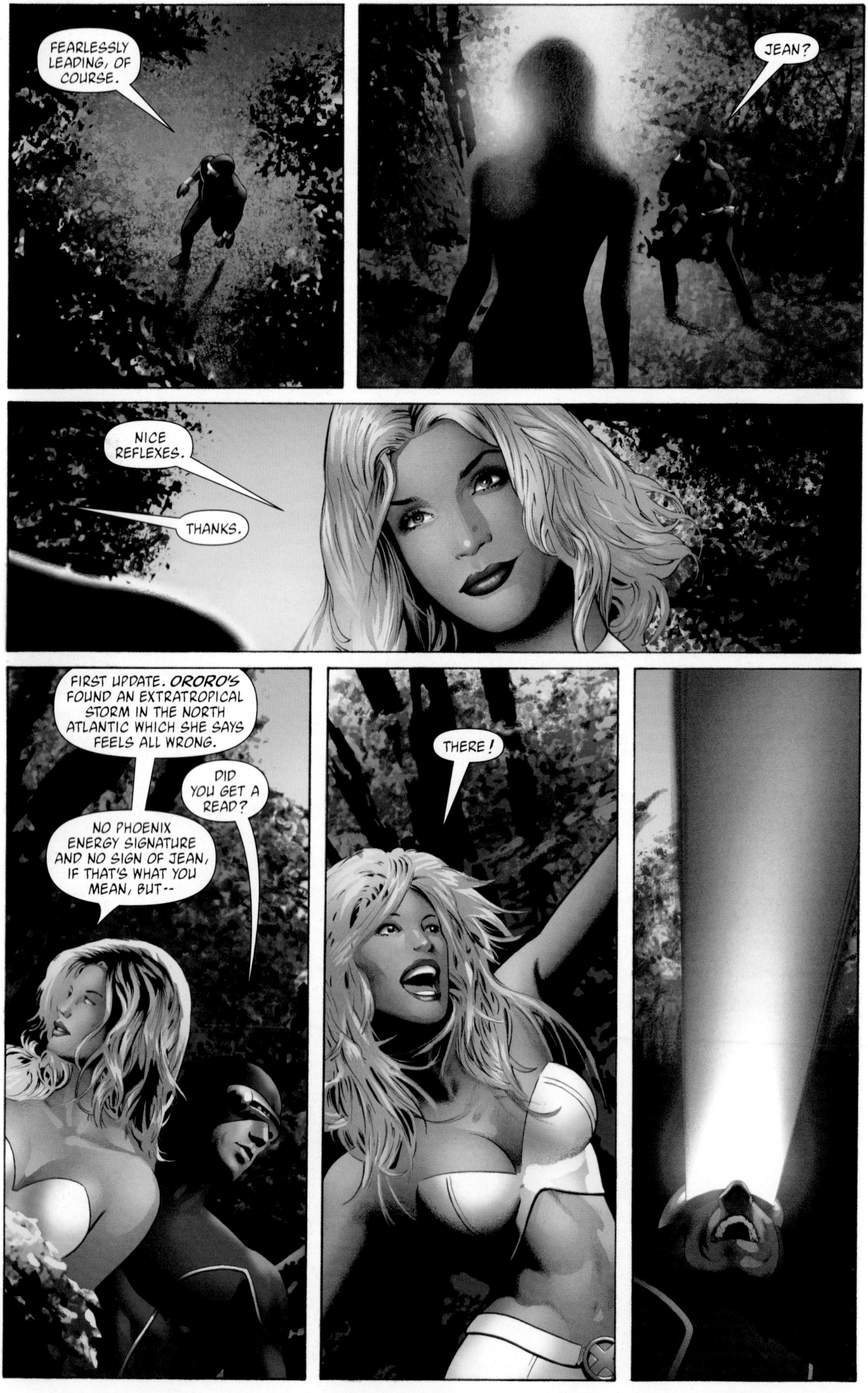
FEARLESSLY LEADING, OF COURSE.
JEAN?
NICE REFLEXES.
THANKS.
FIRST UPDATE. ORORO'S FOUND AN EXTRATROPICAL STORM IN THE NORTH ATLANTIC WHICH SHE SAYS FEELS ALL WRONG.
DID YOU GET A READ?
NO PHOENIX ENERGY SIGNATURE AND NO SIGN OF JEAN, IF THAT'S WHAT YOU MEAN, BUT--
THERE!

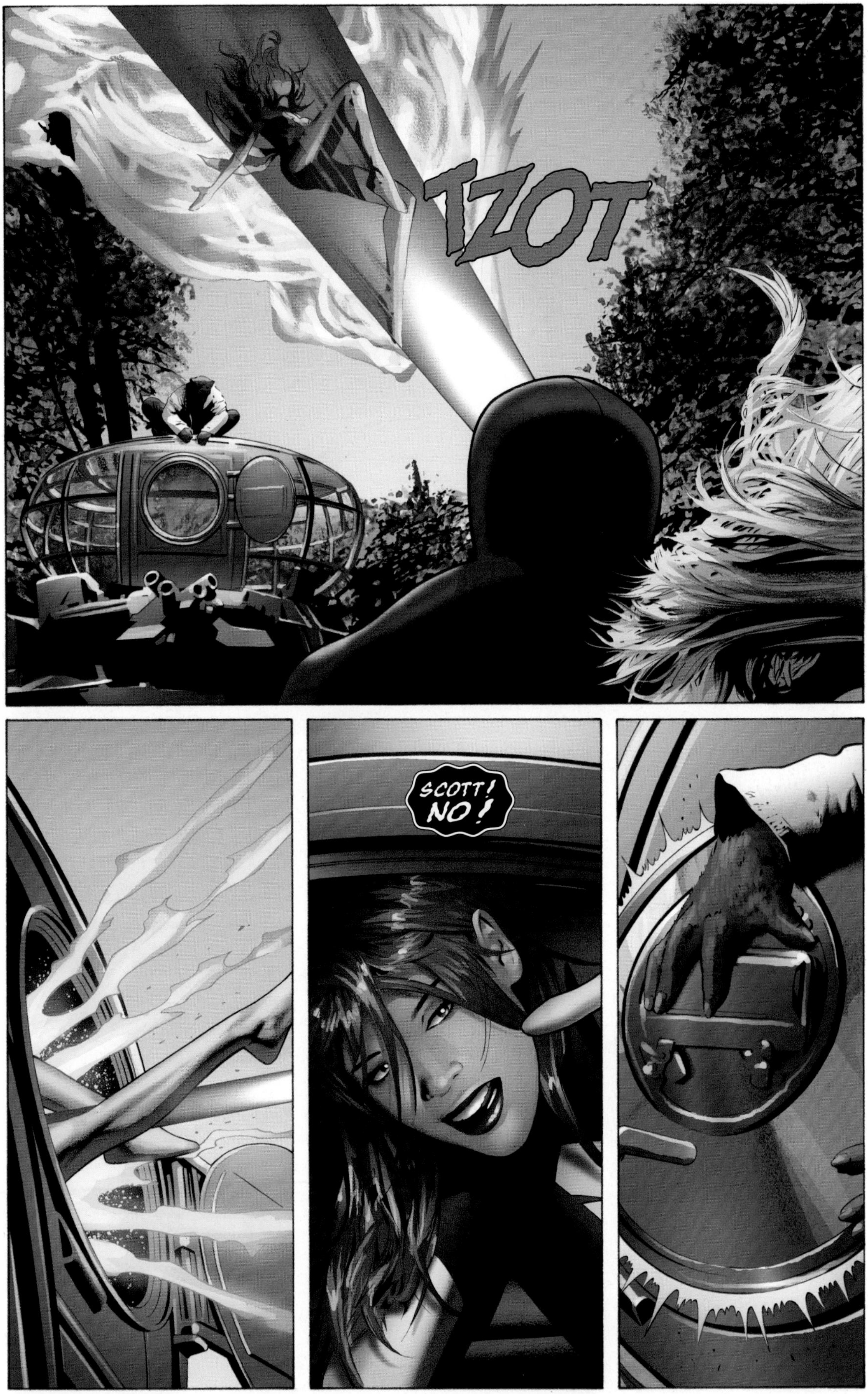
TZOT
SCOTT! NO!

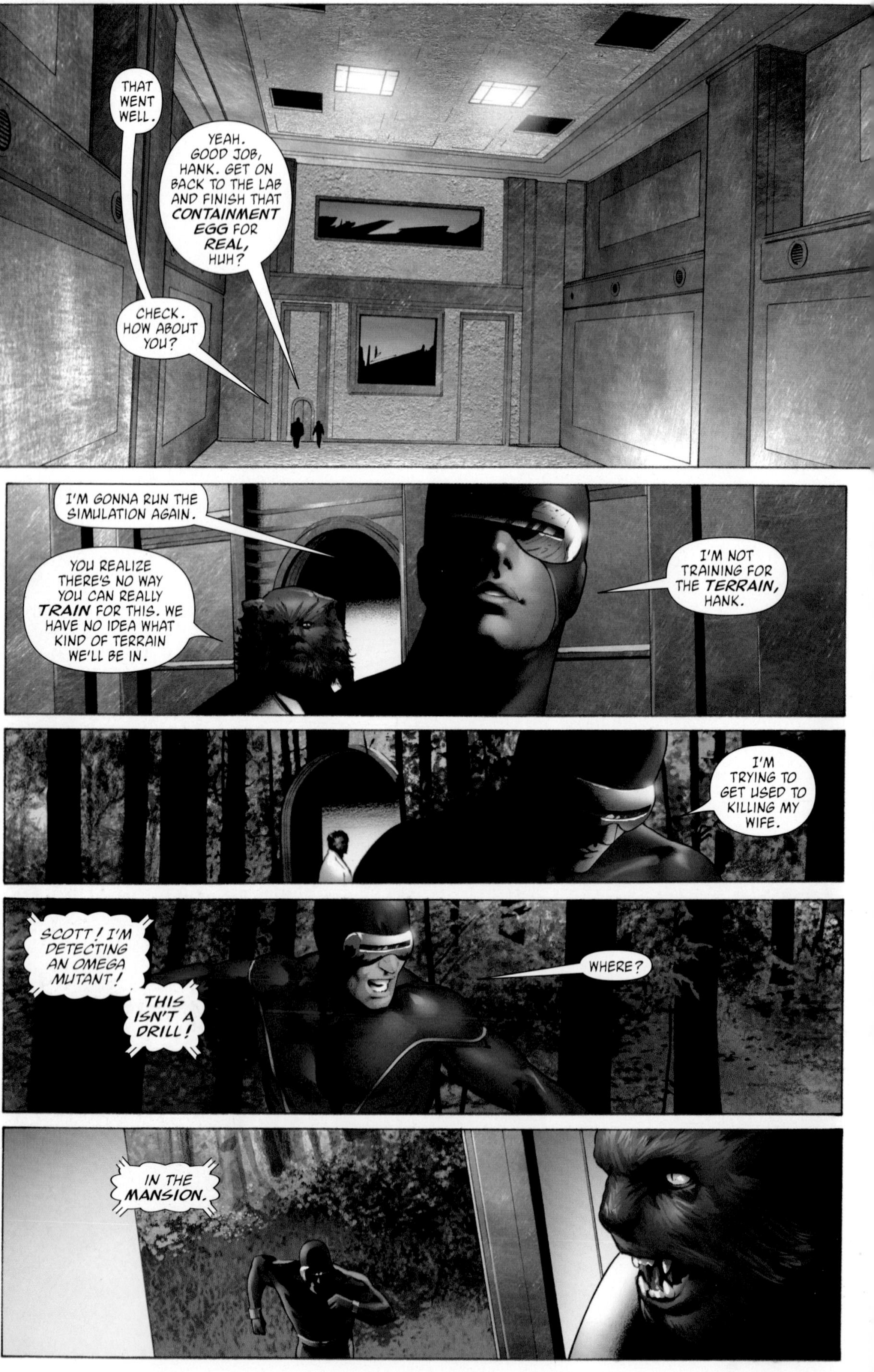
THAT WENT WELL.
YEAH. GOOD JOB, HANK. GET ON BACK TO THE LAB AND FINISH THAT CONTAINMENT EGG FOR REAL, HUH?
CHECK. HOW ABOUT YOU?
I'M GONNA RUN THE SIMULATION AGAIN.
YOU REALIZE THERE'S NO WAY YOU CAN REALLY TRAIN FOR THIS. WE HAVE NO IDEA WHAT KIND OF TERRAIN WE'LL BE IN.
I'M NOT TRAINING FOR THE TERRAIN, HANK.
I'M TRYING TO GET USED TO KILLING MY WIFE.
SCOTT! I'M DETECTING AN OMEGA MUTANT!
THIS ISN'T A DRILL!
WHERE?
IN THE MANSION.

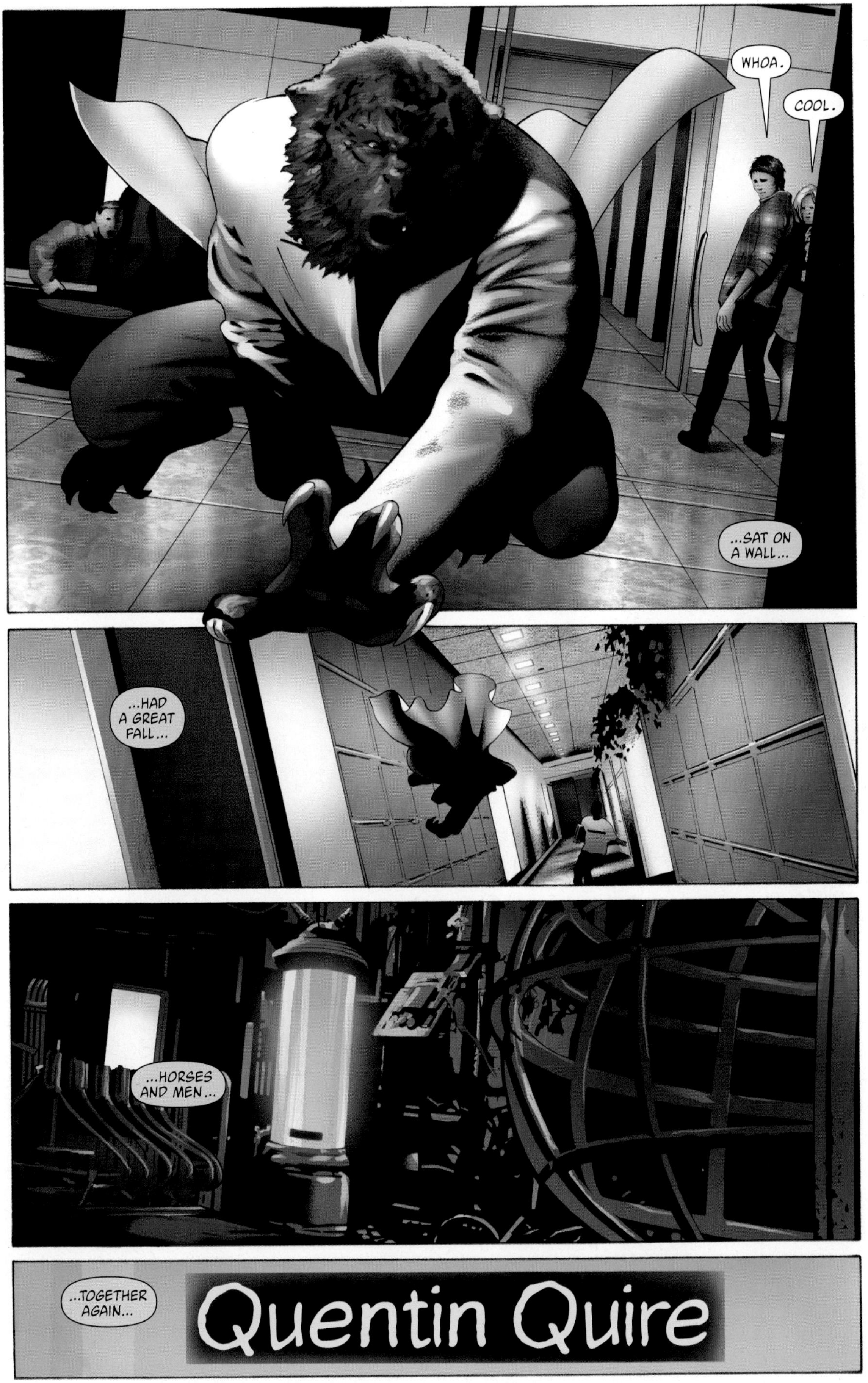
WHOA.
COOL.
...SAT ON A WALL...
...HAD A GREAT FALL...
...HORSES AND MEN...
...TOGETHER AGAIN...
Quentin Quire

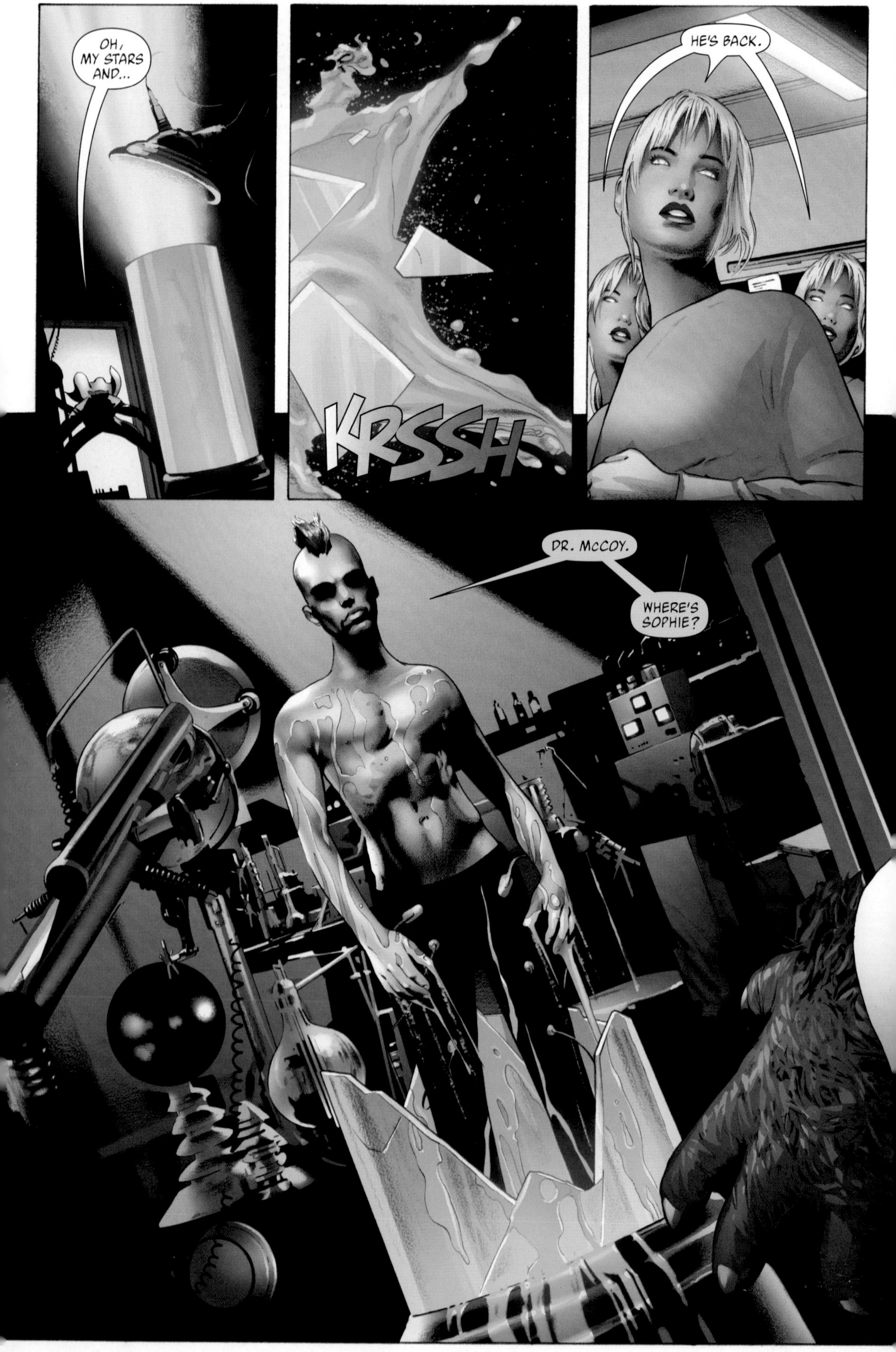
OH, MY STARS AND...
KRSSH
HE'S BACK.
DR. McCOY.
WHERE'S SOPHIE?

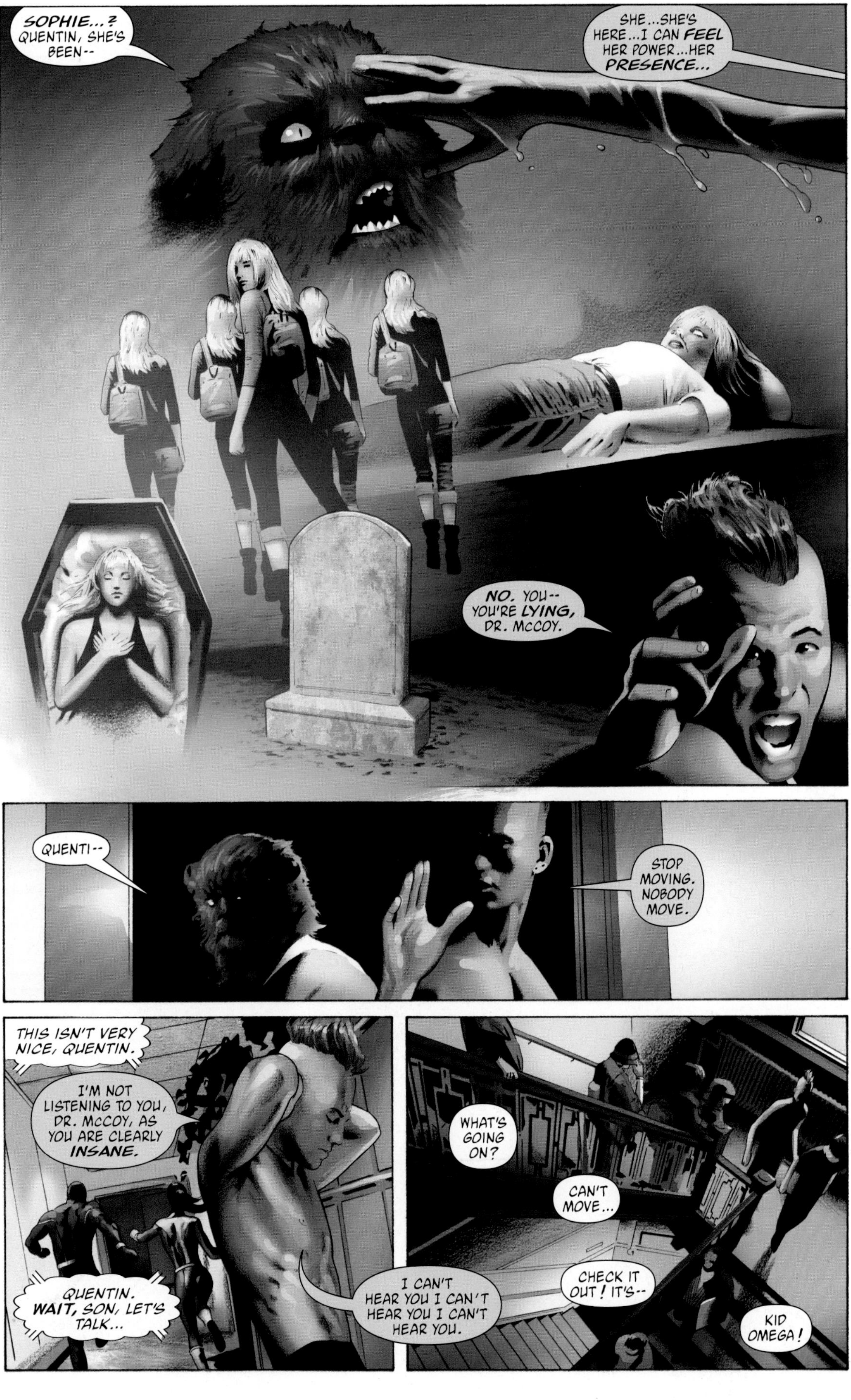
SOPHIE...? QUENTIN, SHE'S BEEN--
SHE...SHE'S HERE...I CAN FEEL HER POWER...HER PRESENCE...
NO. YOU--YOU'RE LYING, DR. McCOY.
QUENTI--
STOP MOVING. NOBODY MOVE.
THIS ISN'T VERY NICE, QUENTIN.
I'M NOT LISTENING TO YOU, DR. McCOY, AS YOU ARE CLEARLY INSANE.
QUENTIN. WAIT, SON, LET'S TALK...
I CAN'T HEAR YOU I CAN'T HEAR YOU I CAN'T HEAR YOU.
WHAT'S GOING ON?
CAN'T MOVE...
CHECK IT OUT! IT'S--
KID OMEGA!

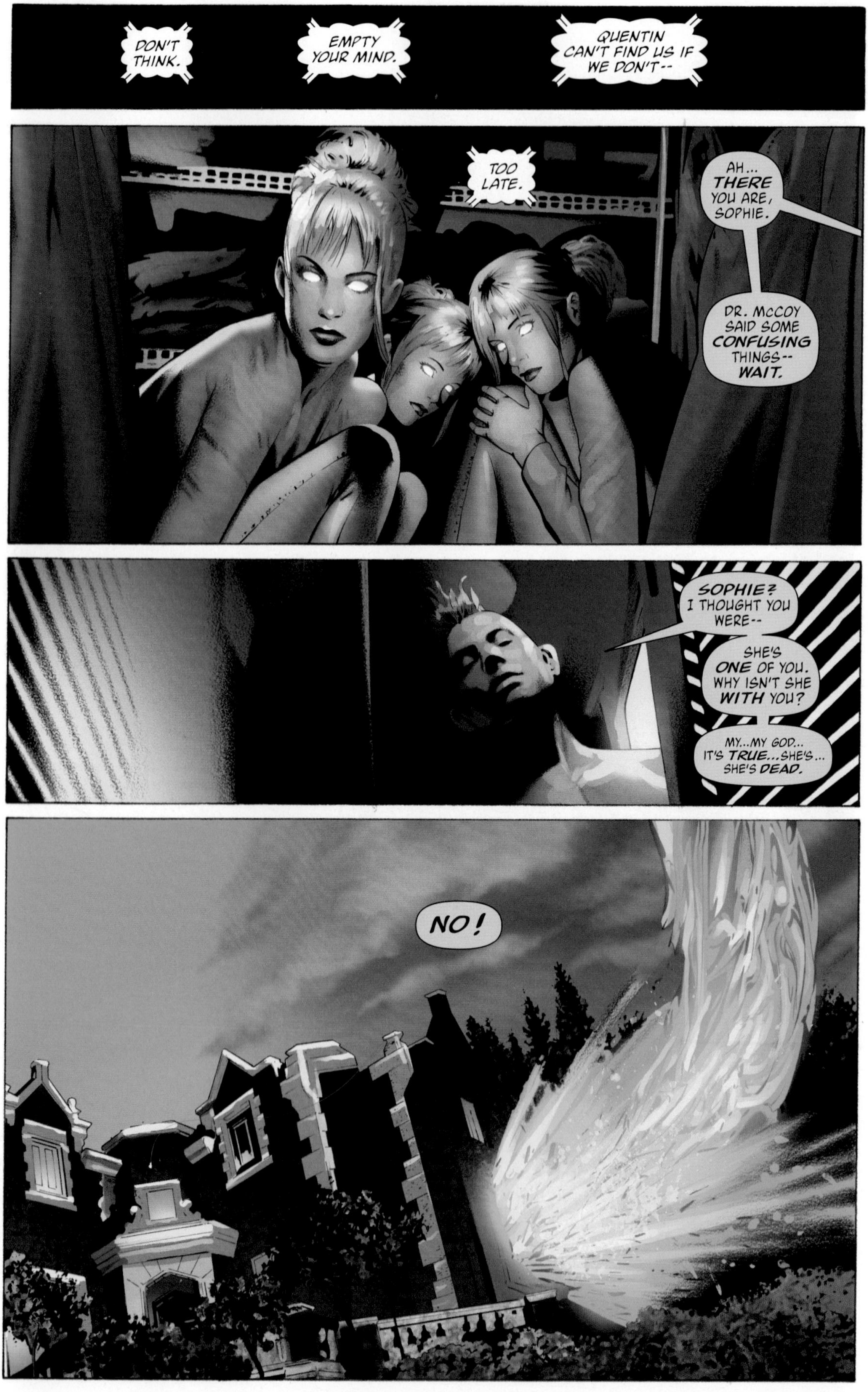
DON'T THINK.
EMPTY YOUR MIND.
QUENTIN CAN'T FIND US IF WE DON'T--
TOO LATE.
AH... THERE YOU ARE, SOPHIE.
DR. McCOY SAID SOME CONFUSING THINGS-- WAIT.
SOPHIE? I THOUGHT YOU WERE--
SHE'S ONE OF YOU. WHY ISN'T SHE WITH YOU?
MY...MY GOD... IT'S TRUE...SHE'S... SHE'S DEAD.
NO!

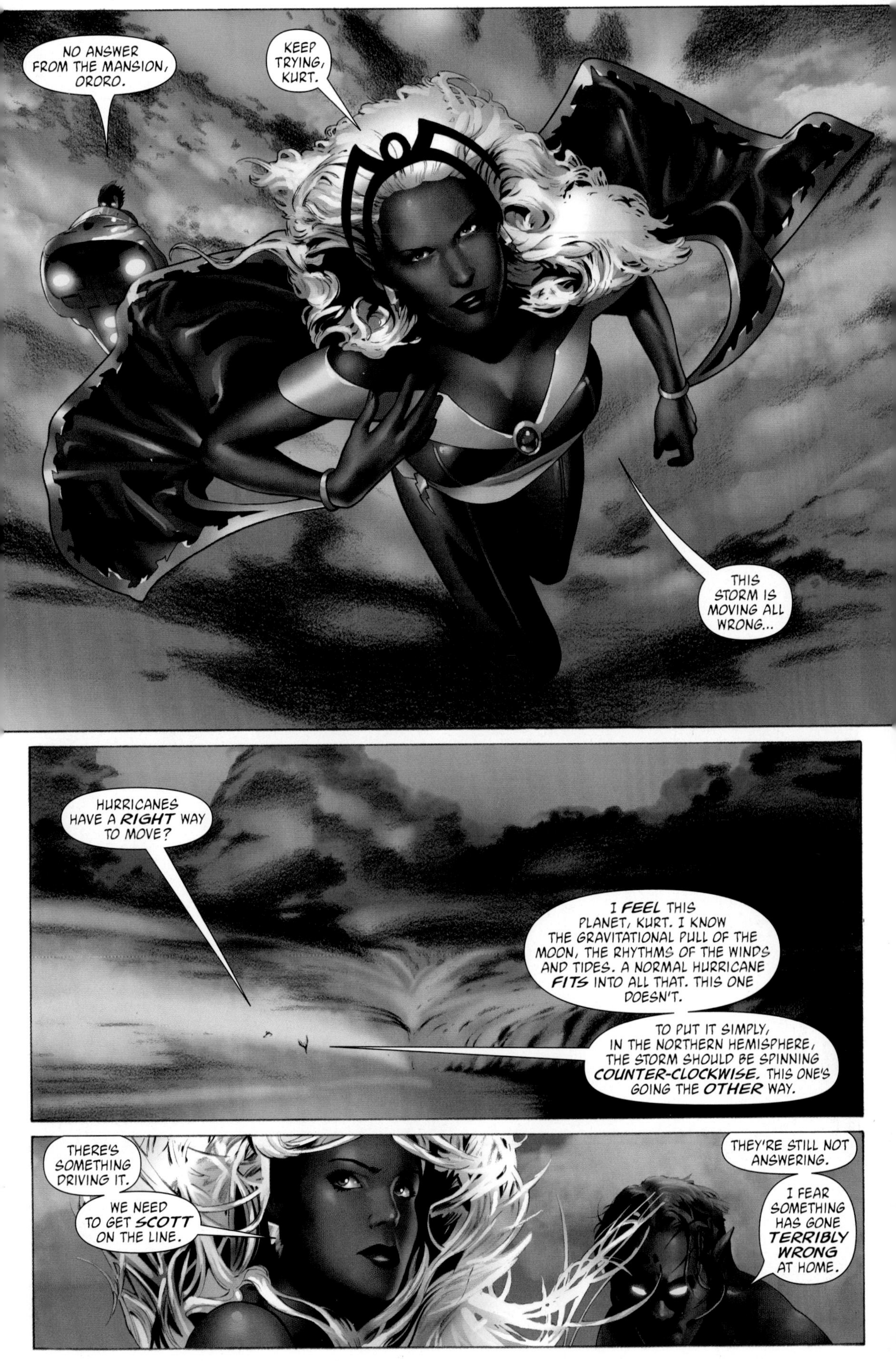
NO ANSWER FROM THE MANSION, ORORO.
KEEP TRYING, KURT.
THIS STORM IS MOVING ALL WRONG...
HURRICANES HAVE A **RIGHT** WAY TO MOVE?
I **FEEL** THIS PLANET, KURT. I KNOW THE GRAVITATIONAL PULL OF THE MOON, THE RHYTHMS OF THE WINDS AND TIDES. A NORMAL HURRICANE **FITS** INTO ALL THAT. THIS ONE DOESN'T.
TO PUT IT SIMPLY, IN THE NORTHERN HEMISPHERE, THE STORM SHOULD BE SPINNING **COUNTER-CLOCKWISE.** THIS ONE'S GOING THE **OTHER** WAY.
THERE'S SOMETHING DRIVING IT.
WE NEED TO GET **SCOTT** ON THE LINE.
THEY'RE STILL NOT ANSWERING.
I FEAR SOMETHING HAS GONE **TERRIBLY WRONG** AT HOME.

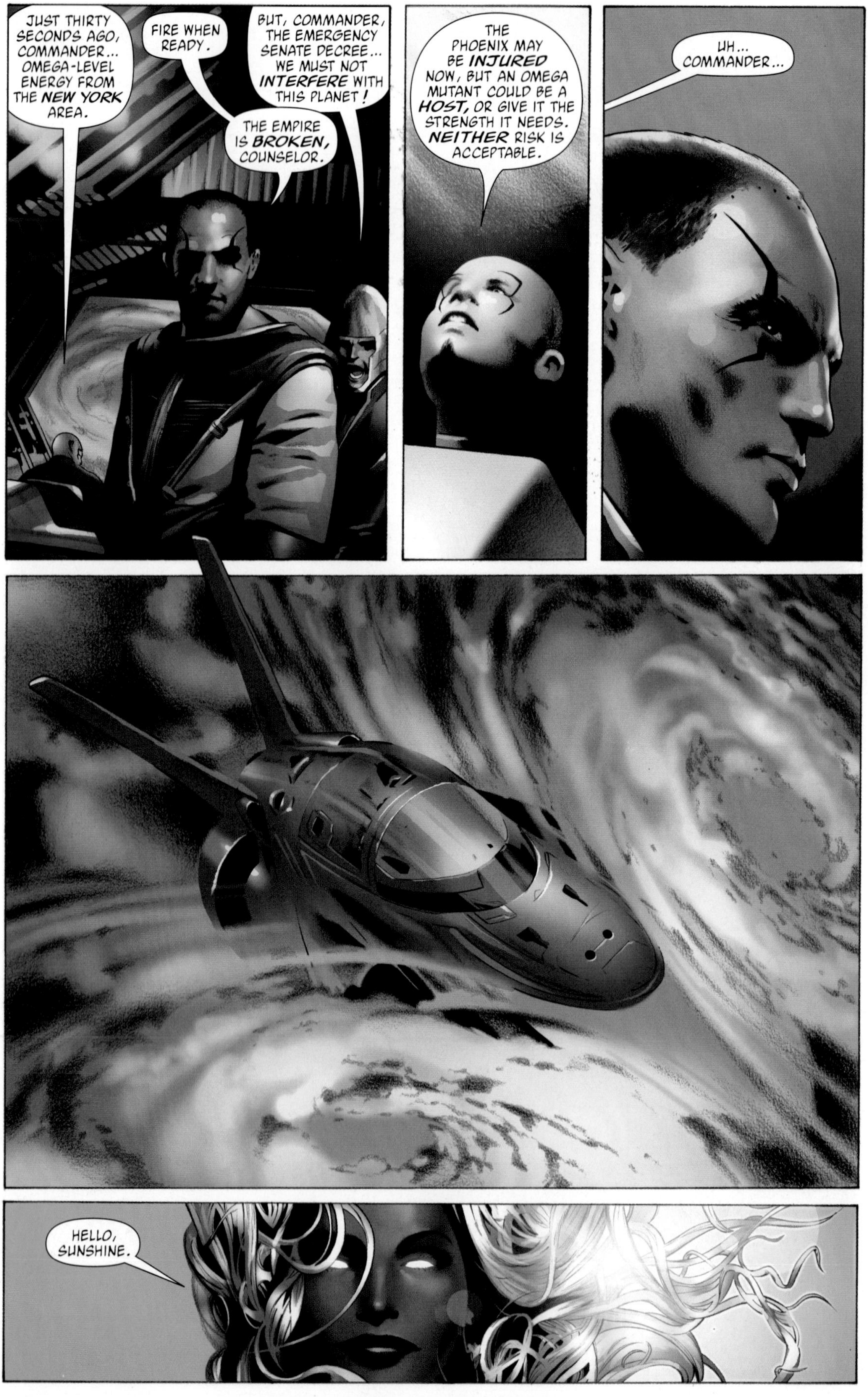
JUST THIRTY SECONDS AGO, COMMANDER... OMEGA-LEVEL ENERGY FROM THE NEW YORK AREA.
FIRE WHEN READY.
BUT, COMMANDER, THE EMERGENCY SENATE DECREE... WE MUST NOT INTERFERE WITH THIS PLANET!
THE EMPIRE IS BROKEN, COUNSELOR.
THE PHOENIX MAY BE INJURED NOW, BUT AN OMEGA MUTANT COULD BE A HOST, OR GIVE IT THE STRENGTH IT NEEDS. NEITHER RISK IS ACCEPTABLE.
UH... COMMANDER...
HELLO, SUNSHINE.

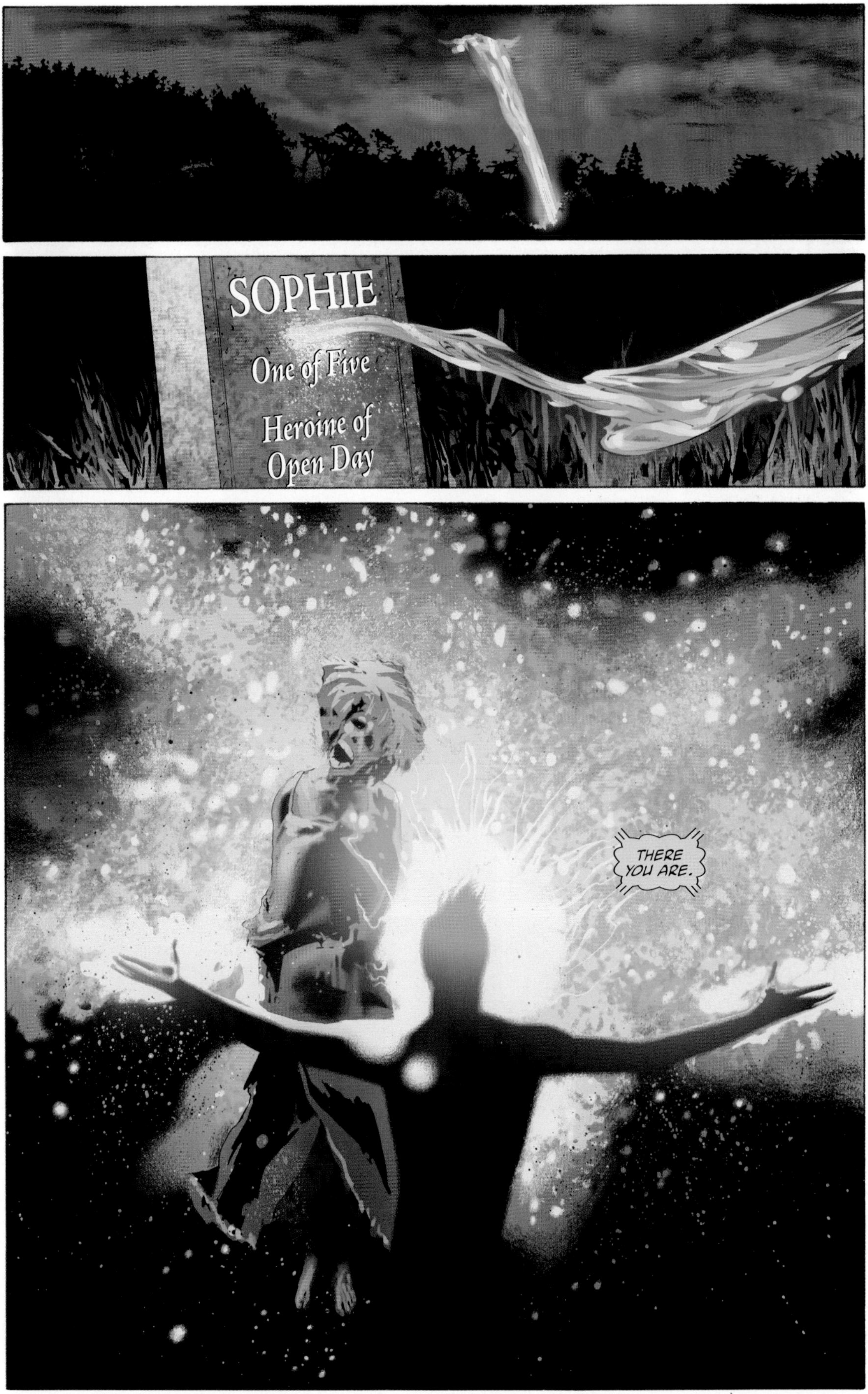
SOPHIE
One of Five
Heroine of Open Day
THERE YOU ARE.

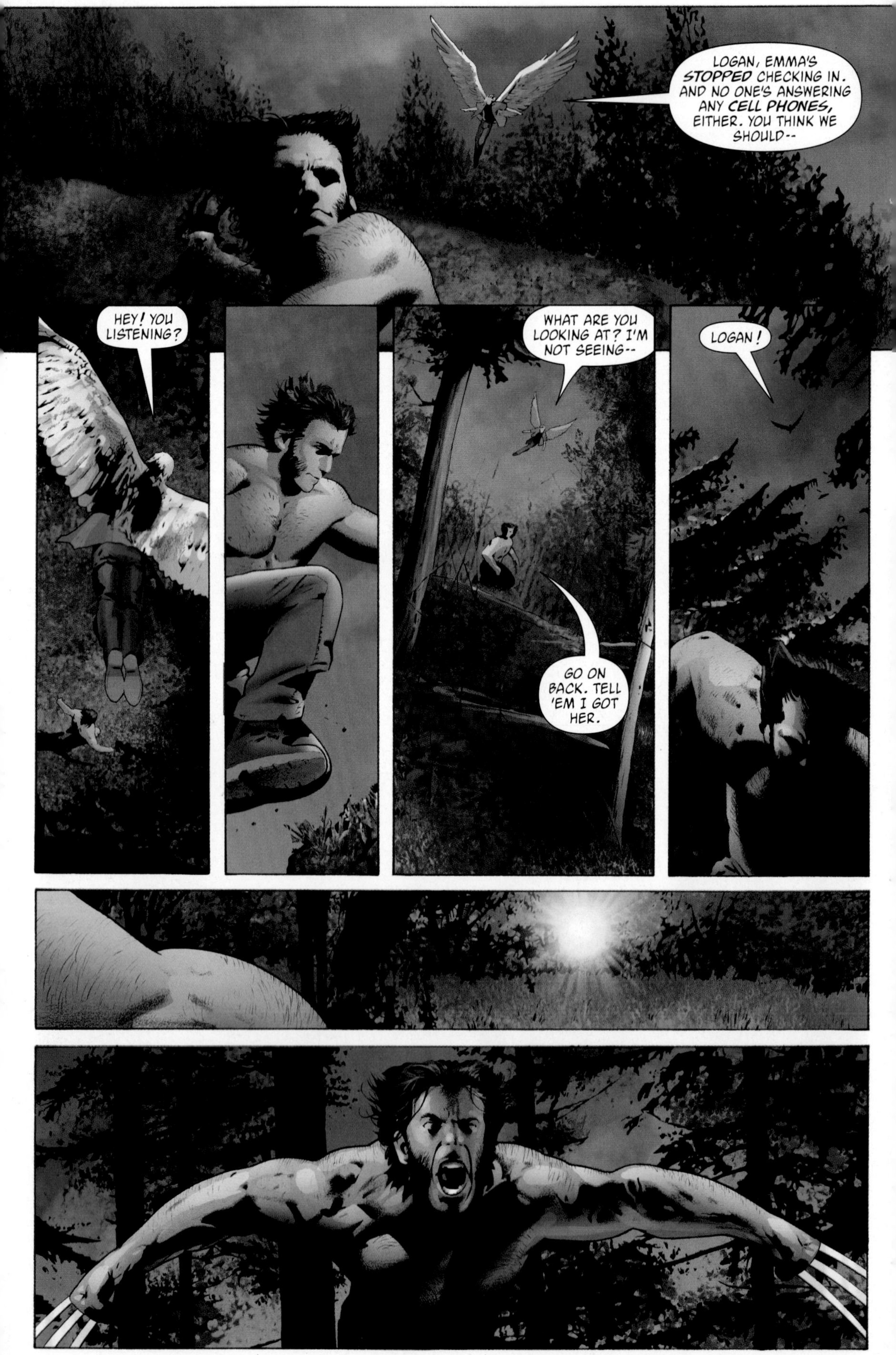
LOGAN, EMMA'S STOPPED CHECKING IN. AND NO ONE'S ANSWERING ANY CELL PHONES, EITHER. YOU THINK WE SHOULD--
HEY! YOU LISTENING?
WHAT ARE YOU LOOKING AT? I'M NOT SEEING--
GO ON BACK. TELL 'EM I GOT HER.
LOGAN!

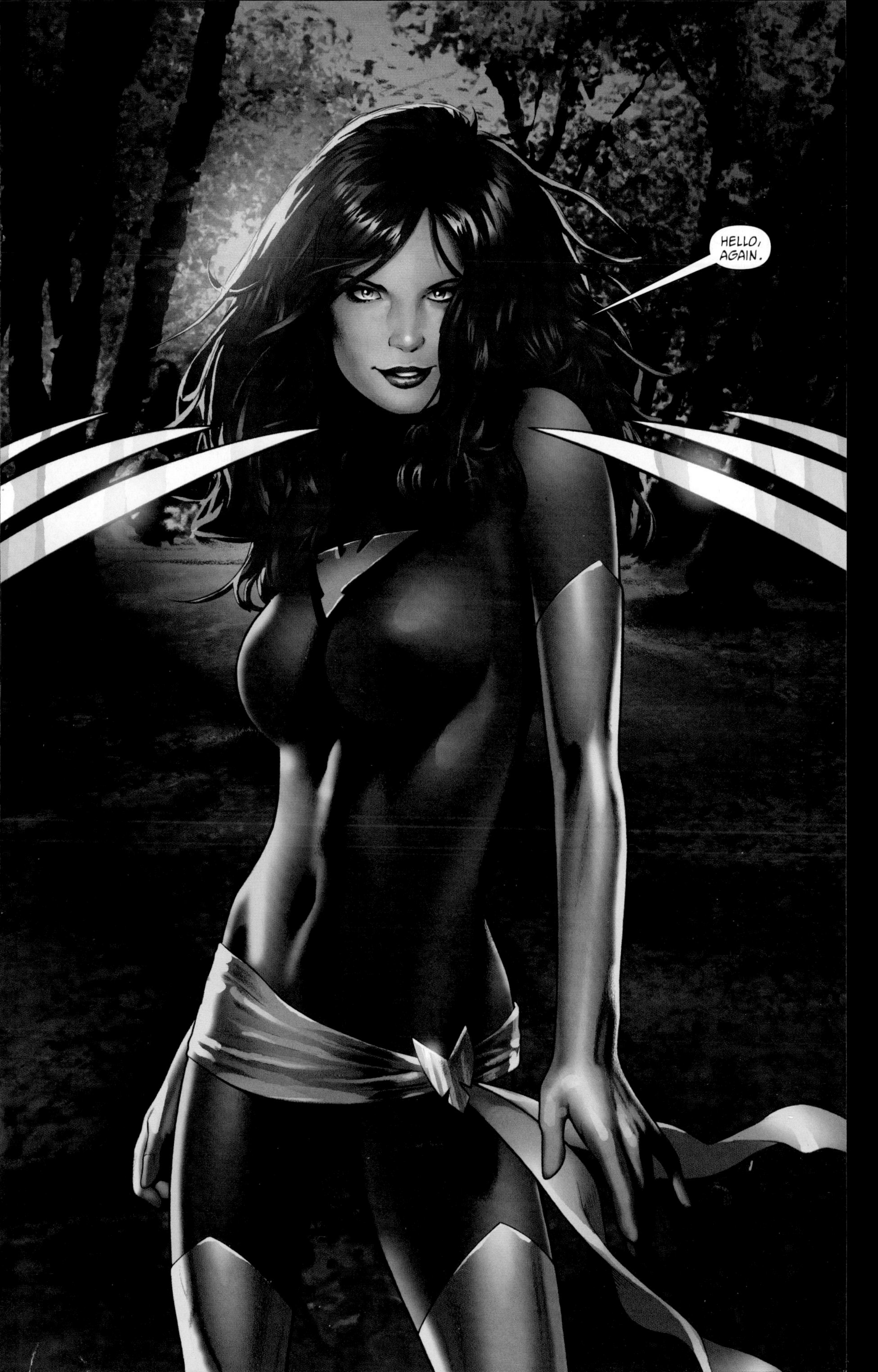
HELLO, AGAIN.

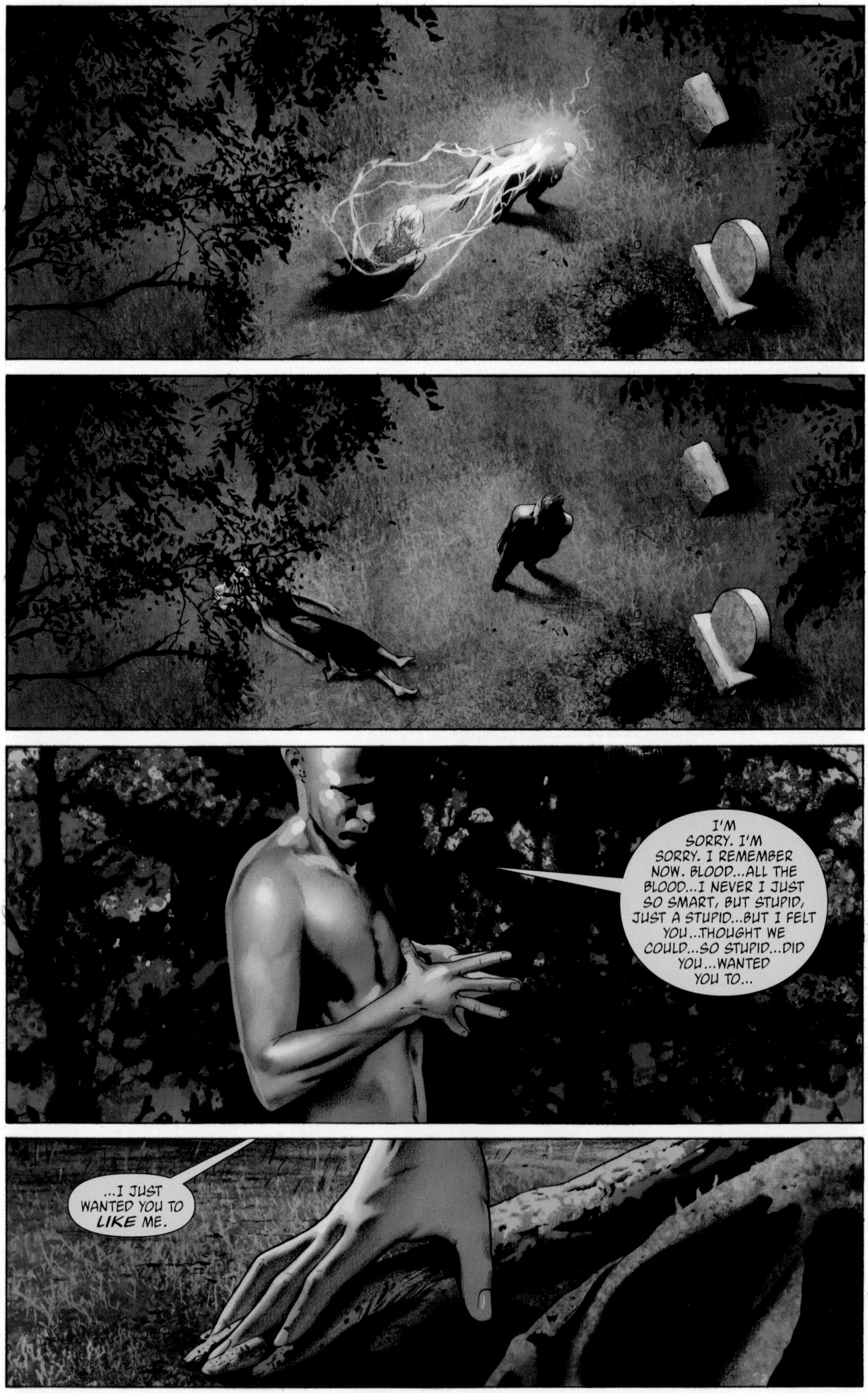
I'M SORRY. I'M SORRY. I REMEMBER NOW. BLOOD...ALL THE BLOOD...I NEVER I JUST SO SMART, BUT STUPID, JUST A STUPID...BUT I FELT YOU...THOUGHT WE COULD...SO STUPID...DID YOU...WANTED YOU TO...
...I JUST WANTED YOU TO LIKE ME.

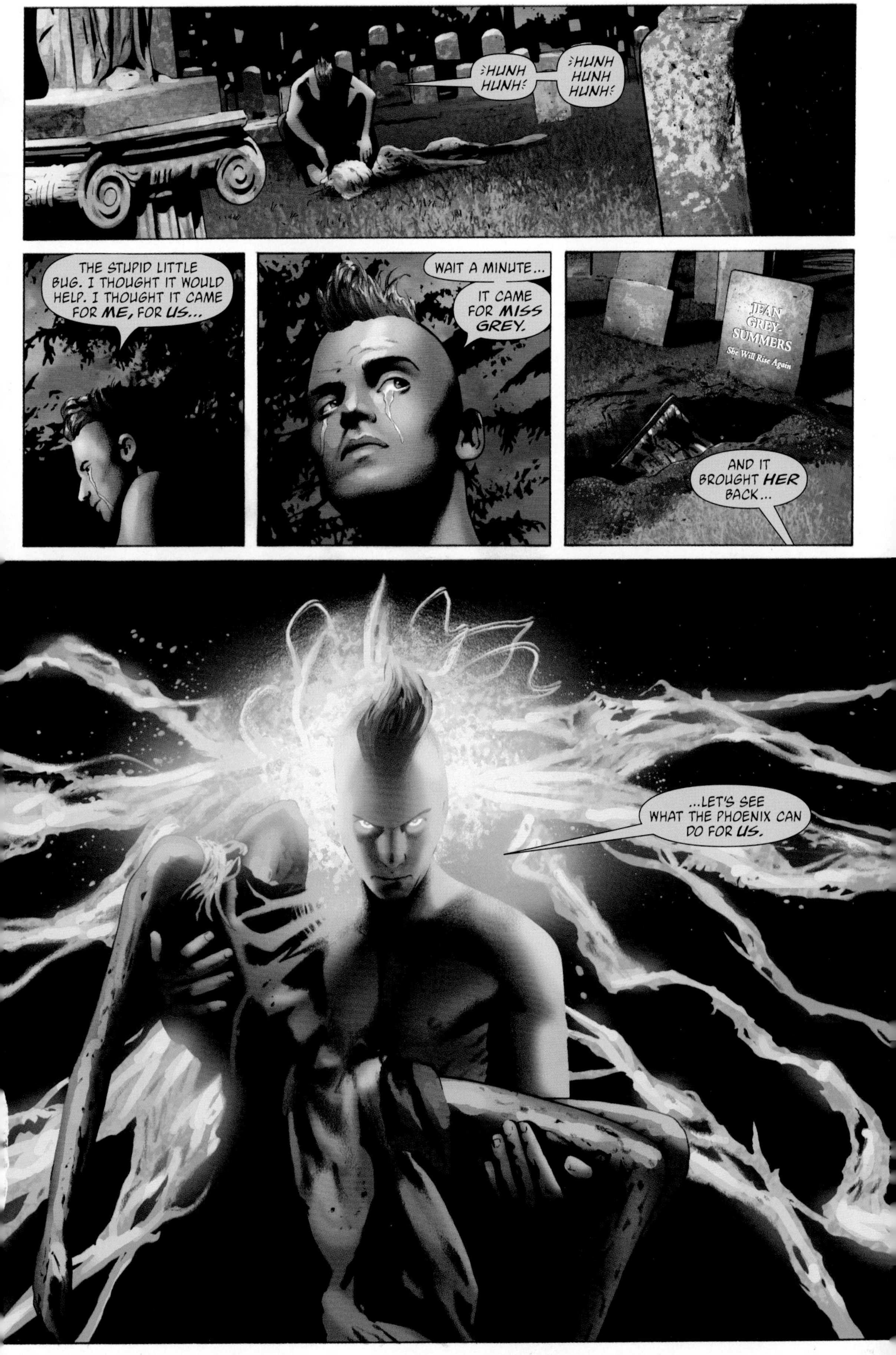
HUNH HUNH
HUNH HUNH HUNH
THE STUPID LITTLE BUG. I THOUGHT IT WOULD HELP. I THOUGHT IT CAME FOR ME, FOR US...
WAIT A MINUTE...
IT CAME FOR MISS GREY.
JEAN GREY-SUMMERS
She Will Rise Again
AND IT BROUGHT HER BACK...
...LET'S SEE WHAT THE PHOENIX CAN DO FOR US.

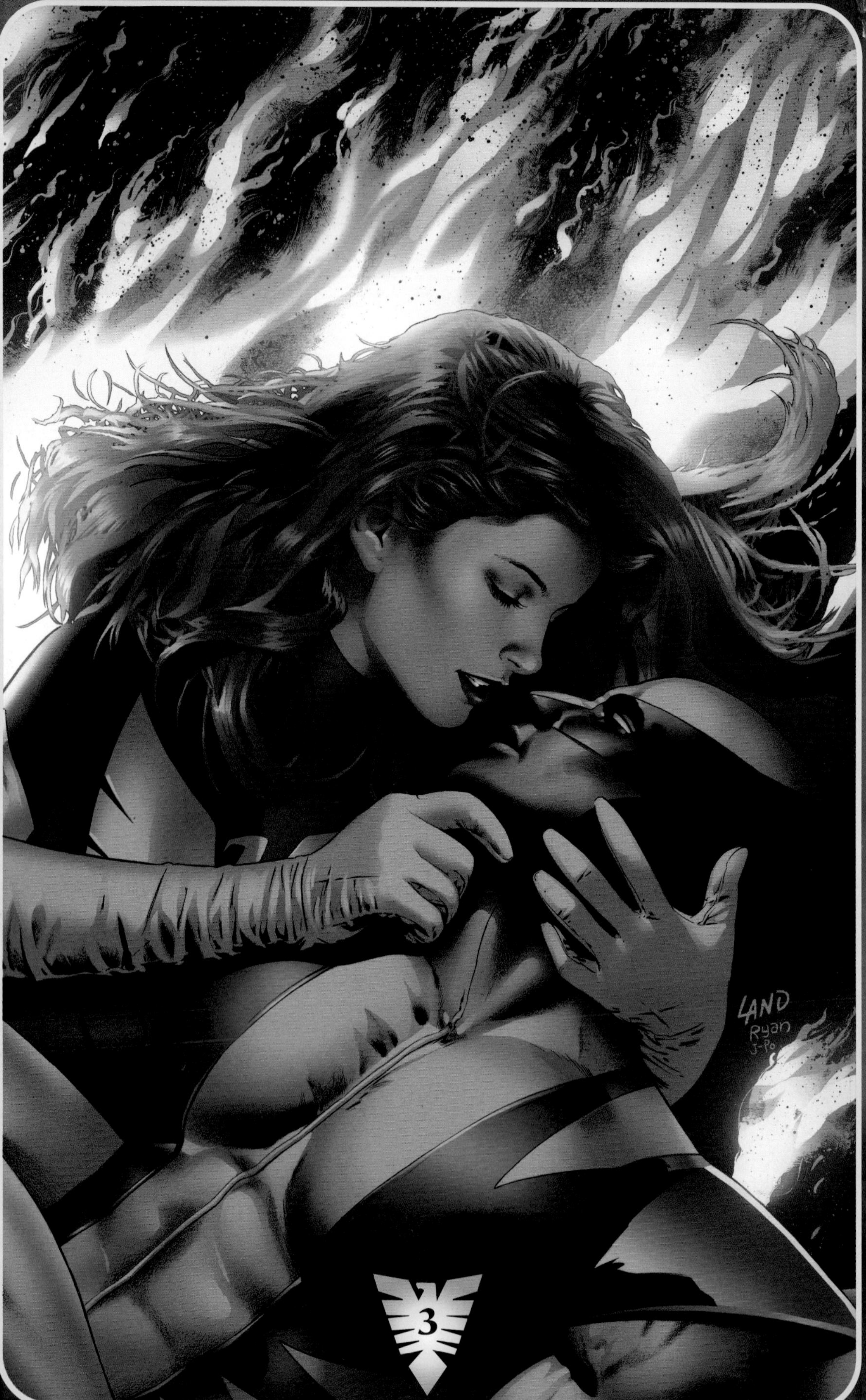
LAND
Ryan
J-Po
3

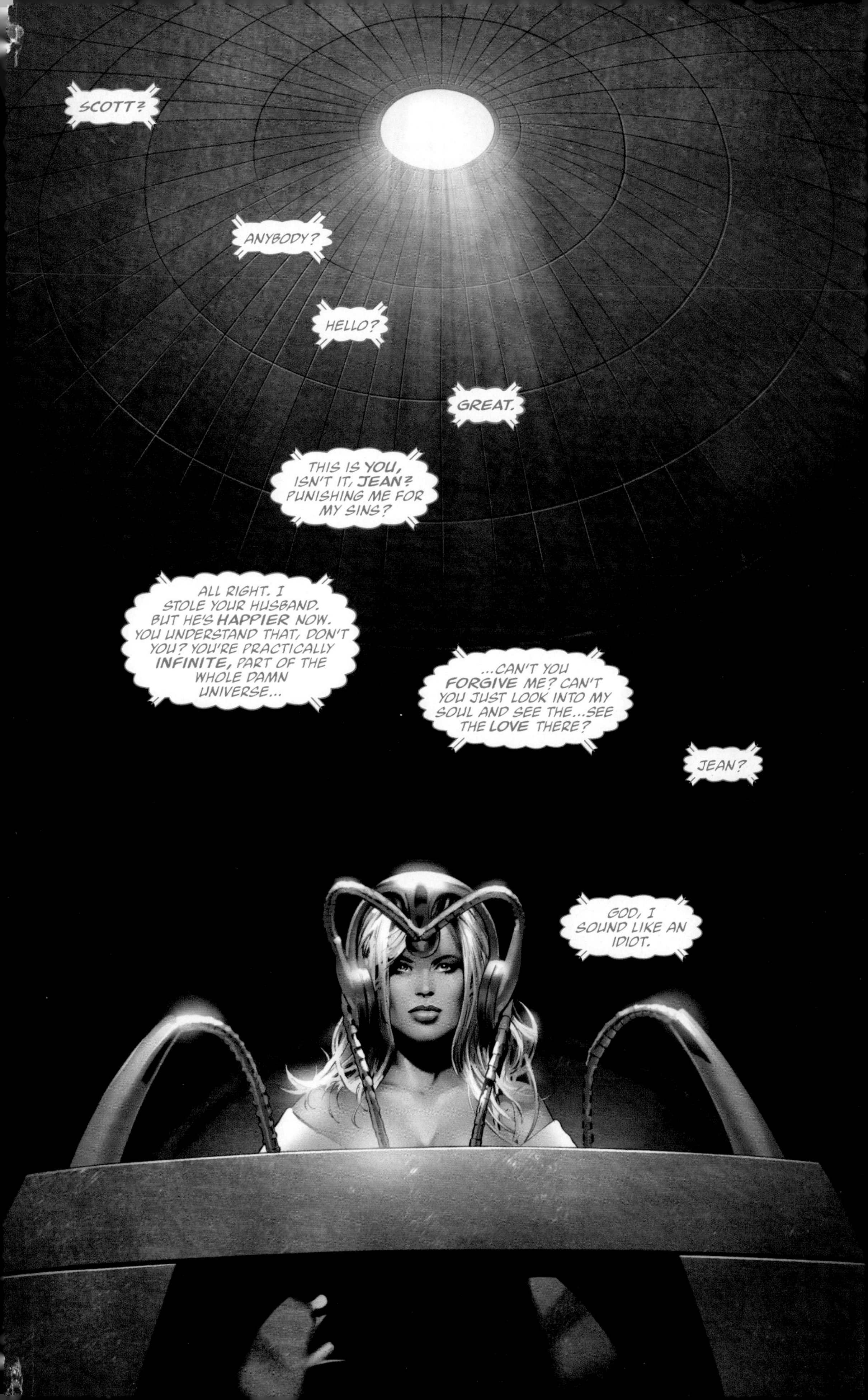
SCOTT?
ANYBODY?
HELLO?
GREAT.
THIS IS YOU, ISN'T IT, JEAN? PUNISHING ME FOR MY SINS?
ALL RIGHT. I STOLE YOUR HUSBAND. BUT HE'S HAPPIER NOW. YOU UNDERSTAND THAT, DON'T YOU? YOU'RE PRACTICALLY INFINITE, PART OF THE WHOLE DAMN UNIVERSE...
...CAN'T YOU FORGIVE ME? CAN'T YOU JUST LOOK INTO MY SOUL AND SEE THE...SEE THE LOVE THERE?
JEAN?
GOD, I SOUND LIKE AN IDIOT.

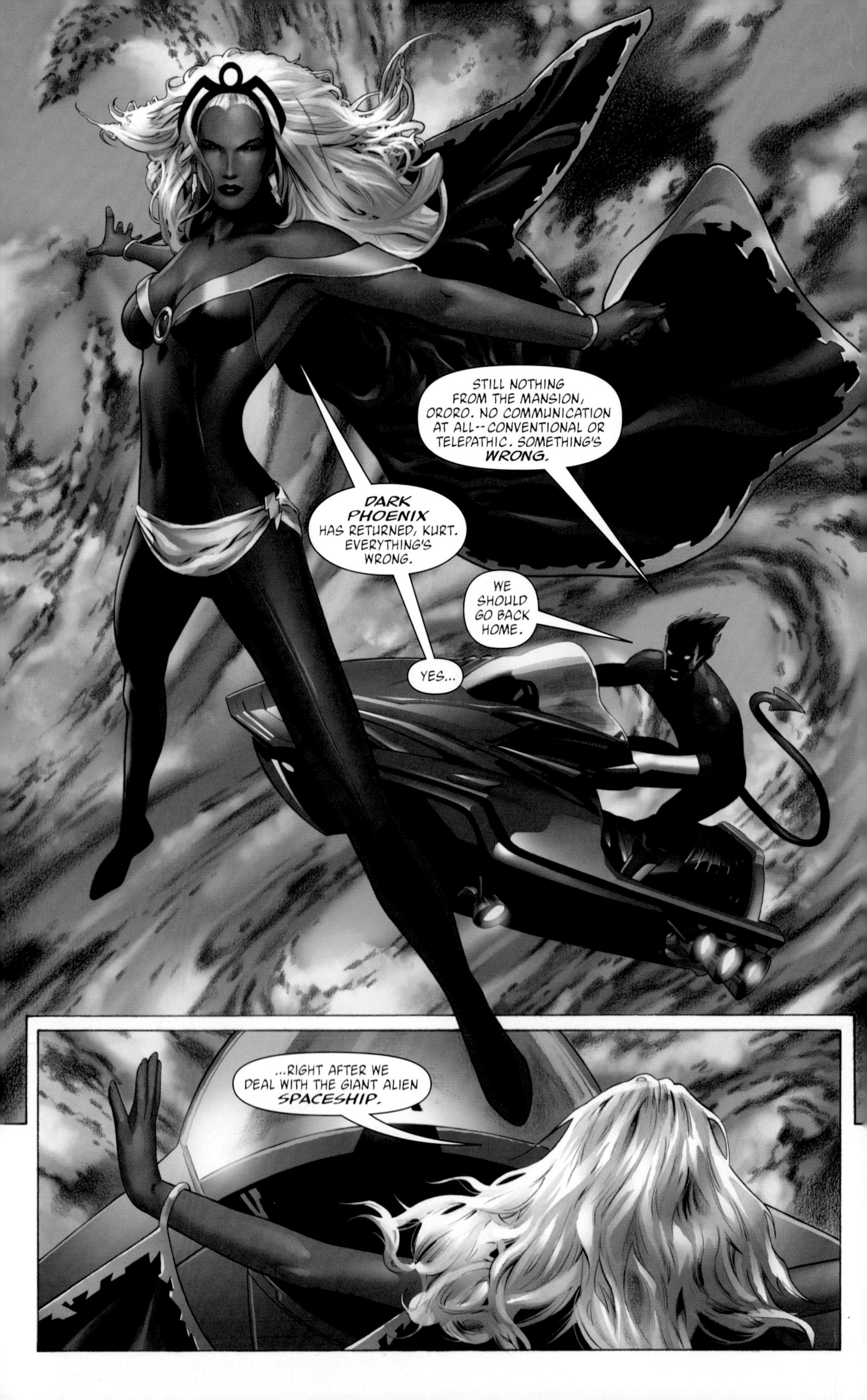
STILL NOTHING FROM THE MANSION, ORORO. NO COMMUNICATION AT ALL--CONVENTIONAL OR TELEPATHIC. SOMETHING'S WRONG.
DARK PHOENIX HAS RETURNED, KURT. EVERYTHING'S WRONG.
WE SHOULD GO BACK HOME.
YES...
...RIGHT AFTER WE DEAL WITH THE GIANT ALIEN SPACESHIP.

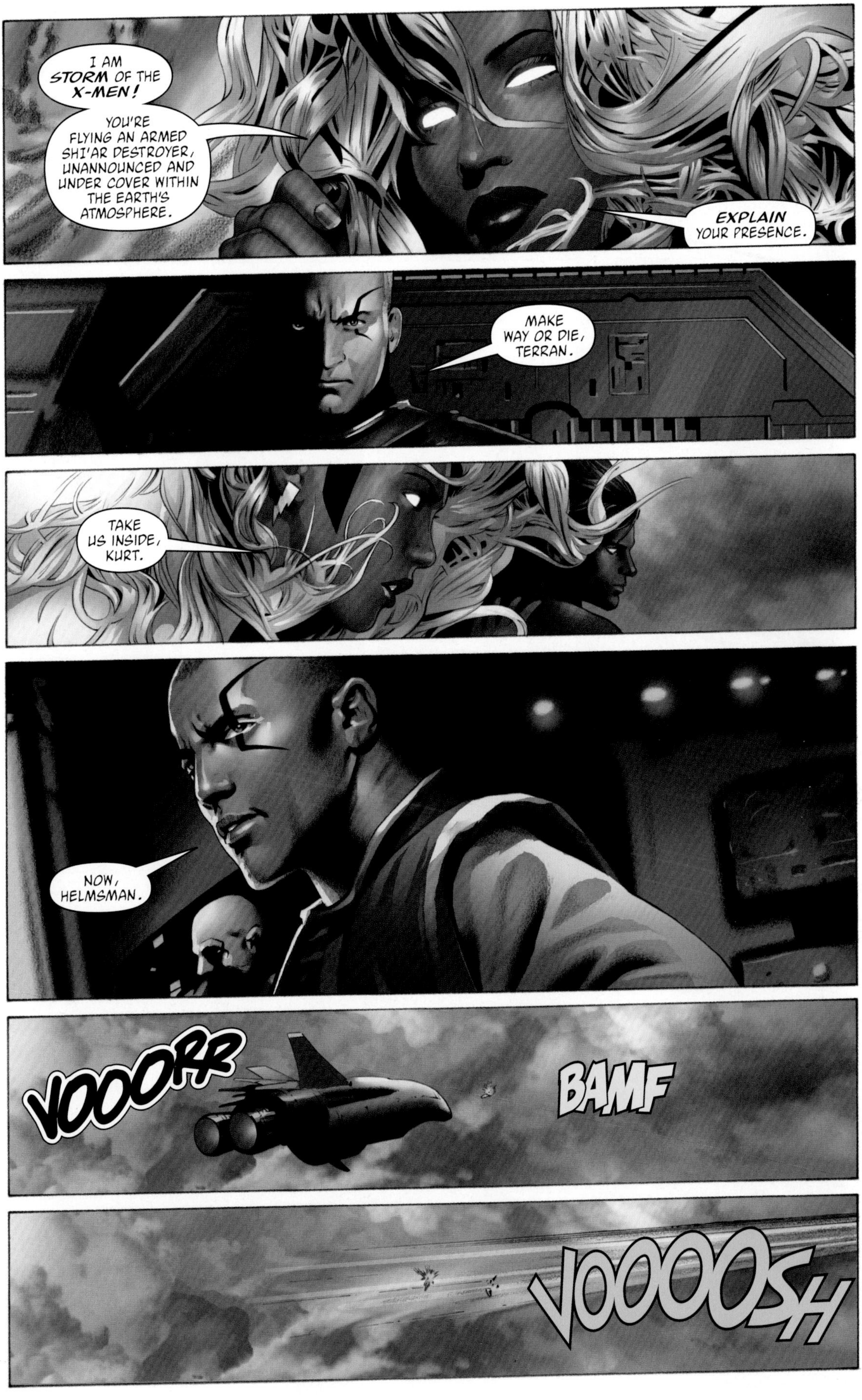
I AM STORM OF THE X-MEN!
YOU'RE FLYING AN ARMED SHI'AR DESTROYER, UNANNOUNCED AND UNDER COVER WITHIN THE EARTH'S ATMOSPHERE.
EXPLAIN YOUR PRESENCE.
MAKE WAY OR DIE, TERRAN.
TAKE US INSIDE, KURT.
NOW, HELMSMAN.
VOOORR
BAMF
VOOOOSH

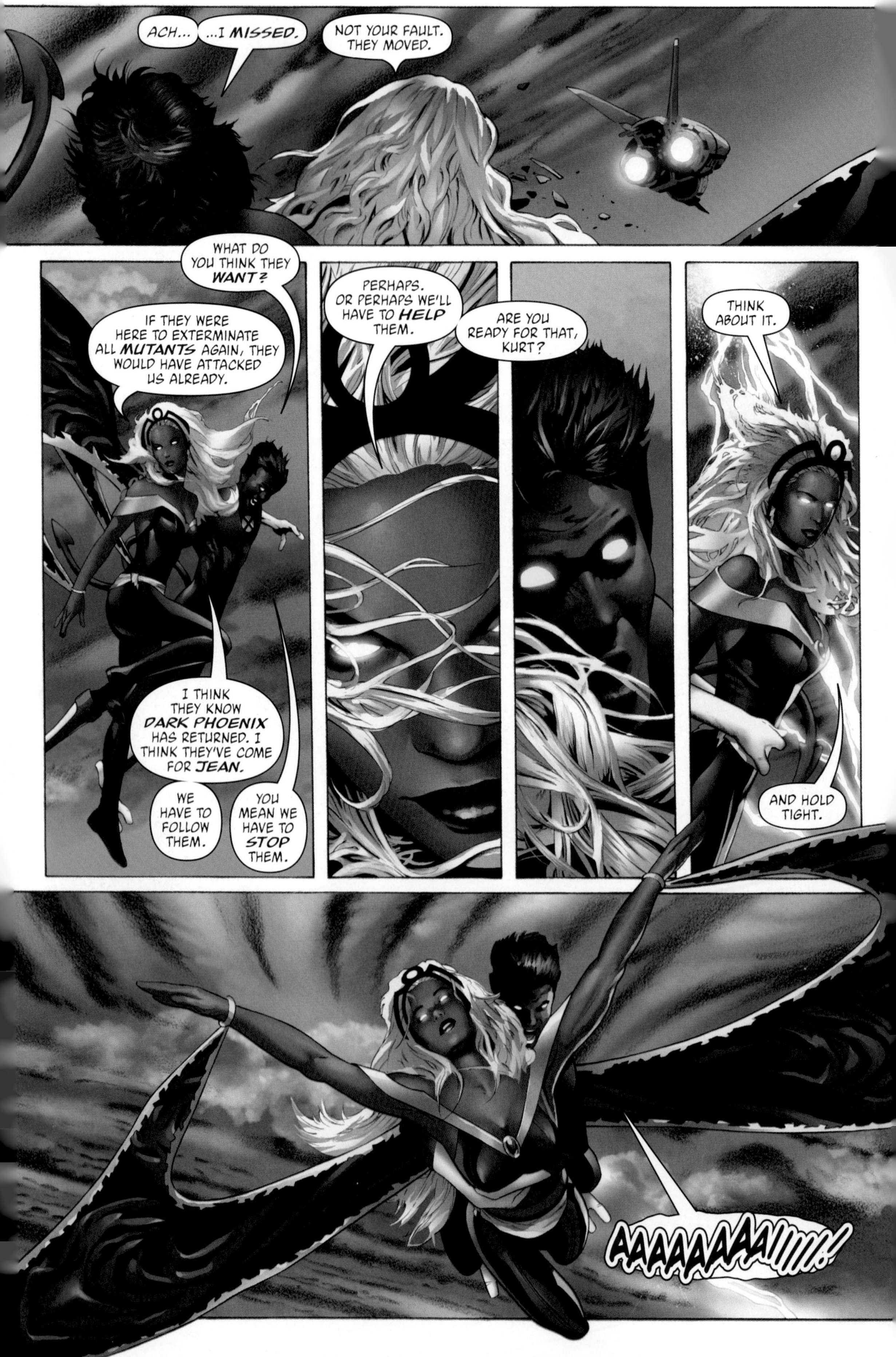
ACH...
...I MISSED.
NOT YOUR FAULT. THEY MOVED.
WHAT DO YOU THINK THEY WANT?
IF THEY WERE HERE TO EXTERMINATE ALL MUTANTS AGAIN, THEY WOULD HAVE ATTACKED US ALREADY.
I THINK THEY KNOW DARK PHOENIX HAS RETURNED. I THINK THEY'VE COME FOR JEAN.
WE HAVE TO FOLLOW THEM.
YOU MEAN WE HAVE TO STOP THEM.
PERHAPS. OR PERHAPS WE'LL HAVE TO HELP THEM.
ARE YOU READY FOR THAT, KURT?
THINK ABOUT IT.
AND HOLD TIGHT.
AAAAAAAA!!!!!!!

THIS IS SO PASSIVE-AGGRESSIVE IT'S ACTUALLY KIND OF EMBARRASSING. IF YOU WANT TO FIGHT, JEAN, WHY DON'T WE JUST *FIGHT*?

OF COURSE, YOU'D ATOMIZE ME WITHIN NANOSECONDS, SO I DON'T KNOW WHY I'M SUGGESTING THIS, BUT MAYBE I'M GOING A LITTLE *INSANE* BEING FROZEN IN THE DARK WITH **NO IDEA** WHEN OR IF I'LL EVER SEE OR HEAR ANOTHER PERSON'S FACE OR THOUGHT EVER AGAIN SO PLEASE **FORGIVE** ME IF--

AAAAH!

EMMA?

SCOTT!

ARE YOU ALL RIGHT?

I'M FINE. STAY THERE-- I NEED YOU IN CEREBRA.

WHERE'S JEAN?

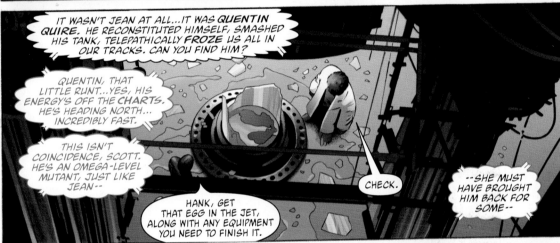

IT WASN'T JEAN AT ALL...IT WAS *QUENTIN QUIRE*. HE RECONSTITUTED HIMSELF, SMASHED HIS TANK, TELEPATHICALLY **FROZE** US ALL IN OUR TRACKS. CAN YOU FIND HIM?

QUENTIN, THAT LITTLE RUNT...YES, HIS ENERGY'S OFF THE **CHARTS**. HE'S HEADING NORTH... INCREDIBLY FAST.

THIS ISN'T COINCIDENCE, SCOTT. HE'S AN OMEGA-LEVEL MUTANT, JUST LIKE JEAN--

HANK, GET THAT EGG IN THE JET, ALONG WITH ANY EQUIPMENT YOU NEED TO FINISH IT.

CHECK.

--SHE MUST HAVE BROUGHT HIM BACK FOR SOME--

AAAAGH!

EMMA, WHAT'S THE MATTER?

ANGEL... SCREAMING IN MY HEAD... MESSAGE FROM LOGAN...

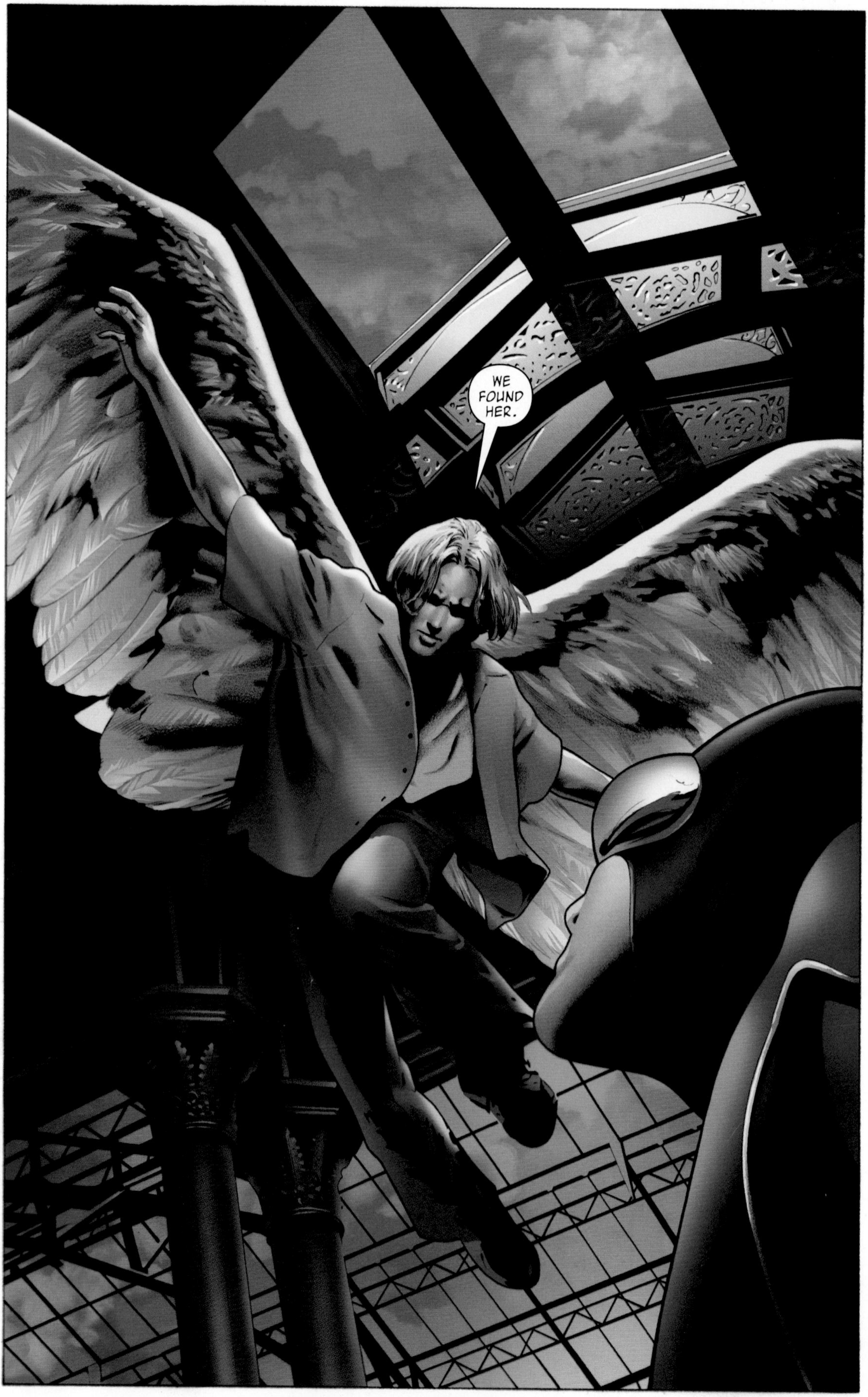
WE FOUND HER.

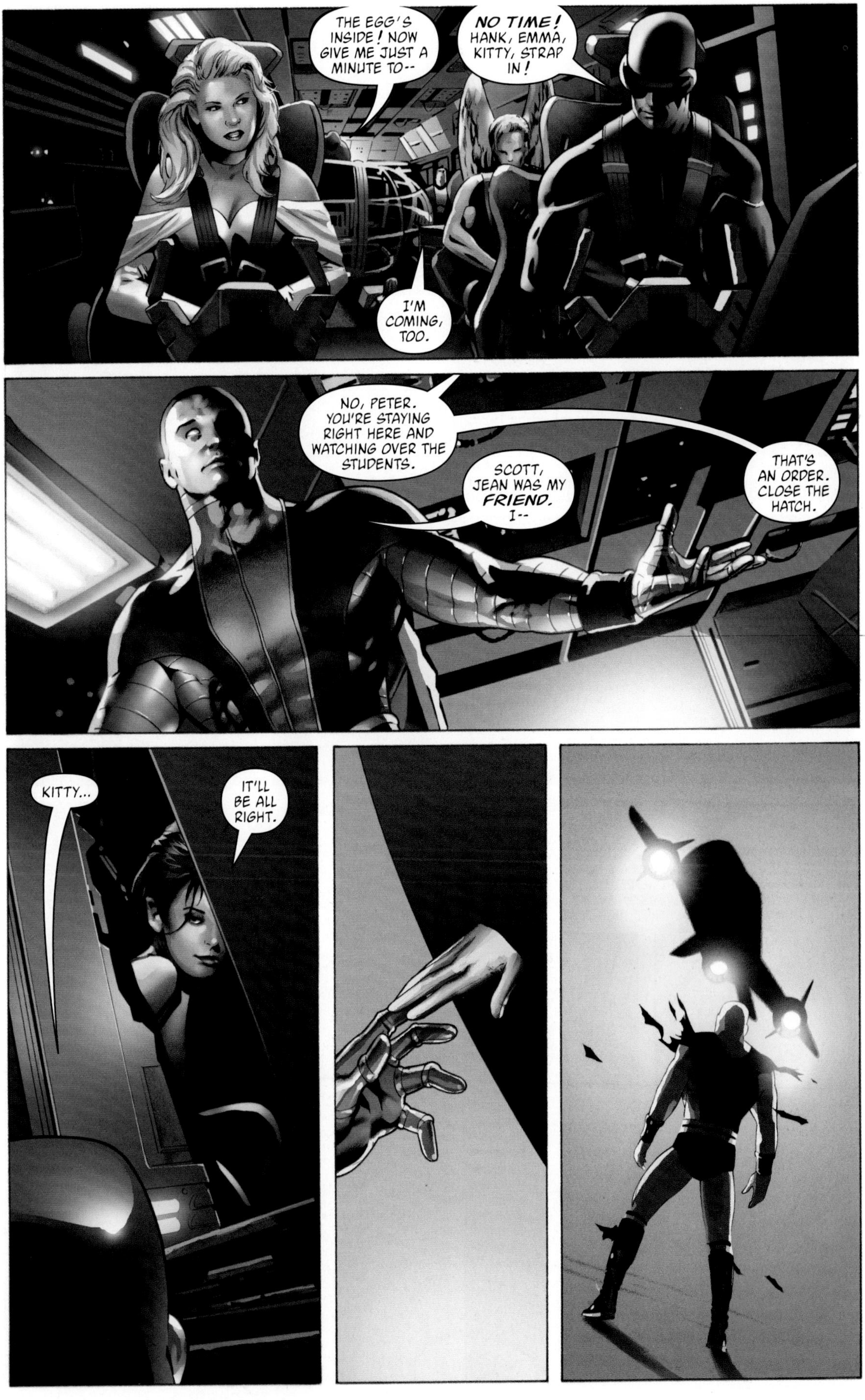
THE EGG'S INSIDE! NOW GIVE ME JUST A MINUTE TO--
NO TIME! HANK, EMMA, KITTY, STRAP IN!
I'M COMING, TOO.
NO, PETER. YOU'RE STAYING RIGHT HERE AND WATCHING OVER THE STUDENTS.
SCOTT, JEAN WAS MY FRIEND. I--
THAT'S AN ORDER. CLOSE THE HATCH.
KITTY...
IT'LL BE ALL RIGHT.

"WE COULD HAVE USED HIM, SCOTT."

"I KNOW, WARREN. I'D WANT HIM AT MY SIDE IN ANY OTHER FIGHT. BUT HE HAD A CHANCE TO KILL DARK PHOENIX THE LAST TIME AROUND.

"AND HE PULLED HIS PUNCH."

HE WASN'T THE ONLY ONE.

WE CAN'T MAKE THOSE KINDS OF MISTAKES AGAIN. OR ALL OF US--EVERY LIVING CREATURE ON THIS PLANET--COULD PAY THE PRICE.

I KNOW WHAT YOU'RE THINKING. MAYBE IT'S REALLY JEAN WE'RE FACING. MAYBE WE CAN REACH HER. MAYBE WE CAN SAVE HER.

AND MAYBE YOUR FEARLESS LEADER KEEPS INSISTING IT'S DARK PHOENIX BECAUSE HE'D RATHER FIGHT A MONSTER THAN FACE HIS WIFE.

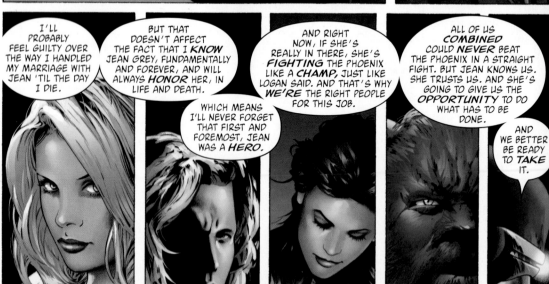

I'LL PROBABLY FEEL GUILTY OVER THE WAY I HANDLED MY MARRIAGE WITH JEAN 'TIL THE DAY I DIE.

BUT THAT DOESN'T AFFECT THE FACT THAT I KNOW JEAN GREY, FUNDAMENTALLY AND FOREVER, AND WILL ALWAYS HONOR HER, IN LIFE AND DEATH.

WHICH MEANS I'LL NEVER FORGET THAT FIRST AND FOREMOST, JEAN WAS A HERO.

AND RIGHT NOW, IF SHE'S REALLY IN THERE, SHE'S FIGHTING THE PHOENIX LIKE A CHAMP, JUST LIKE LOGAN SAID. AND THAT'S WHY WE'RE THE RIGHT PEOPLE FOR THIS JOB.

ALL OF US COMBINED COULD NEVER BEAT THE PHOENIX IN A STRAIGHT FIGHT. BUT JEAN KNOWS US. SHE TRUSTS US. AND SHE'S GOING TO GIVE US THE OPPORTUNITY TO DO WHAT HAS TO BE DONE.

AND WE BETTER BE READY TO TAKE IT.

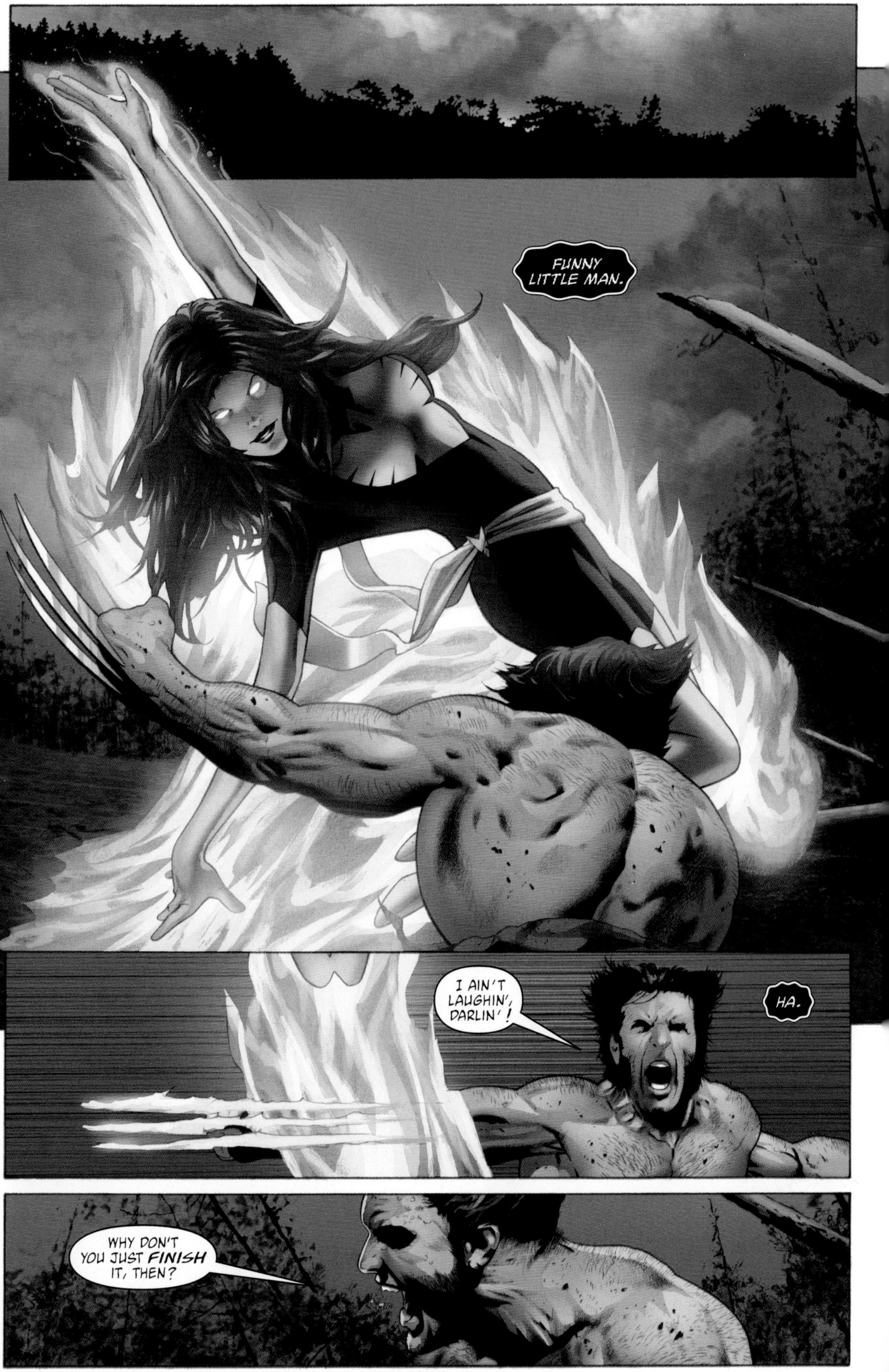
FUNNY LITTLE MAN.
I AIN'T LAUGHIN', DARLIN'!
HA.
WHY DON'T YOU JUST FINISH IT, THEN?

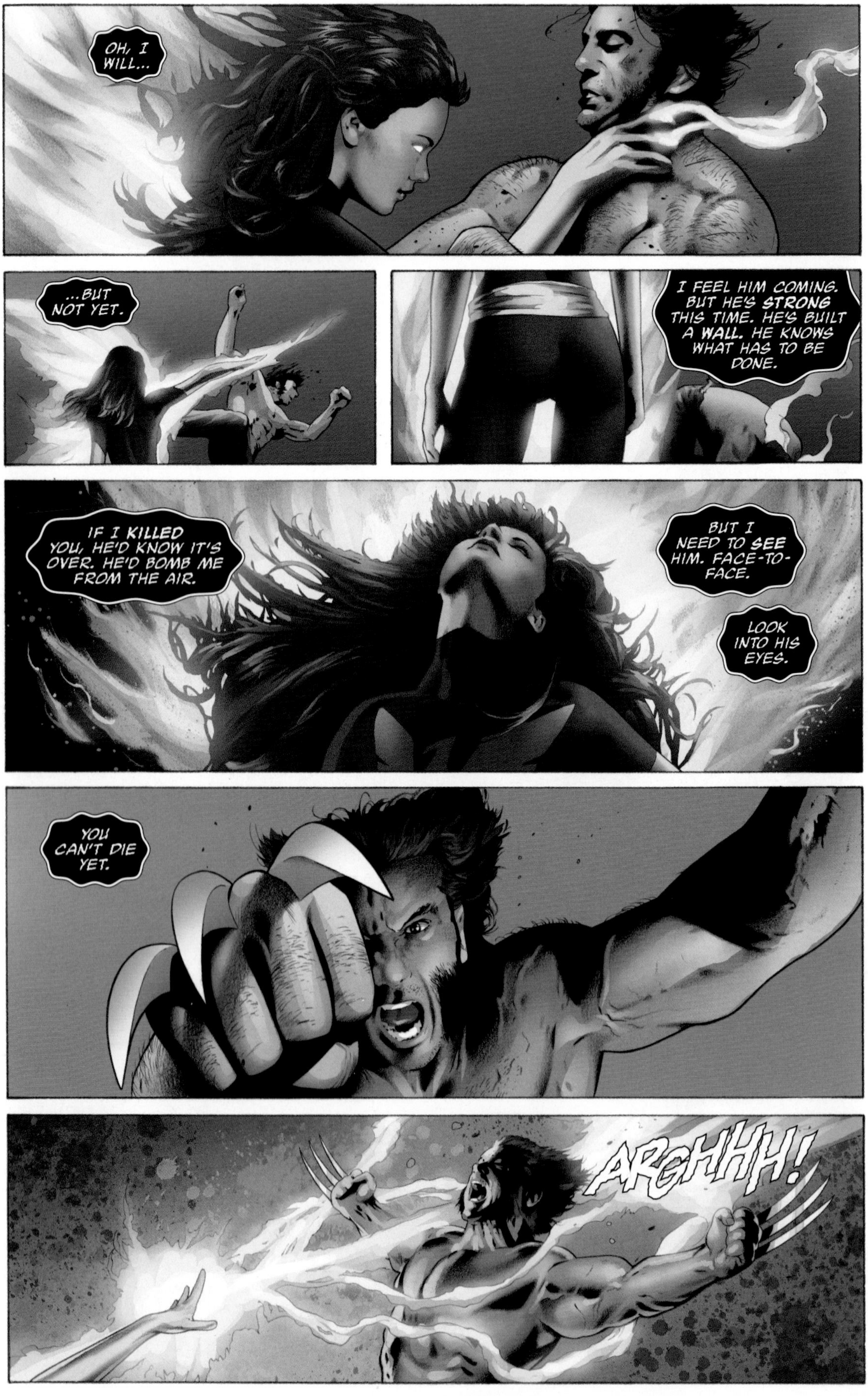
OH, I WILL...
...BUT NOT YET.
I FEEL HIM COMING. BUT HE'S STRONG THIS TIME. HE'S BUILT A WALL. HE KNOWS WHAT HAS TO BE DONE.
IF I KILLED YOU, HE'D KNOW IT'S OVER. HE'D BOMB ME FROM THE AIR.
BUT I NEED TO SEE HIM. FACE-TO-FACE.
LOOK INTO HIS EYES.
YOU CAN'T DIE YET.
ARGHHH!

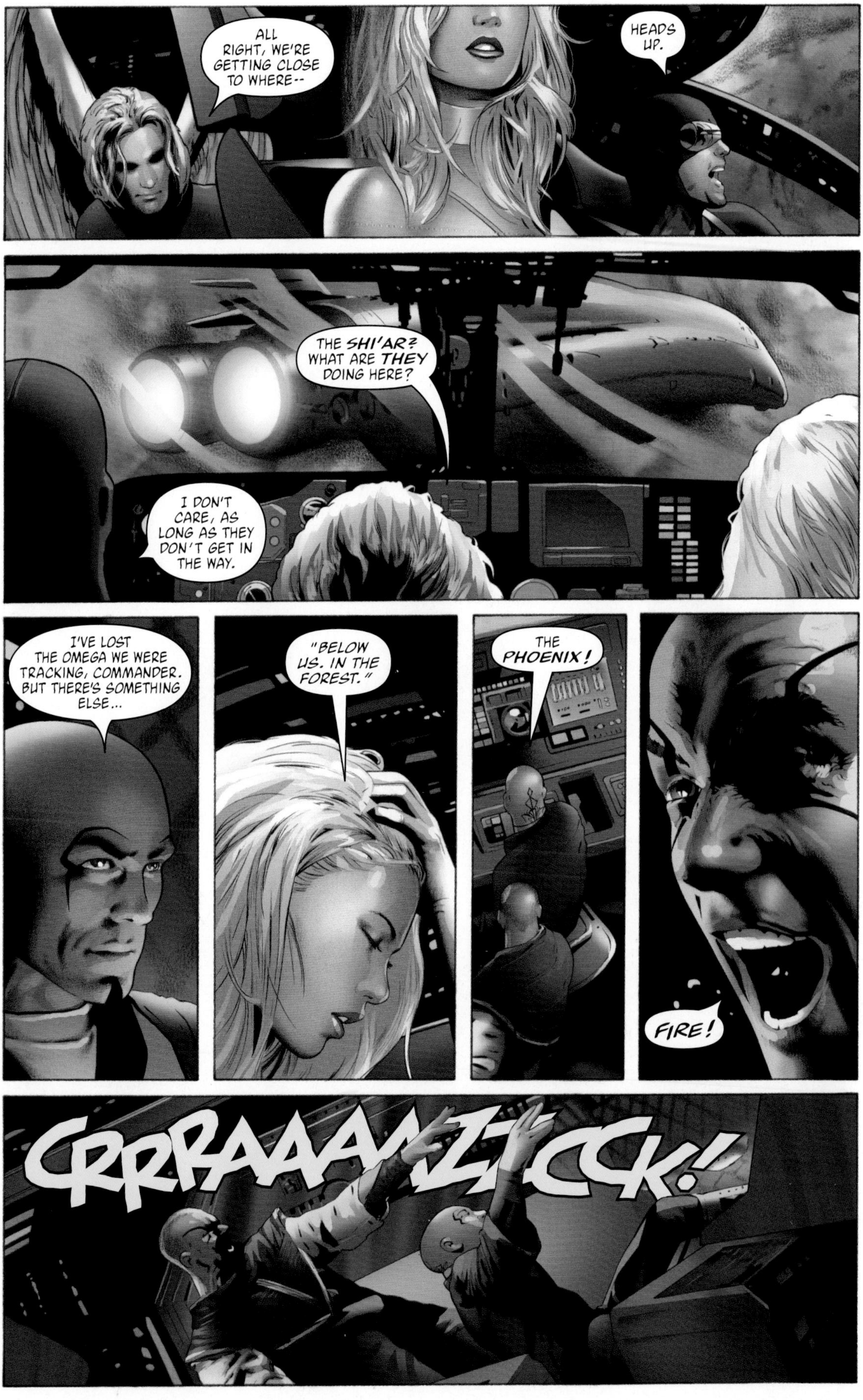
ALL RIGHT, WE'RE GETTING CLOSE TO WHERE--
HEADS UP.
THE SHI'AR? WHAT ARE THEY DOING HERE?
I DON'T CARE, AS LONG AS THEY DON'T GET IN THE WAY.
I'VE LOST THE OMEGA WE WERE TRACKING, COMMANDER. BUT THERE'S SOMETHING ELSE...
"BELOW US. IN THE FOREST."
THE PHOENIX!
FIRE!
CRRRAAANZZCCK!!

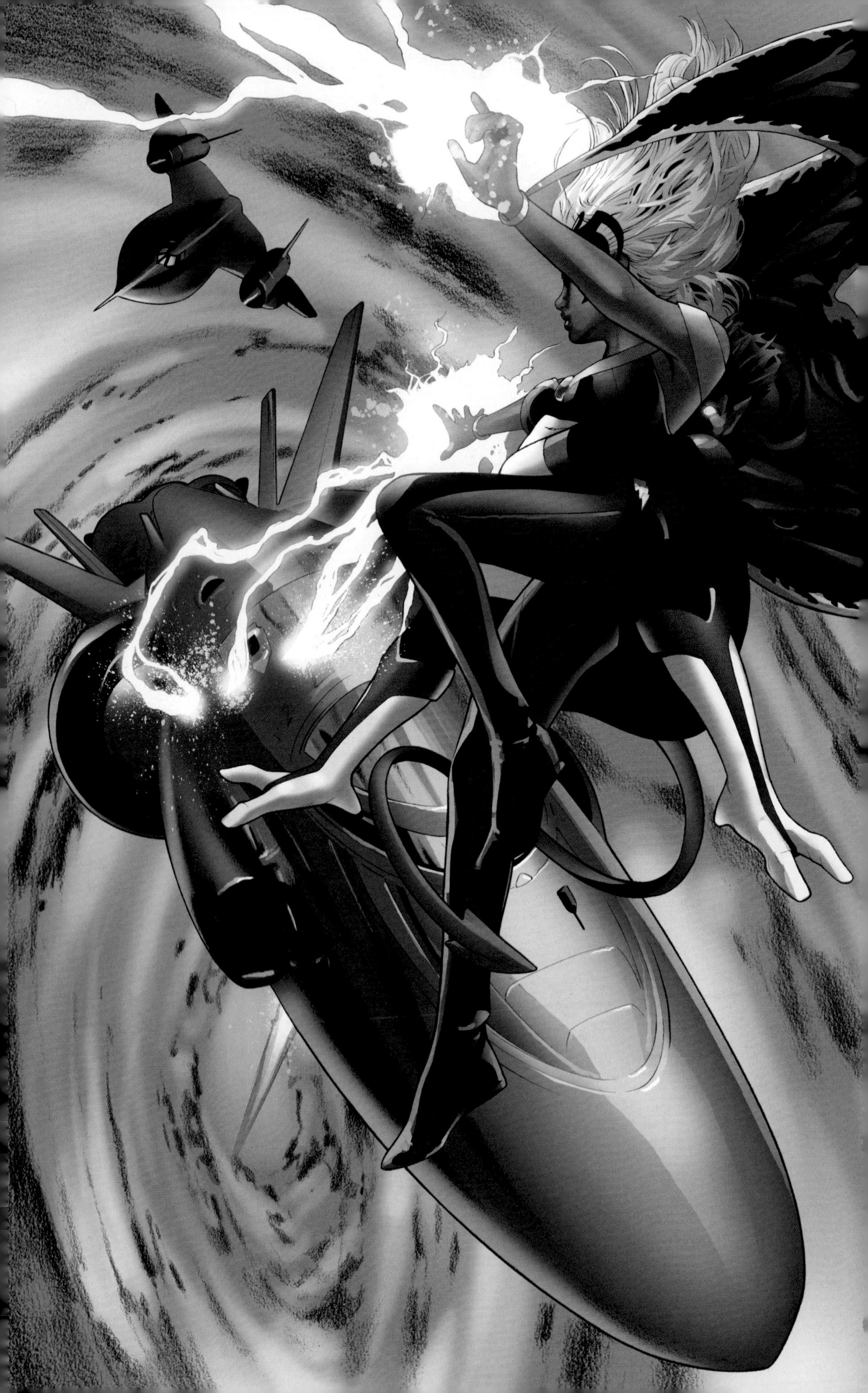

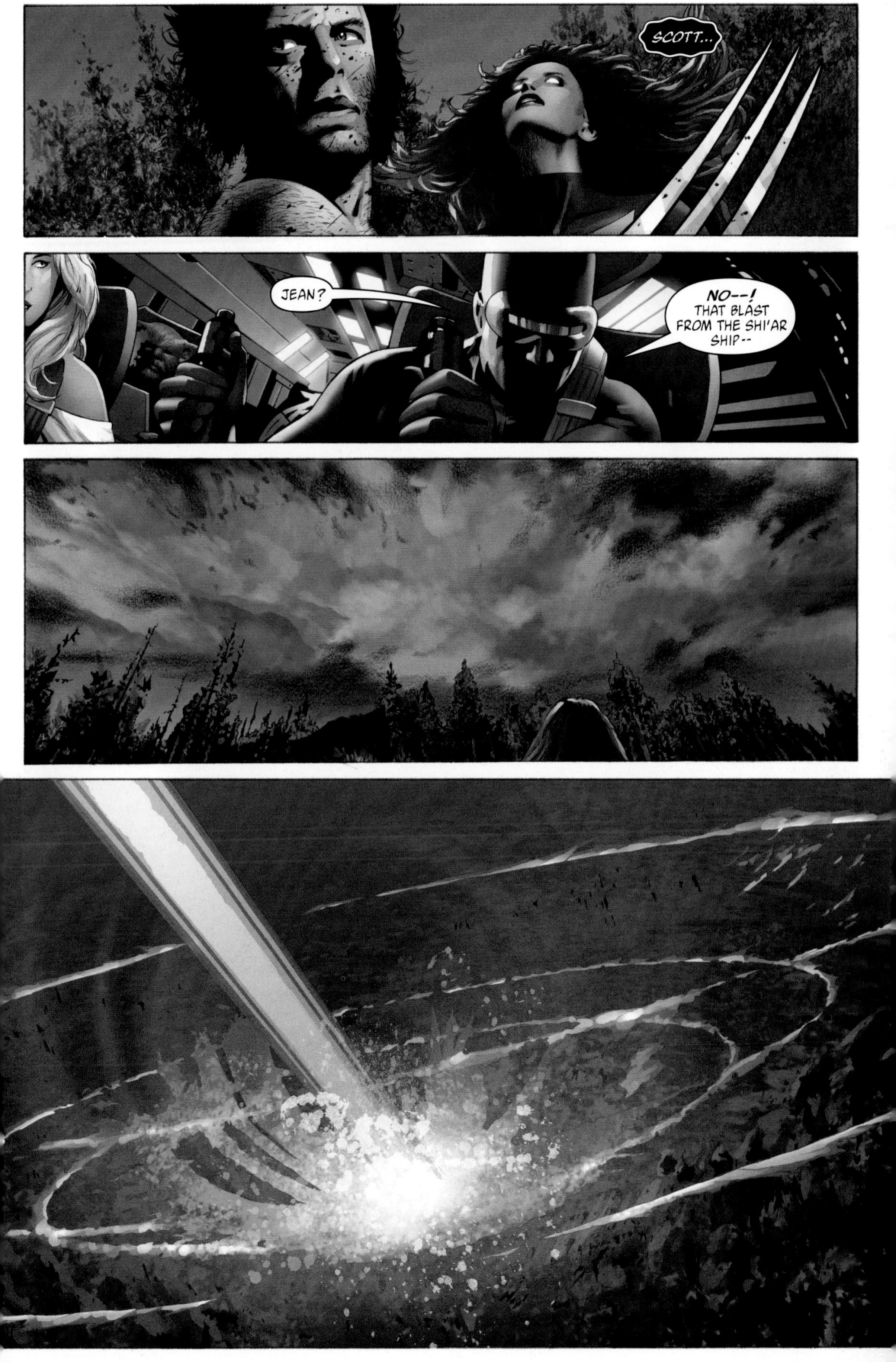
SCOTT...
JEAN?
NO--! THAT BLAST FROM THE SHI'AR SHIP--

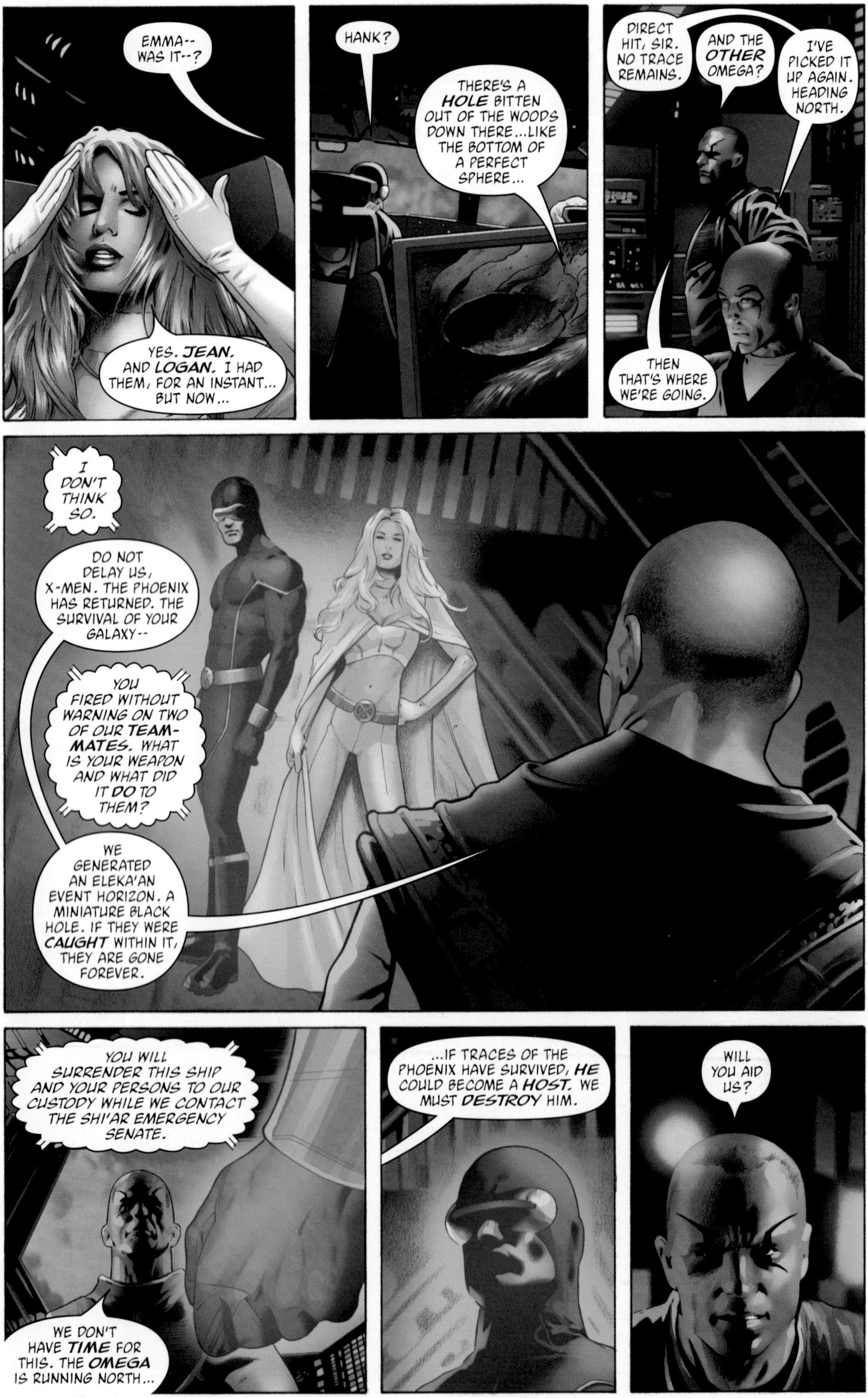
EMMA--
WAS IT--?
YES. JEAN. AND LOGAN. I HAD THEM, FOR AN INSTANT... BUT NOW...
HANK?
THERE'S A HOLE BITTEN OUT OF THE WOODS DOWN THERE...LIKE THE BOTTOM OF A PERFECT SPHERE...
DIRECT HIT, SIR. NO TRACE REMAINS.
AND THE OTHER OMEGA?
I'VE PICKED IT UP AGAIN. HEADING NORTH.
THEN THAT'S WHERE WE'RE GOING.
I DON'T THINK SO.
DO NOT DELAY US, X-MEN. THE PHOENIX HAS RETURNED. THE SURVIVAL OF YOUR GALAXY--
YOU FIRED WITHOUT WARNING ON TWO OF OUR TEAMMATES. WHAT IS YOUR WEAPON AND WHAT DID IT DO TO THEM?
WE GENERATED AN ELEKA'AN EVENT HORIZON. A MINIATURE BLACK HOLE. IF THEY WERE CAUGHT WITHIN IT, THEY ARE GONE FOREVER.
YOU WILL SURRENDER THIS SHIP AND YOUR PERSONS TO OUR CUSTODY WHILE WE CONTACT THE SHI'AR EMERGENCY SENATE.
WE DON'T HAVE TIME FOR THIS. THE OMEGA IS RUNNING NORTH...
...IF TRACES OF THE PHOENIX HAVE SURVIVED, HE COULD BECOME A HOST. WE MUST DESTROY HIM.
WILL YOU AID US?

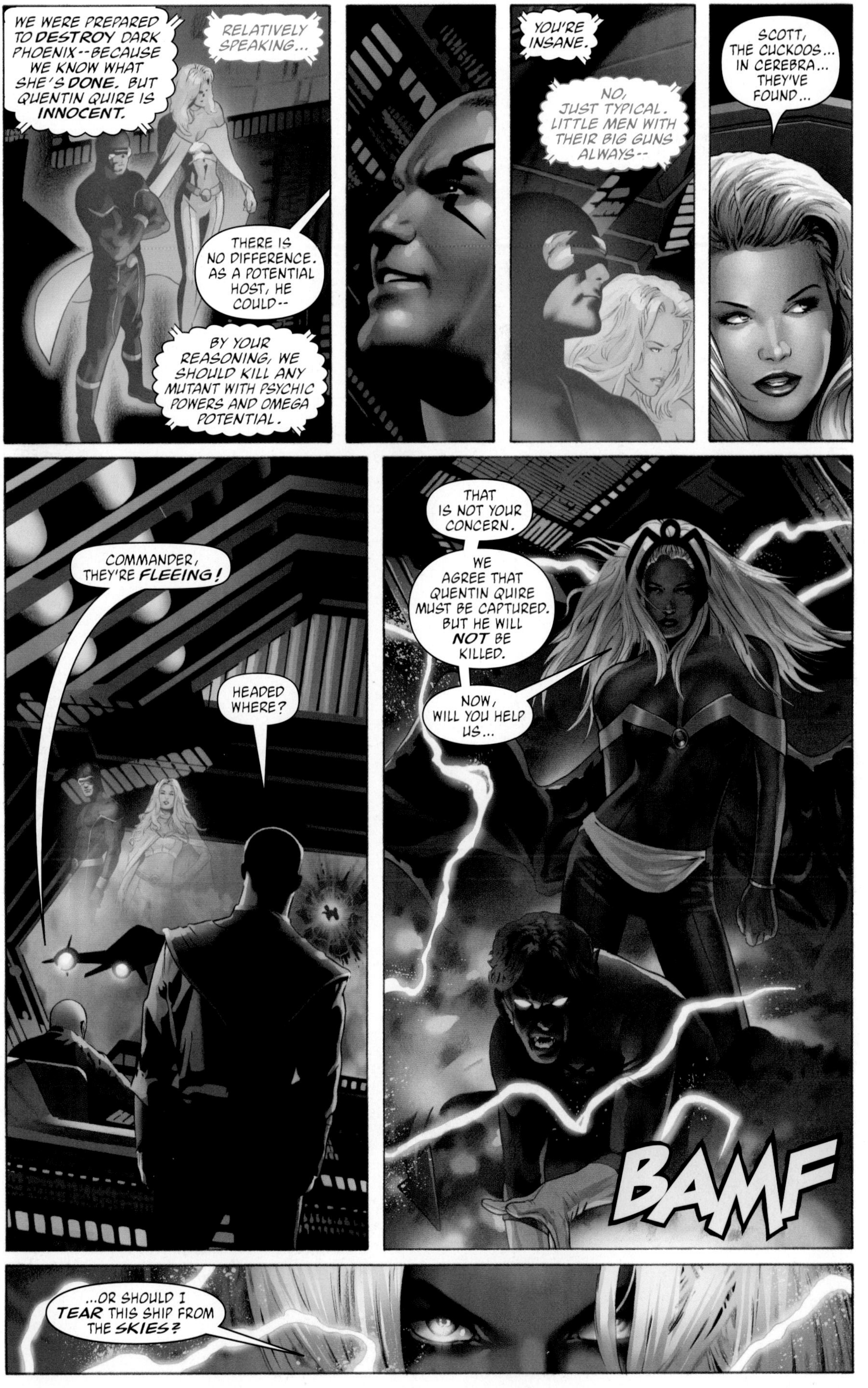
WE WERE PREPARED TO DESTROY DARK PHOENIX--BECAUSE WE KNOW WHAT SHE'S DONE. BUT QUENTIN QUIRE IS INNOCENT.
RELATIVELY SPEAKING...
THERE IS NO DIFFERENCE. AS A POTENTIAL HOST, HE COULD--
BY YOUR REASONING, WE SHOULD KILL ANY MUTANT WITH PSYCHIC POWERS AND OMEGA POTENTIAL.
YOU'RE INSANE.
NO, JUST TYPICAL. LITTLE MEN WITH THEIR BIG GUNS ALWAYS--
SCOTT, THE CUCKOOS... IN CEREBRA... THEY'VE FOUND...
COMMANDER, THEY'RE FLEEING!
HEADED WHERE?
THAT IS NOT YOUR CONCERN.
WE AGREE THAT QUENTIN QUIRE MUST BE CAPTURED. BUT HE WILL NOT BE KILLED.
NOW, WILL YOU HELP US...
BAMF
...OR SHOULD I TEAR THIS SHIP FROM THE SKIES?

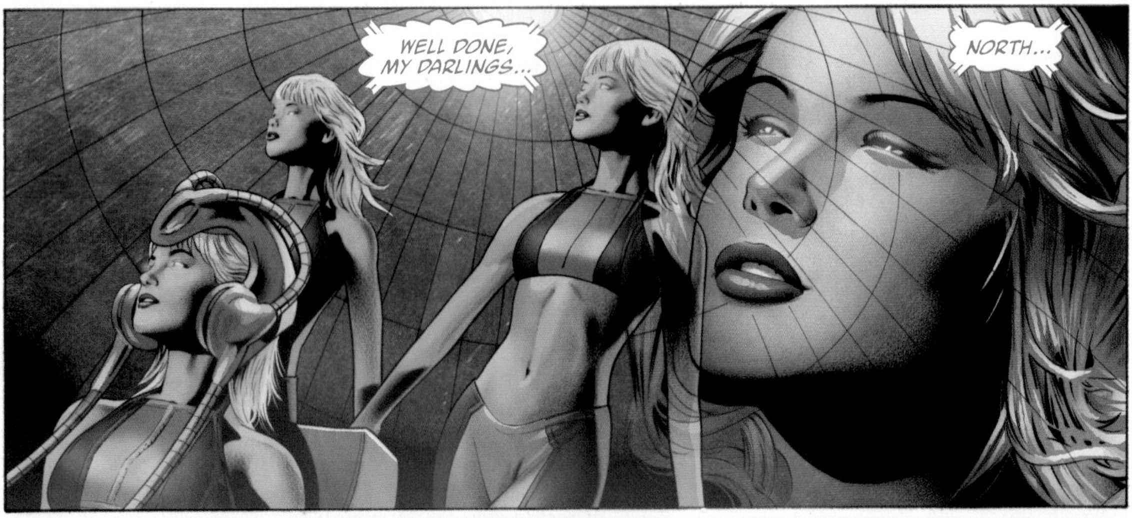
WELL DONE, MY DARLINGS...
NORTH...

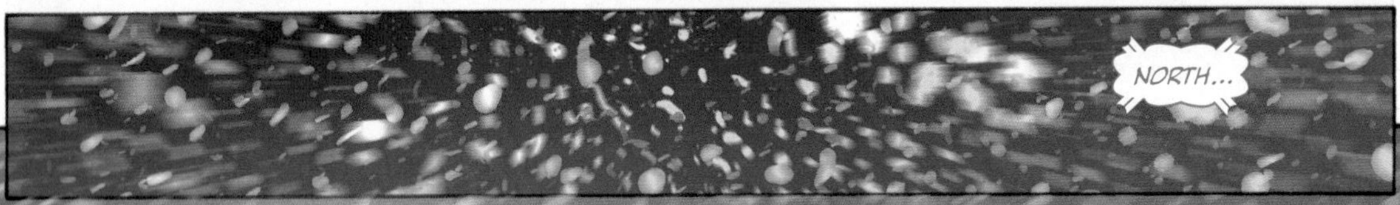
NORTH...

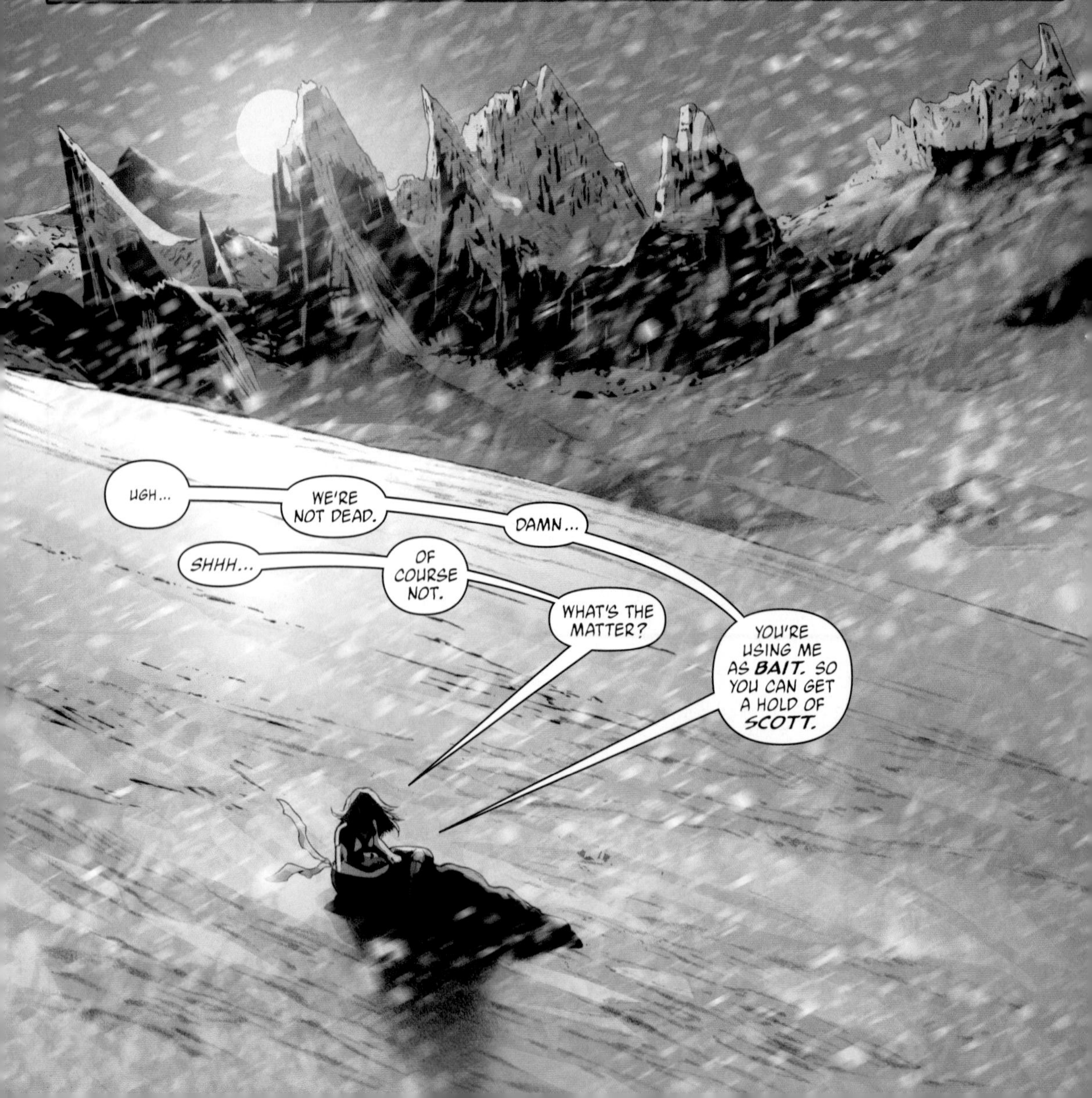
UGH...
WE'RE NOT DEAD.
DAMN...
SHHH...
OF COURSE NOT.
WHAT'S THE MATTER?
YOU'RE USING ME AS BAIT. SO YOU CAN GET A HOLD OF SCOTT.

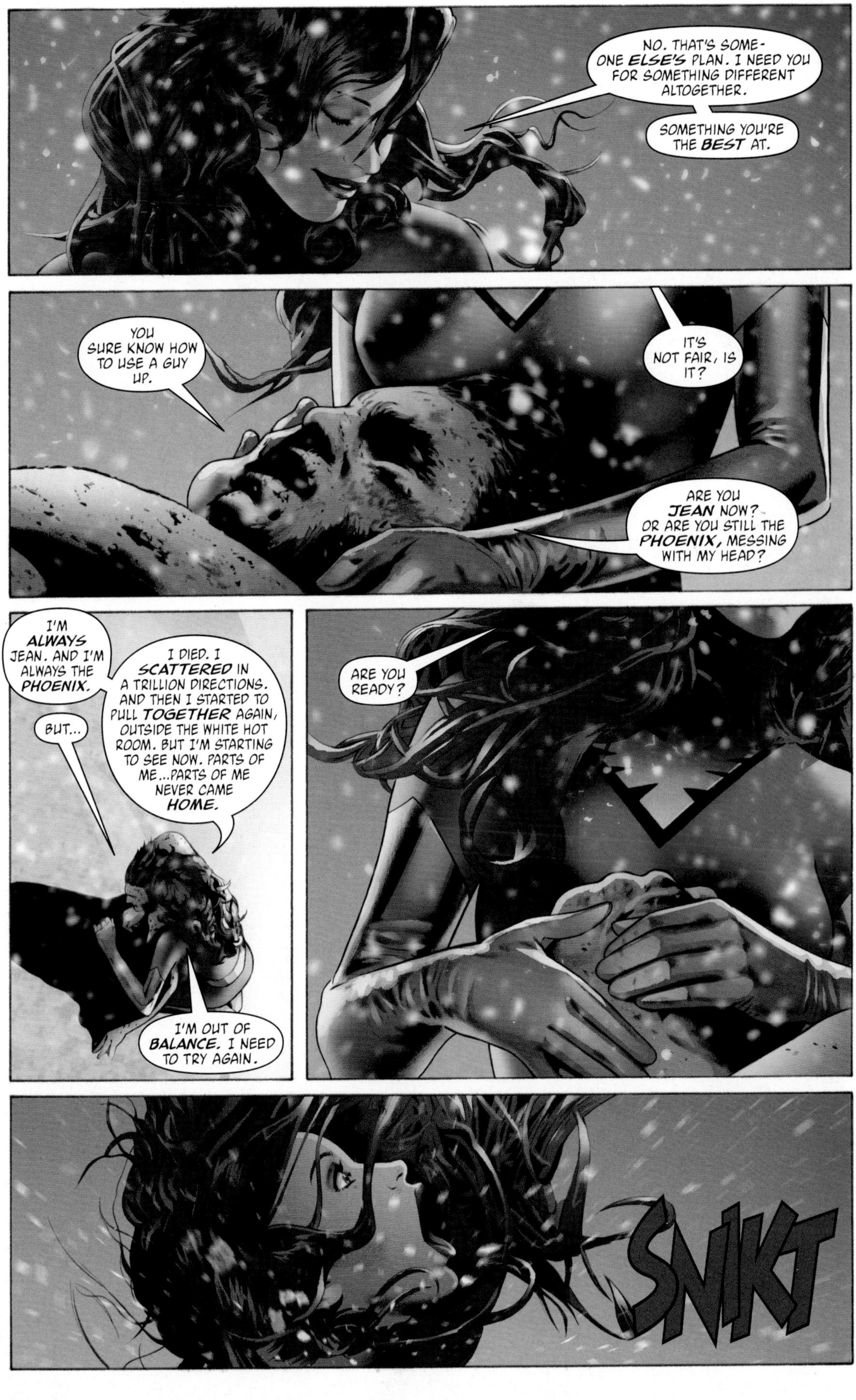
NO. THAT'S SOME-ONE ELSE'S PLAN. I NEED YOU FOR SOMETHING DIFFERENT ALTOGETHER.
SOMETHING YOU'RE THE BEST AT.
YOU SURE KNOW HOW TO USE A GUY UP.
IT'S NOT FAIR, IS IT?
ARE YOU JEAN NOW? OR ARE YOU STILL THE PHOENIX, MESSING WITH MY HEAD?
I'M ALWAYS JEAN. AND I'M ALWAYS THE PHOENIX.
BUT...
I DIED. I SCATTERED IN A TRILLION DIRECTIONS. AND THEN I STARTED TO PULL TOGETHER AGAIN, OUTSIDE THE WHITE HOT ROOM. BUT I'M STARTING TO SEE NOW. PARTS OF ME...PARTS OF ME NEVER CAME HOME.
I'M OUT OF BALANCE. I NEED TO TRY AGAIN.
ARE YOU READY?
SNIKT

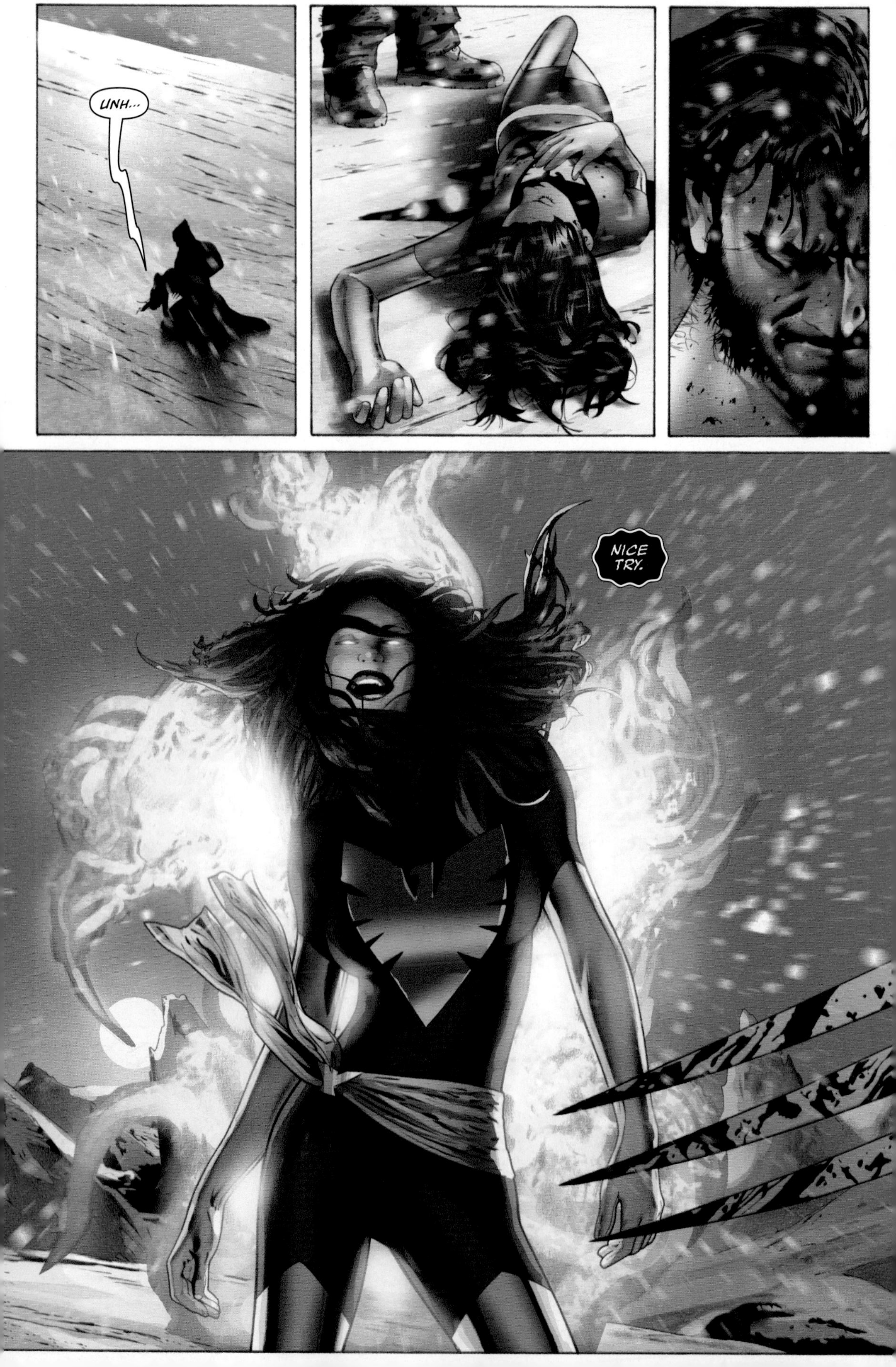
UNH...
NICE TRY.

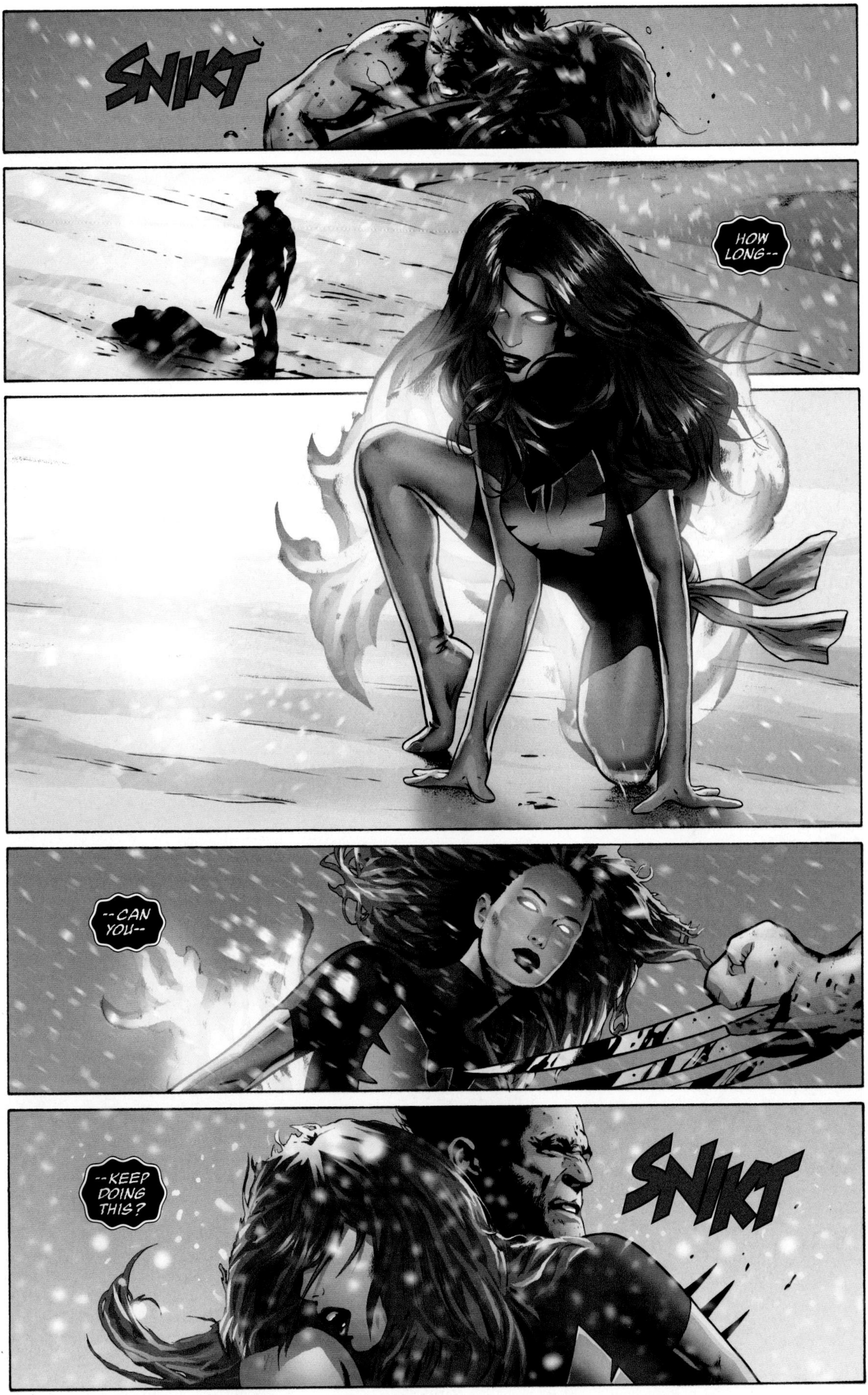
SNIKT
HOW LONG--
--CAN YOU--
--KEEP DOING THIS?
SNIKT

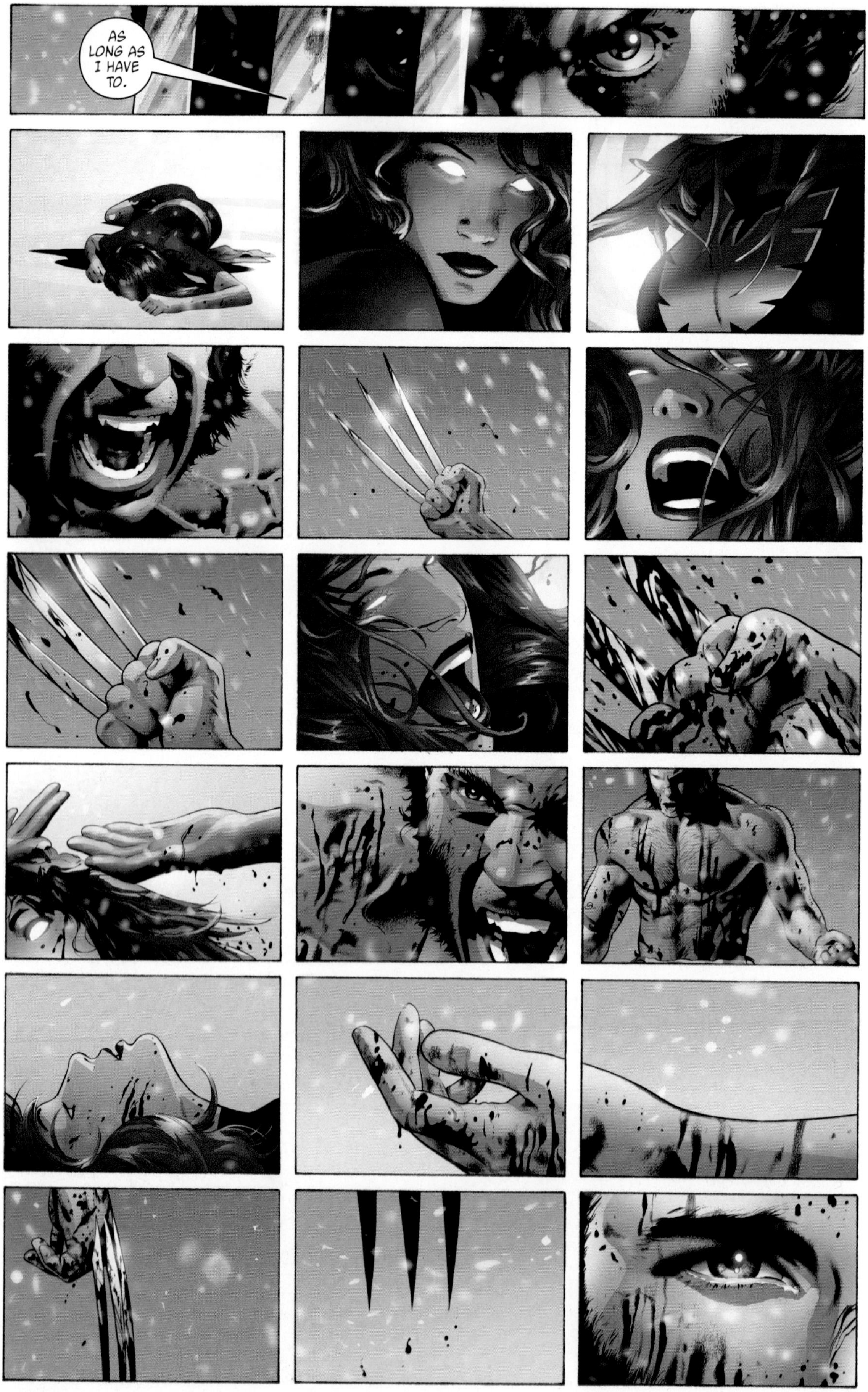
AS LONG AS I HAVE TO.

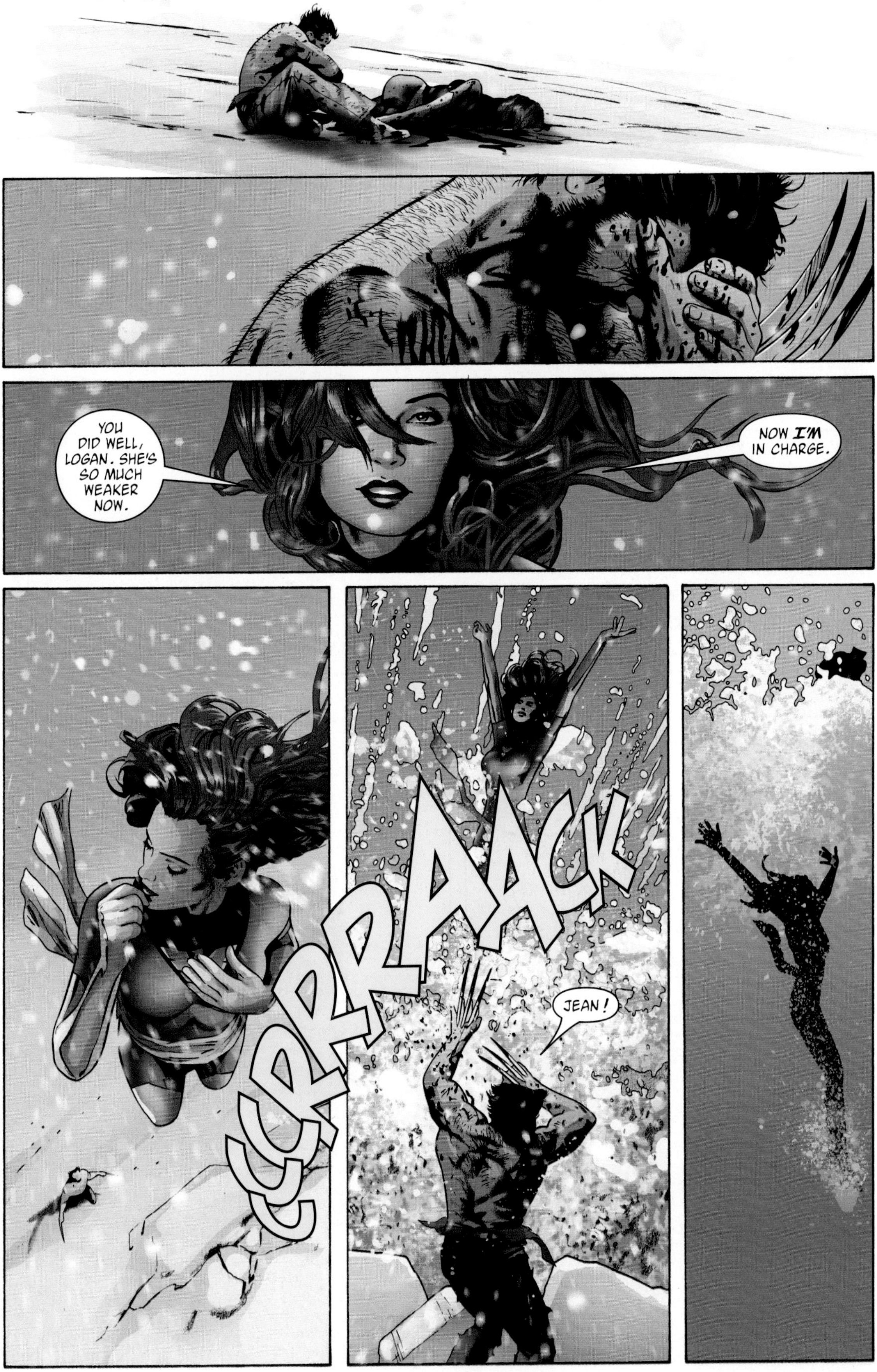
YOU DID WELL, LOGAN. SHE'S SO MUCH WEAKER NOW.
NOW I'M IN CHARGE.
CCCRRRAACK
JEAN!

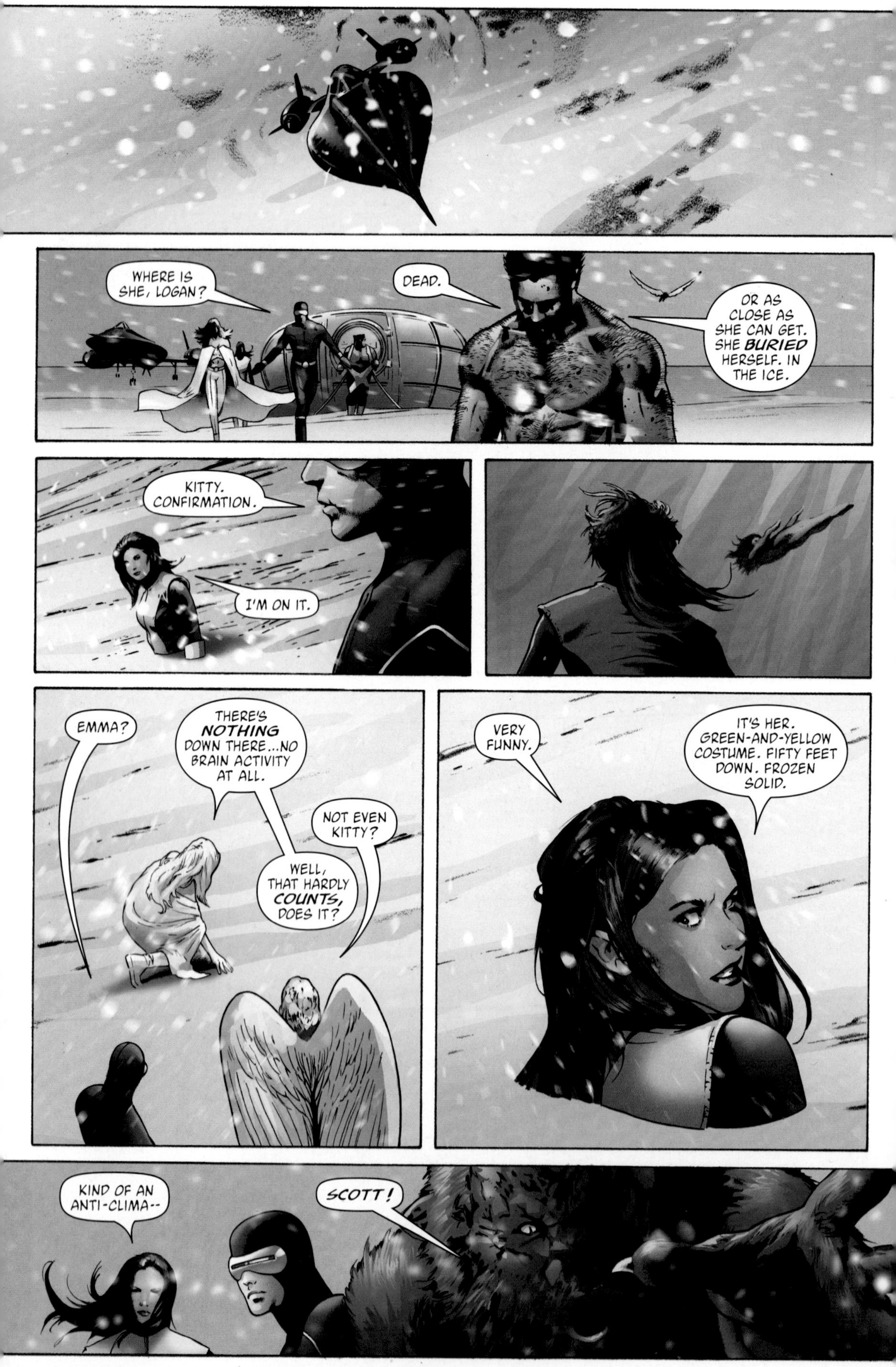
WHERE IS SHE, LOGAN?
DEAD.
OR AS CLOSE AS SHE CAN GET. SHE BURIED HERSELF. IN THE ICE.
KITTY. CONFIRMATION.
I'M ON IT.
EMMA?
THERE'S NOTHING DOWN THERE...NO BRAIN ACTIVITY AT ALL.
NOT EVEN KITTY?
WELL, THAT HARDLY COUNTS, DOES IT?
VERY FUNNY.
IT'S HER. GREEN-AND-YELLOW COSTUME. FIFTY FEET DOWN. FROZEN SOLID.
KIND OF AN ANTI-CLIMA--
SCOTT!

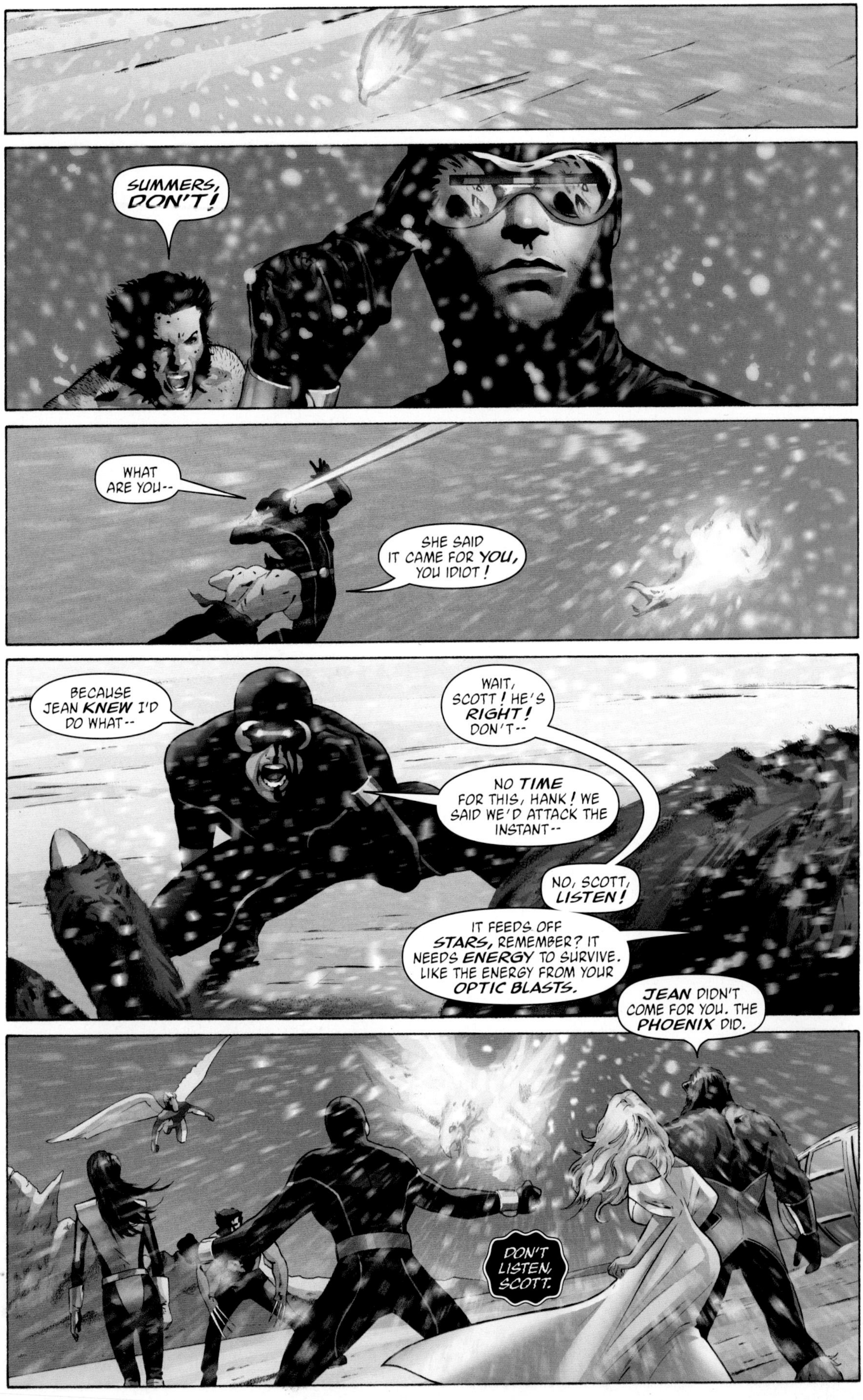

SUMMERS, DON'T!
WHAT ARE YOU--
SHE SAID IT CAME FOR YOU, YOU IDIOT!
BECAUSE JEAN KNEW I'D DO WHAT--
WAIT, SCOTT! HE'S RIGHT! DON'T--
NO TIME FOR THIS, HANK! WE SAID WE'D ATTACK THE INSTANT--
NO, SCOTT, LISTEN!
IT FEEDS OFF STARS, REMEMBER? IT NEEDS ENERGY TO SURVIVE. LIKE THE ENERGY FROM YOUR OPTIC BLASTS.
JEAN DIDN'T COME FOR YOU. THE PHOENIX DID.
DON'T LISTEN, SCOTT.

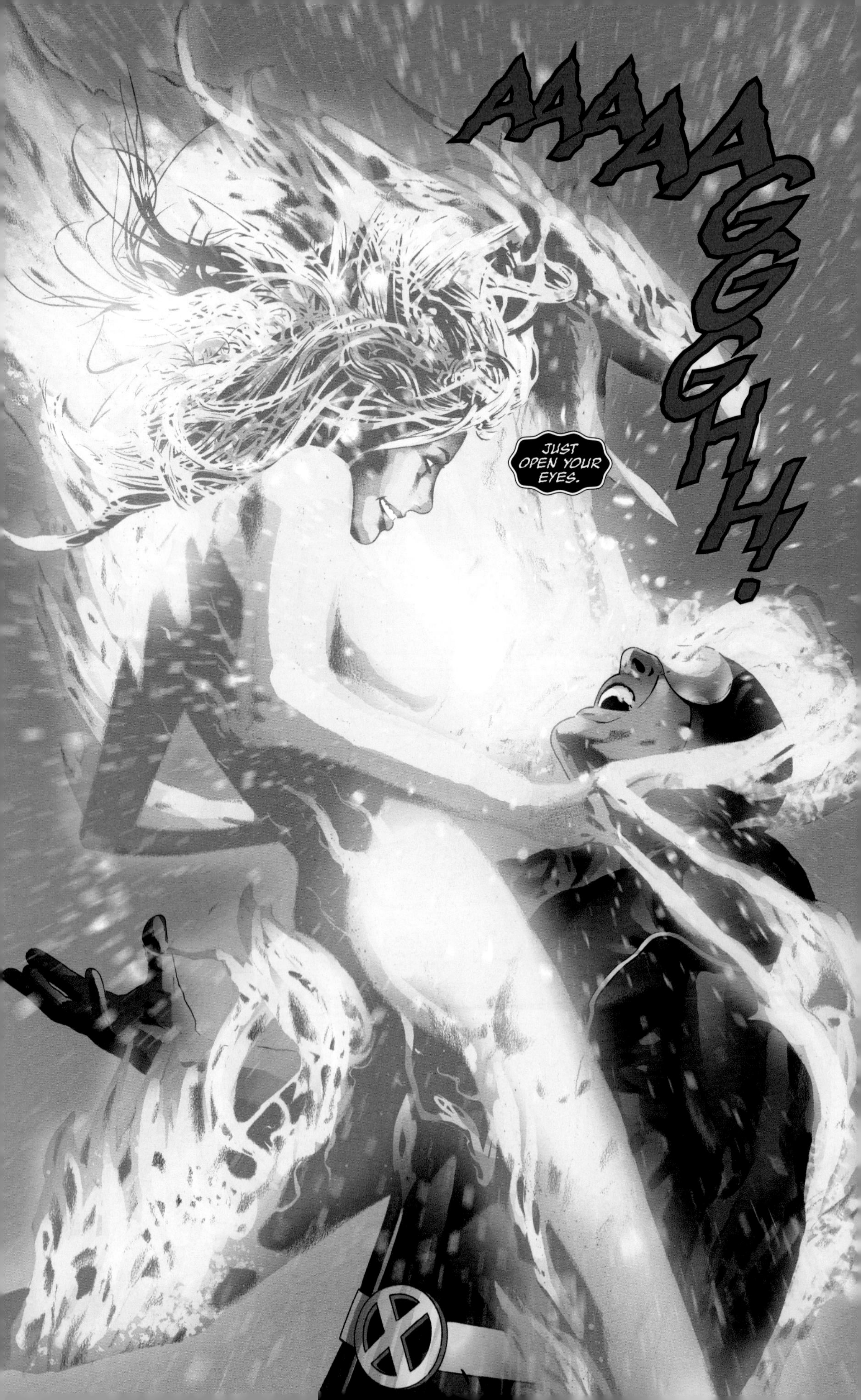
AAAAAGGGHH!
JUST OPEN YOUR EYES.

VARIANT COVERS

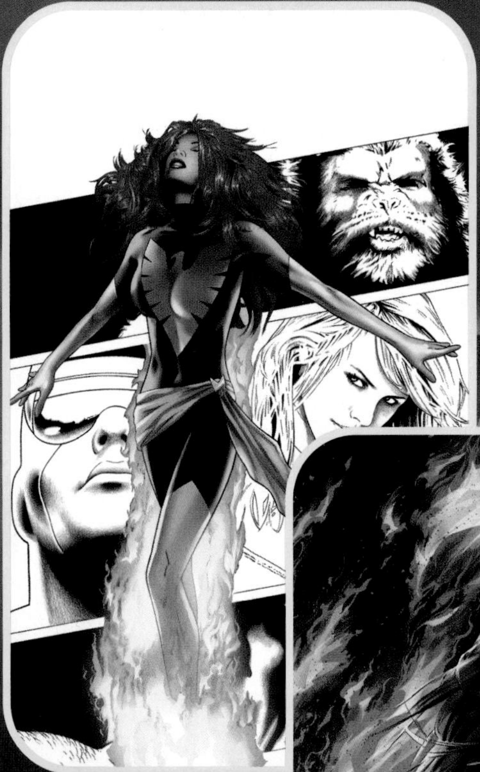

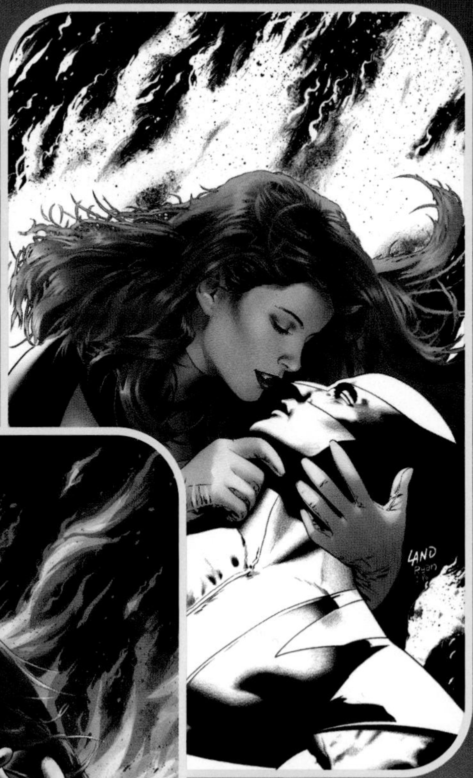

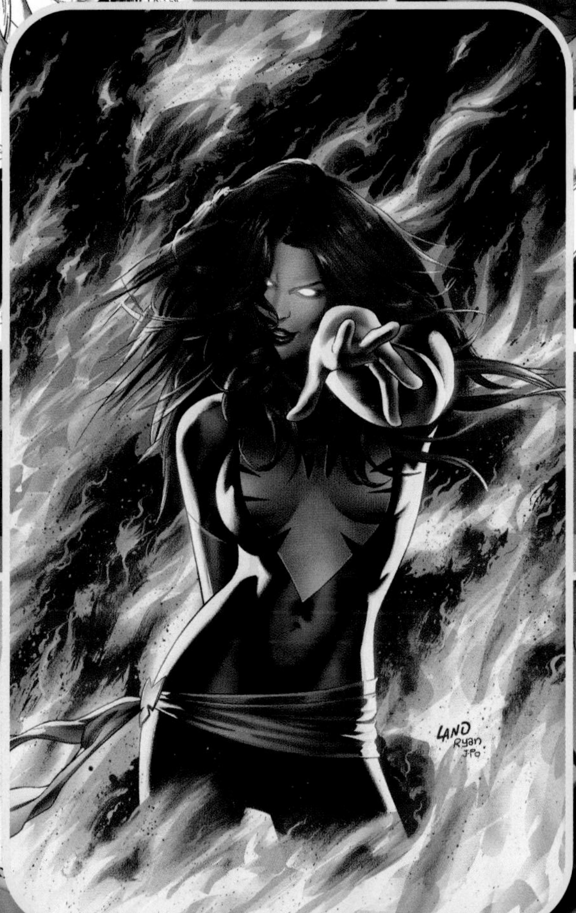

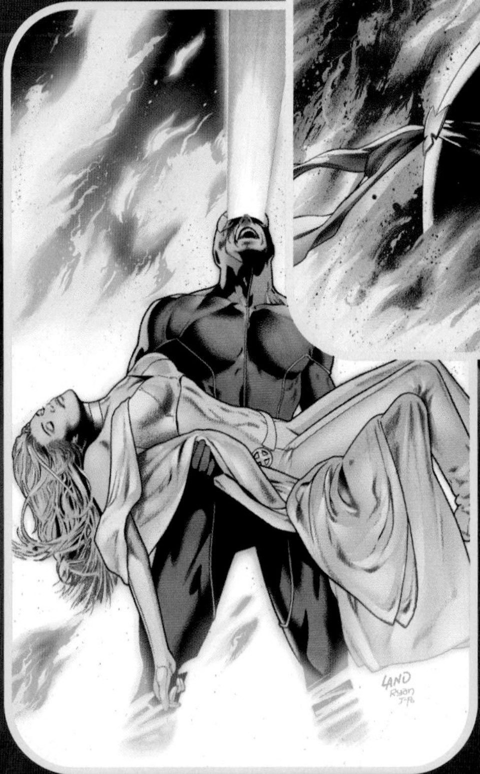

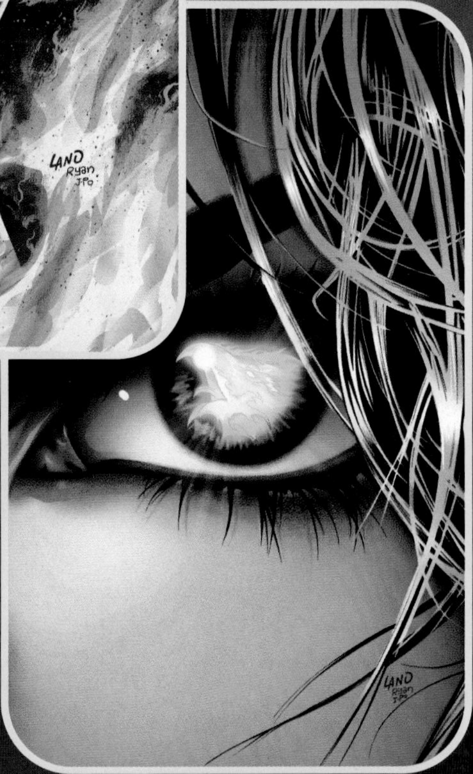

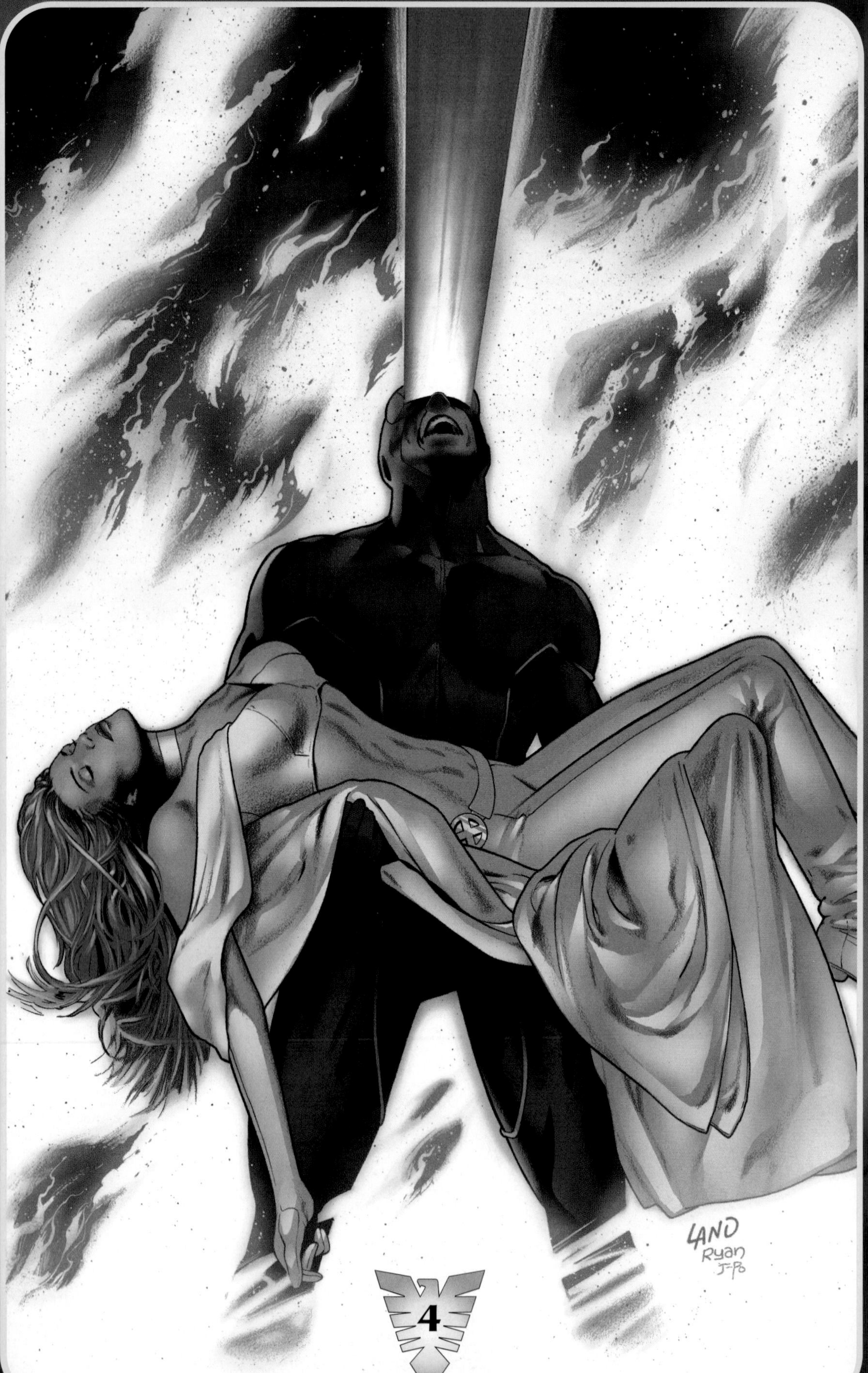
LAND
Ryan
J-Po
4

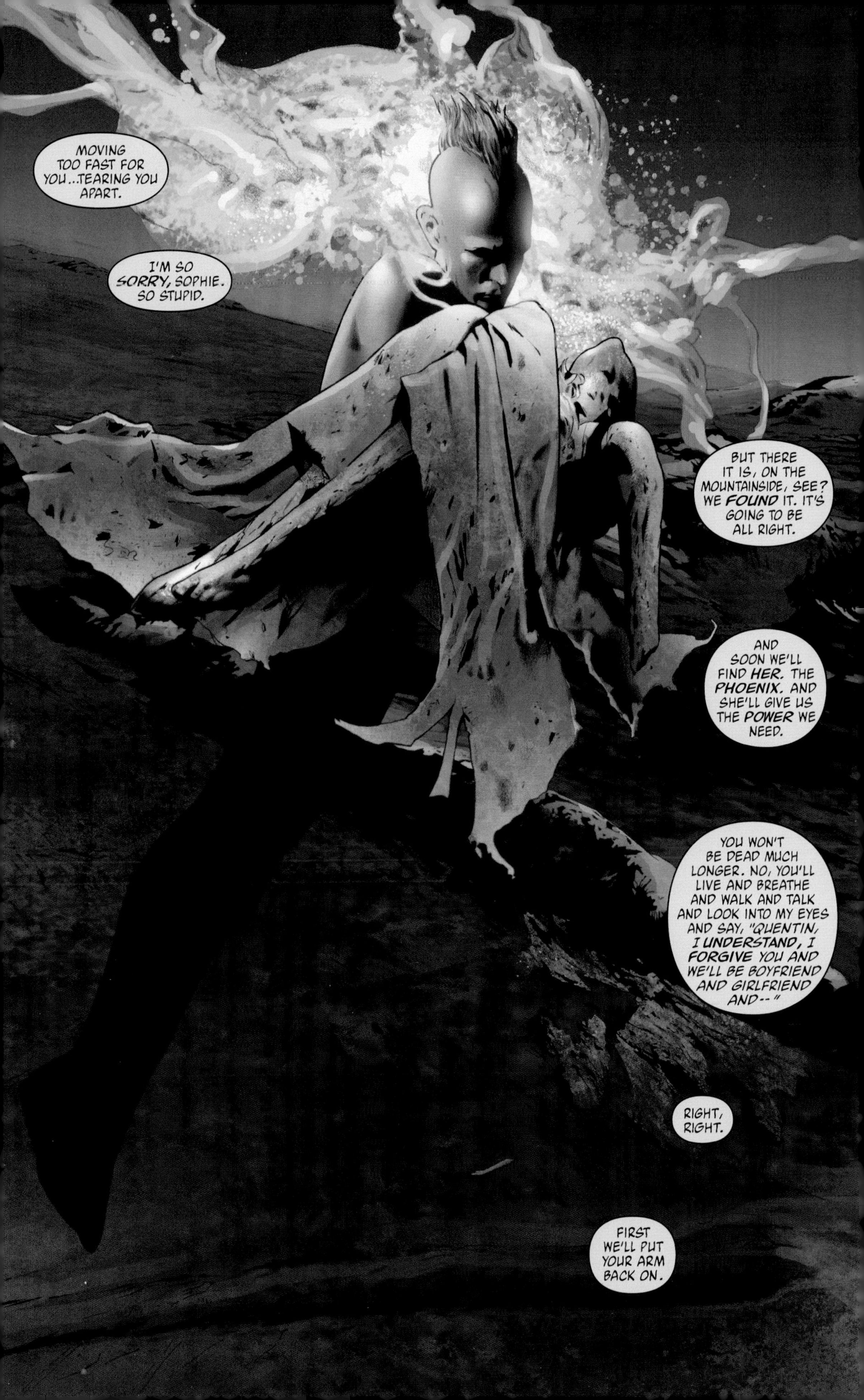
MOVING TOO FAST FOR YOU...TEARING YOU APART.
I'M SO SORRY, SOPHIE. SO STUPID.
BUT THERE IT IS, ON THE MOUNTAINSIDE, SEE? WE FOUND IT. IT'S GOING TO BE ALL RIGHT.
AND SOON WE'LL FIND HER. THE PHOENIX. AND SHE'LL GIVE US THE POWER WE NEED.
YOU WON'T BE DEAD MUCH LONGER. NO, YOU'LL LIVE AND BREATHE AND WALK AND TALK AND LOOK INTO MY EYES AND SAY, "QUENTIN, I UNDERSTAND, I FORGIVE YOU AND WE'LL BE BOYFRIEND AND GIRLFRIEND AND--"
RIGHT, RIGHT.
FIRST WE'LL PUT YOUR ARM BACK ON.

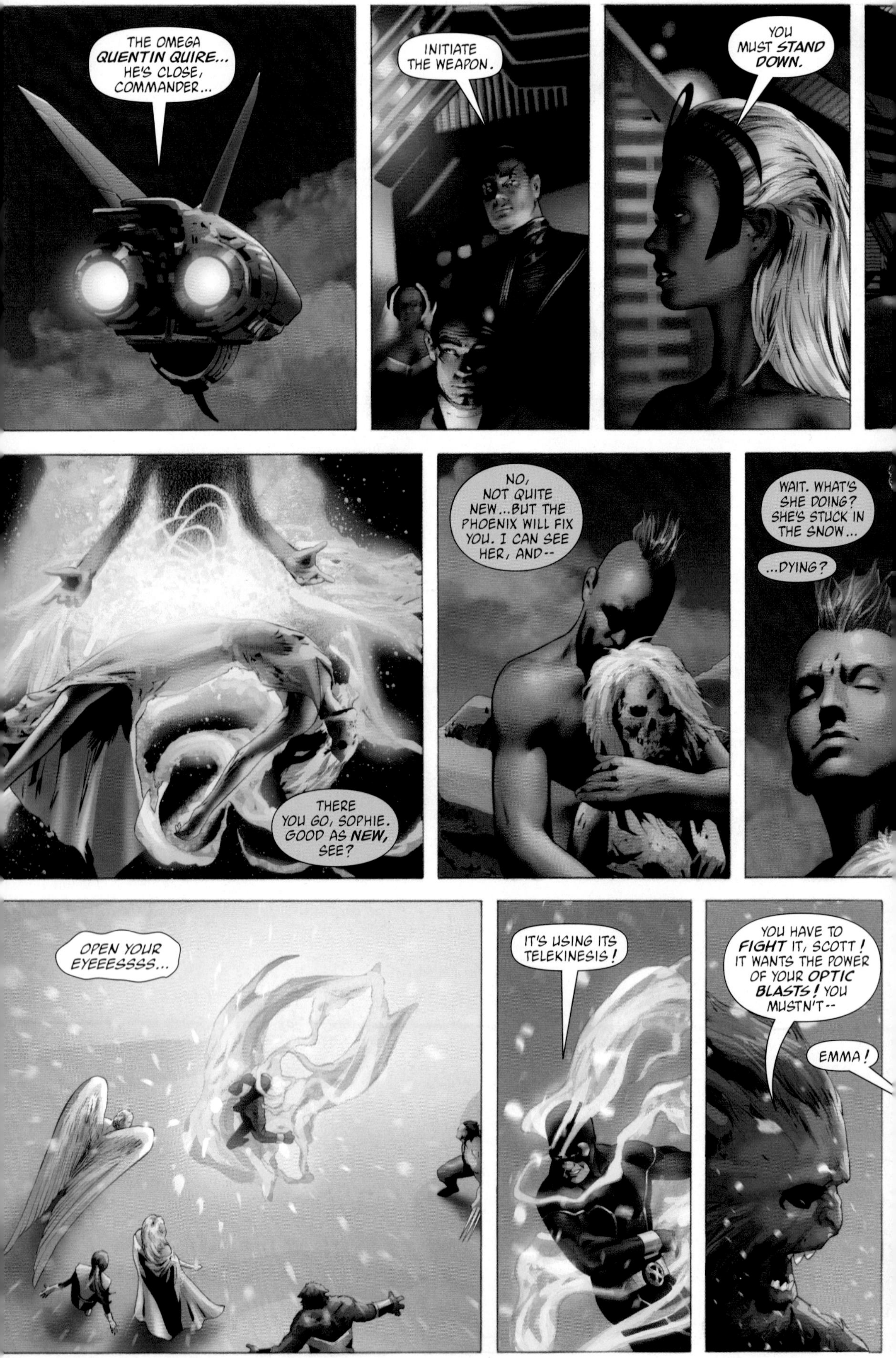
THE OMEGA QUENTIN QUIRE... HE'S CLOSE, COMMANDER...
INITIATE THE WEAPON.
YOU MUST STAND DOWN.
THERE YOU GO, SOPHIE. GOOD AS NEW, SEE?
NO, NOT QUITE NEW...BUT THE PHOENIX WILL FIX YOU. I CAN SEE HER, AND--
WAIT. WHAT'S SHE DOING? SHE'S STUCK IN THE SNOW...
...DYING?
OPEN YOUR EYEEESSSS...
IT'S USING ITS TELEKINESIS!
YOU HAVE TO FIGHT IT, SCOTT! IT WANTS THE POWER OF YOUR OPTIC BLASTS! YOU MUSTN'T--
EMMA!

HE COULD HOST THE *PHOENIX.* HE COULD DESTROY YOUR *ENTIRE* GALAXY!

YOU CANNOT *KILL* HIM FOR WHAT HE HAS *NOT* YET DONE.

ALMOST UPON HIM, SIR...

FIRE WHEN READY.

SHE WARNED YOU!

I CAN HEAR THEM, SOPHIE.

THEY'RE FIGHTING HER. *HURTING* HER...

I'M HERE, SCOTT. BACKING YOU UP.

DON'T WORRY--THE PHOENIX IS WEAK. IT CAN'T BEAT US.

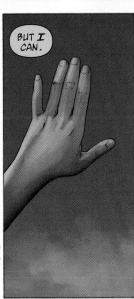

BUT *I* CAN.

HA!

I'M HERE, SCOTT. PROTECTING YOU.

DON'T WORRY--IT'S WEAK. IT CAN'T BEAT US.

BUT *I* CAN.

QUENTIN? *AAAH--!*

NOW OPEN YOUR *EYES,* MR. SUMMERS!

NO! IT'S FORCING ME TO--

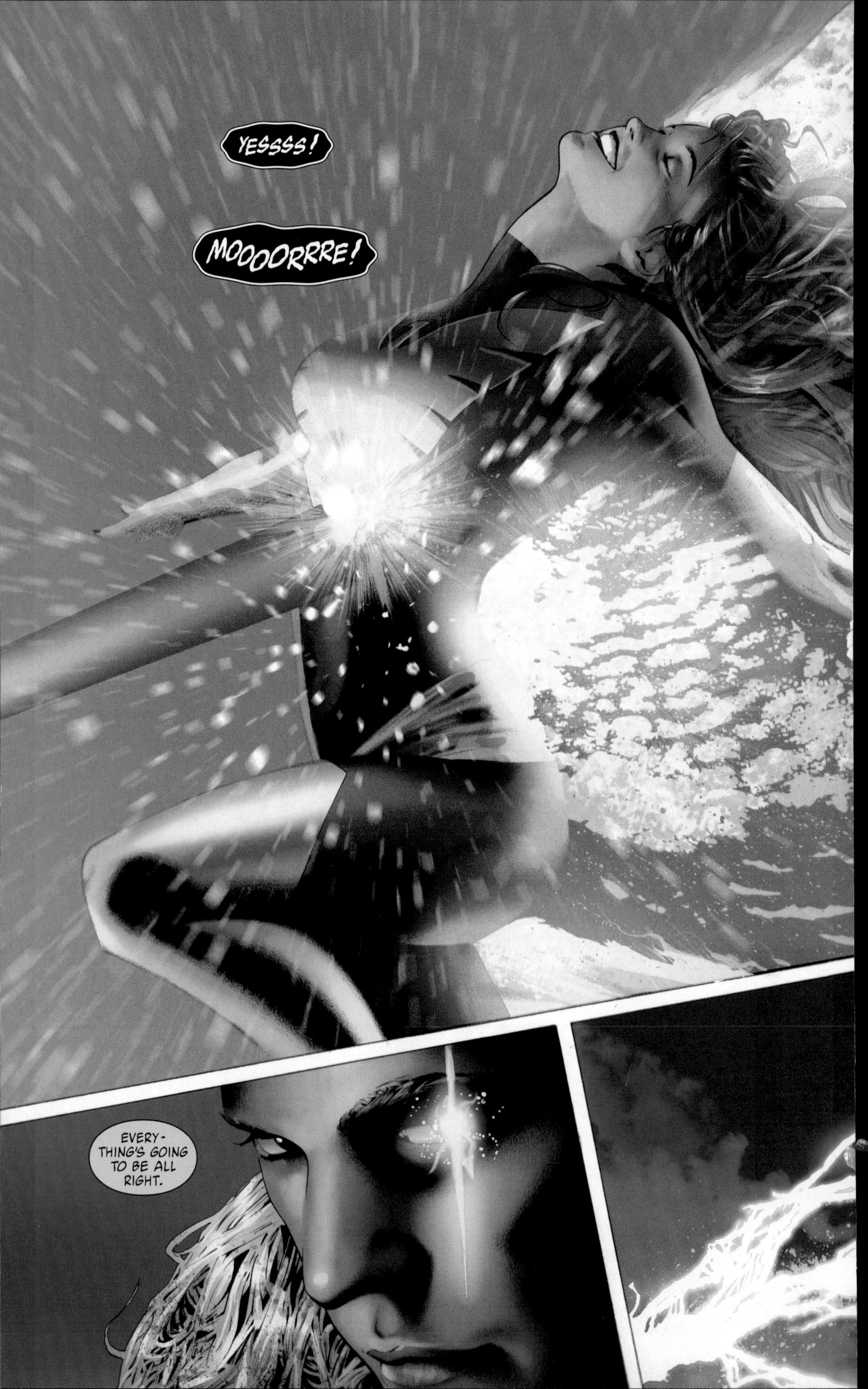
YESSSS!
MOOOORRRE!
EVERY-THING'S GOING TO BE ALL RIGHT.

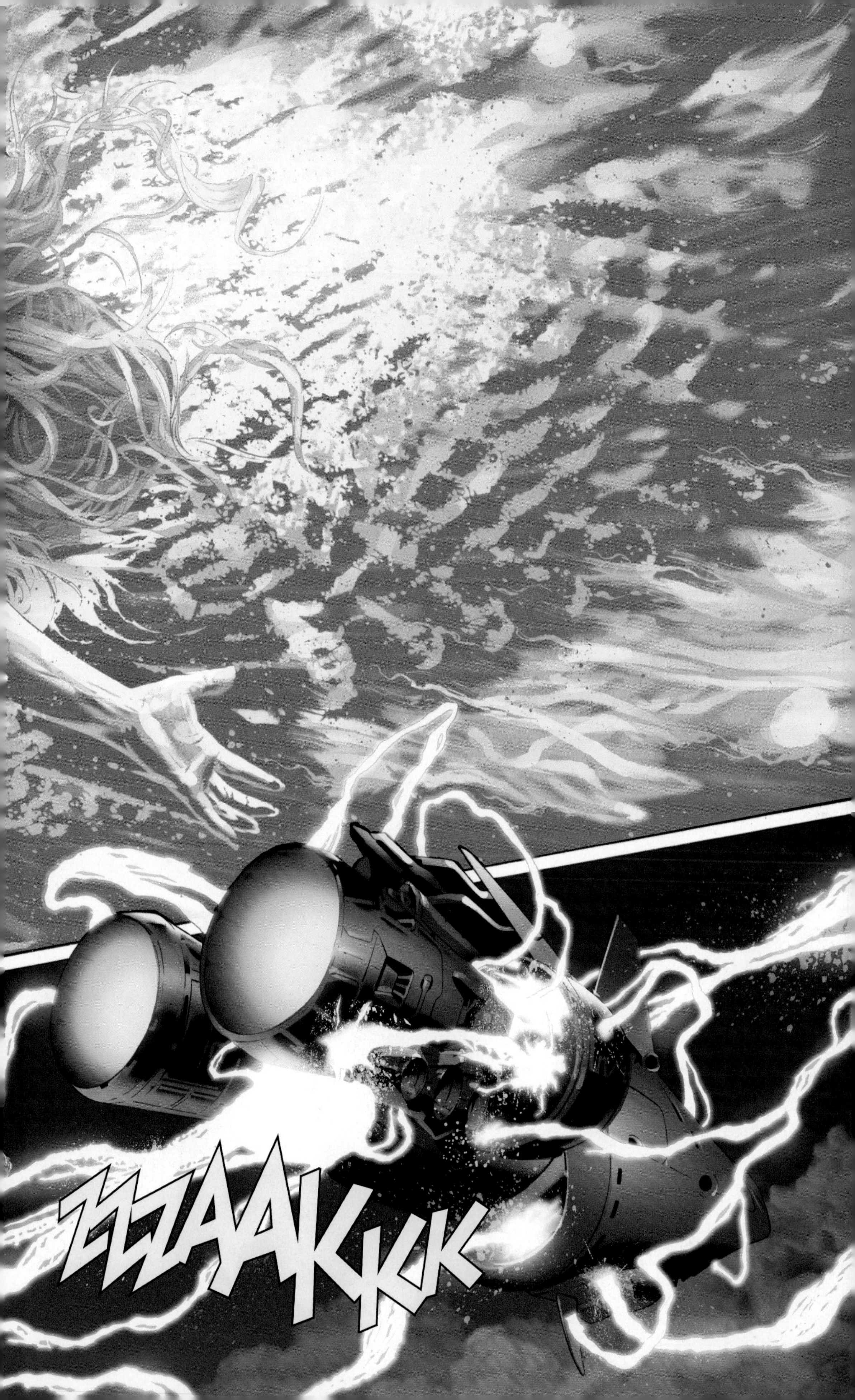
ZZZAAKKK

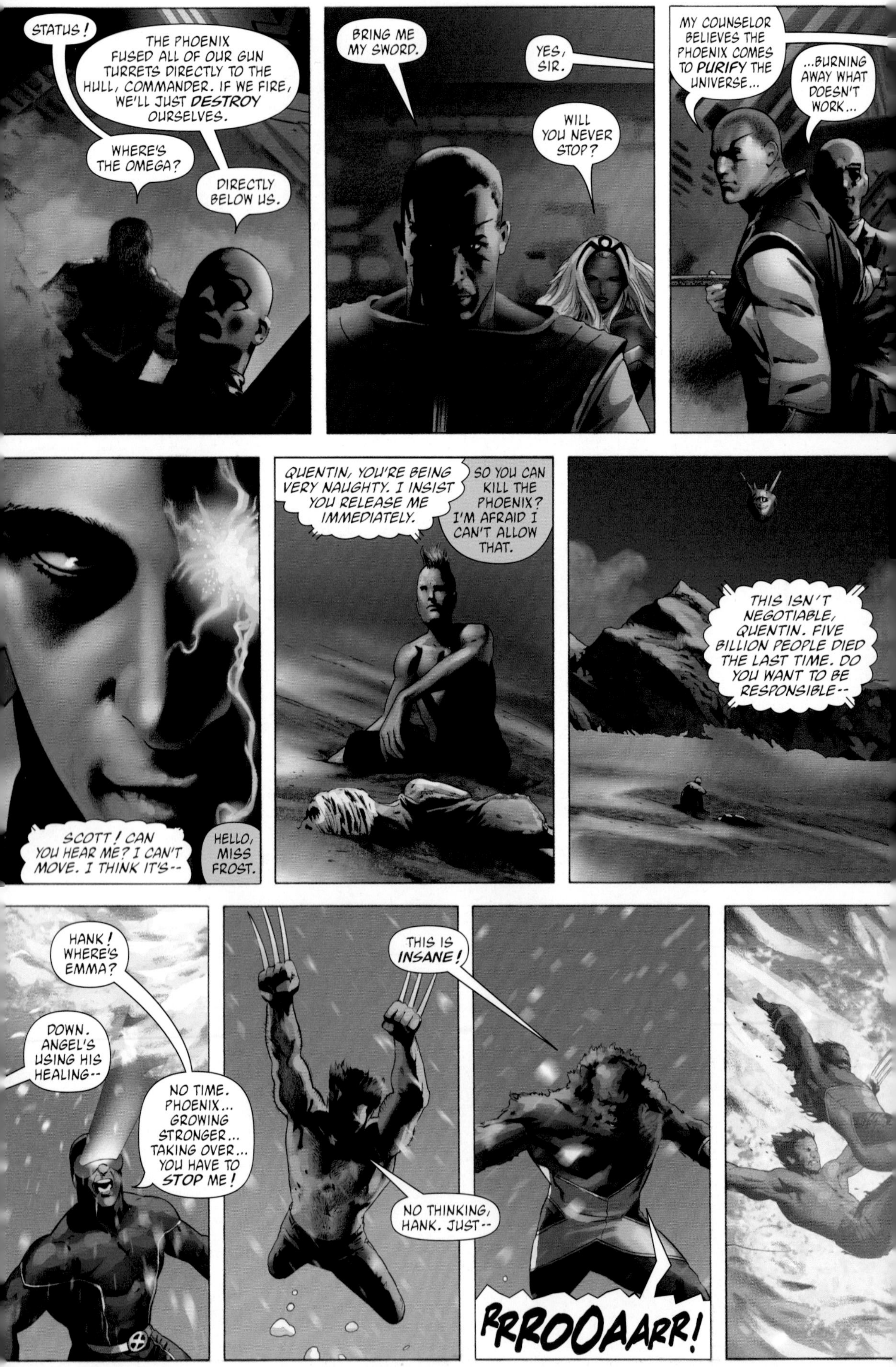

STATUS!
THE PHOENIX FUSED ALL OF OUR GUN TURRETS DIRECTLY TO THE HULL, COMMANDER. IF WE FIRE, WE'LL JUST DESTROY OURSELVES.
WHERE'S THE OMEGA?
DIRECTLY BELOW US.
BRING ME MY SWORD.
YES, SIR.
WILL YOU NEVER STOP?
MY COUNSELOR BELIEVES THE PHOENIX COMES TO PURIFY THE UNIVERSE...
...BURNING AWAY WHAT DOESN'T WORK...
SCOTT! CAN YOU HEAR ME? I CAN'T MOVE. I THINK IT'S--
HELLO, MISS FROST.
QUENTIN, YOU'RE BEING VERY NAUGHTY. I INSIST YOU RELEASE ME IMMEDIATELY.
SO YOU CAN KILL THE PHOENIX? I'M AFRAID I CAN'T ALLOW THAT.
THIS ISN'T NEGOTIABLE, QUENTIN. FIVE BILLION PEOPLE DIED THE LAST TIME. DO YOU WANT TO BE RESPONSIBLE--
HANK! WHERE'S EMMA?
DOWN. ANGEL'S USING HIS HEALING--
NO TIME. PHOENIX... GROWING STRONGER... TAKING OVER... YOU HAVE TO STOP ME!
THIS IS INSANE!
NO THINKING, HANK. JUST--
RRROOAARR!

MY WIFE. MY CHILDREN. MY PARENTS AND THEIR PARENTS. THEY DIED WITH FIVE BILLION OTHERS WHEN DARK PHOENIX ATE D'BARI'S STAR!

AND IF YOU WANT TO TELL ME *THEY* WERE A GENETIC OBSOLESCENCE, A COSMIC BLOT, PART OF AN UNRAVELING THAT THE PHOENIX WAS DESIGNED TO CORRECT?

THEN YOU'RE AS INSANE AS THE *PHOENIX* HERSELF.

YOU DON'T UNDER-STAND, MISS FROST. I'M TRYING--

REMEMBER *OPEN DAY,* QUENTIN?

YES...NO! FOR SOPHIE, I'M GOING TO MAKE IT *ALL BETTER.*

QUENTIN, SHE'S KILLING THEM! *LET ME GO!*

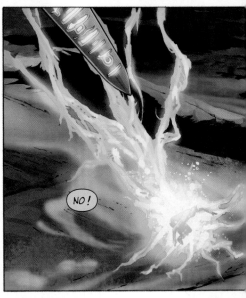

NO!

HENRY!

NNNN...

YES...

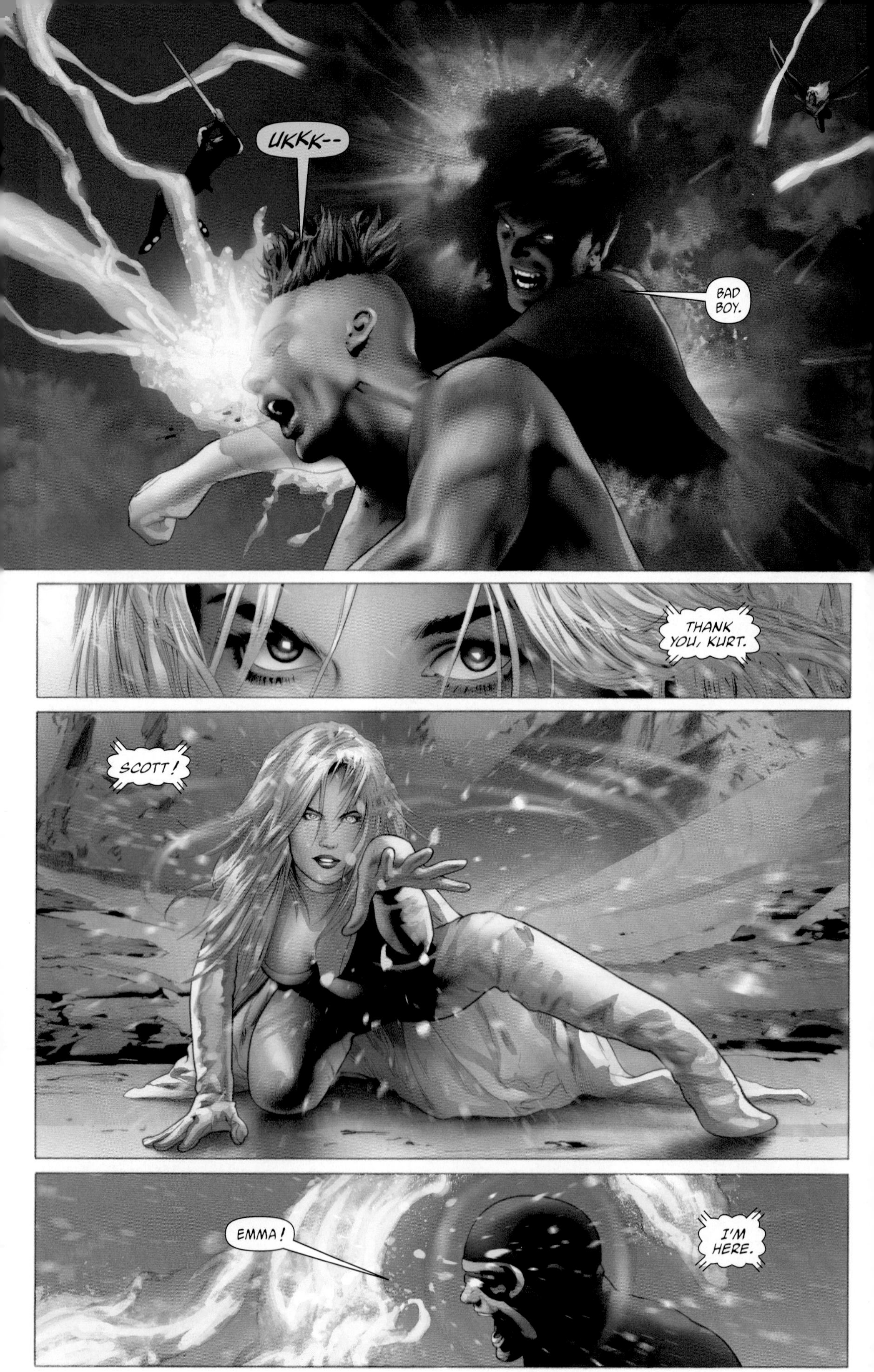
UKKK--
BAD BOY.
THANK YOU, KURT.
SCOTT!
EMMA!
I'M HERE.

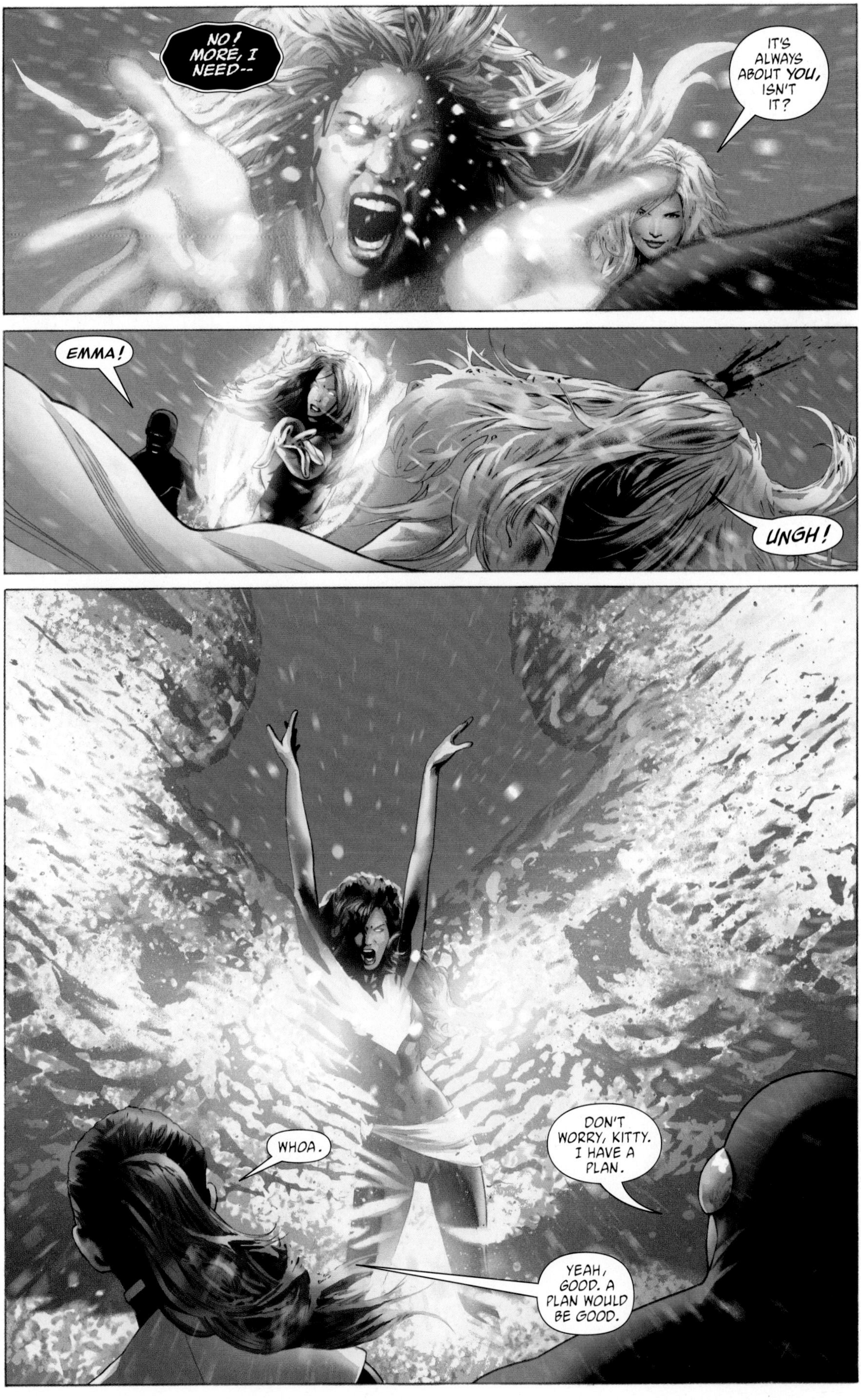

NO! MORE, I NEED--
IT'S ALWAYS ABOUT YOU, ISN'T IT?
EMMA!
UNGH!
WHOA.
DON'T WORRY, KITTY. I HAVE A PLAN.
YEAH, GOOD. A PLAN WOULD BE GOOD.

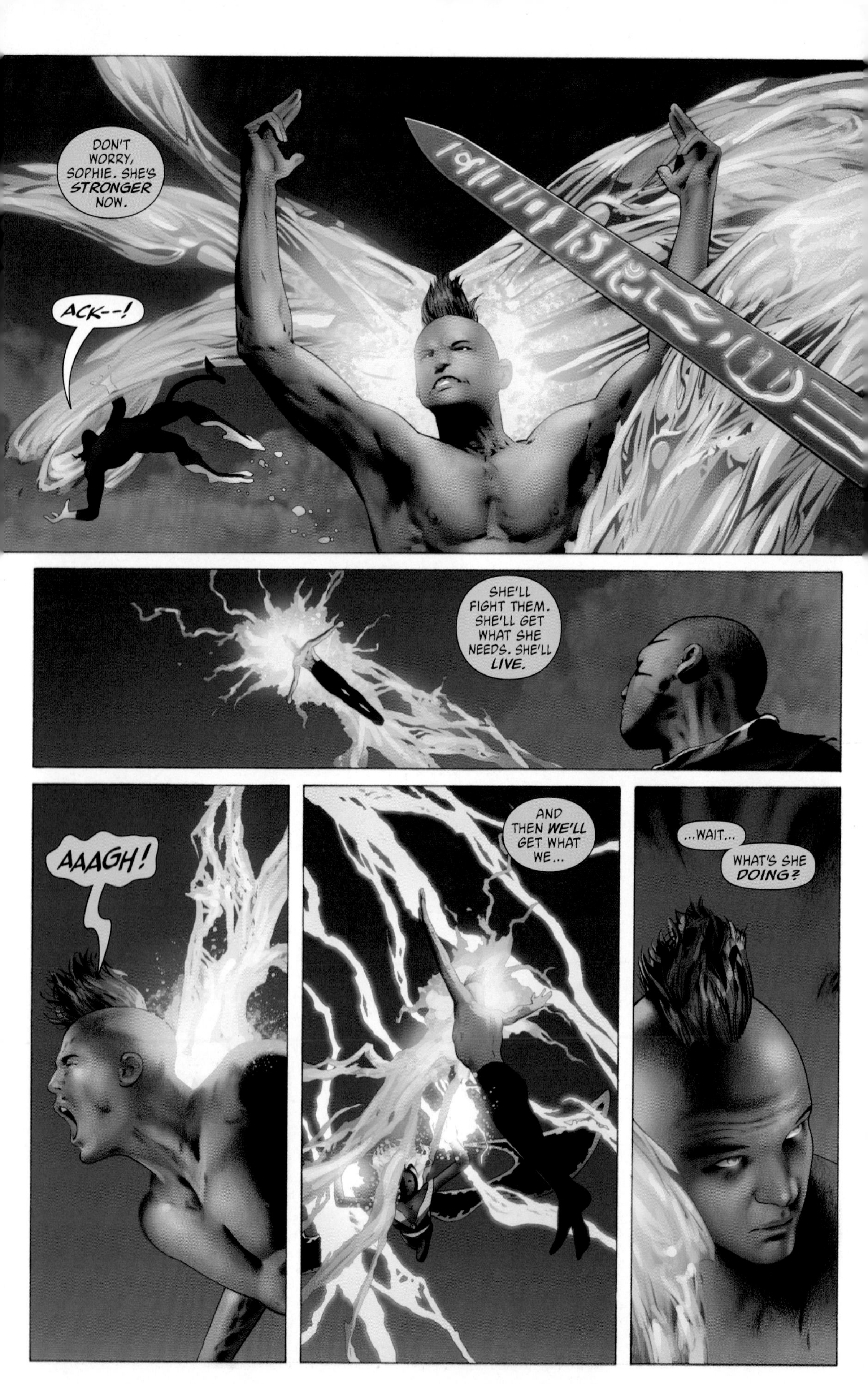
DON'T WORRY, SOPHIE. SHE'S STRONGER NOW.
ACK--!
SHE'LL FIGHT THEM. SHE'LL GET WHAT SHE NEEDS. SHE'LL LIVE.
AAAGH!
AND THEN WE'LL GET WHAT WE...
...WAIT...
WHAT'S SHE DOING?

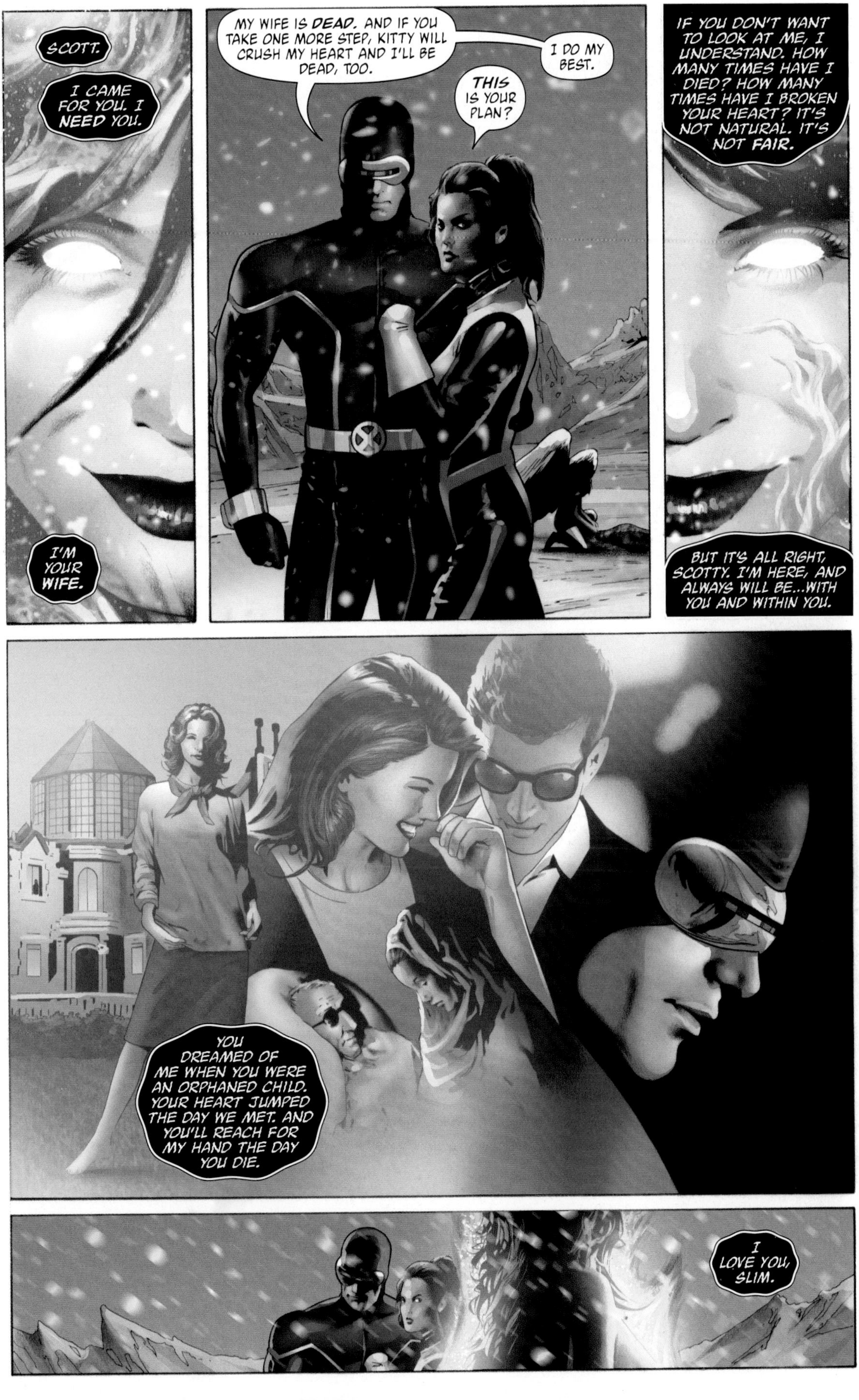
SCOTT.
I CAME FOR YOU. I NEED YOU.
I'M YOUR WIFE.
MY WIFE IS DEAD. AND IF YOU TAKE ONE MORE STEP, KITTY WILL CRUSH MY HEART AND I'LL BE DEAD, TOO.
THIS IS YOUR PLAN?
I DO MY BEST.
IF YOU DON'T WANT TO LOOK AT ME, I UNDERSTAND. HOW MANY TIMES HAVE I DIED? HOW MANY TIMES HAVE I BROKEN YOUR HEART? IT'S NOT NATURAL. IT'S NOT FAIR.
BUT IT'S ALL RIGHT, SCOTTY. I'M HERE, AND ALWAYS WILL BE...WITH YOU AND WITHIN YOU.
YOU DREAMED OF ME WHEN YOU WERE AN ORPHANED CHILD. YOUR HEART JUMPED THE DAY WE MET. AND YOU'LL REACH FOR MY HAND THE DAY YOU DIE.
I LOVE YOU, SLIM.

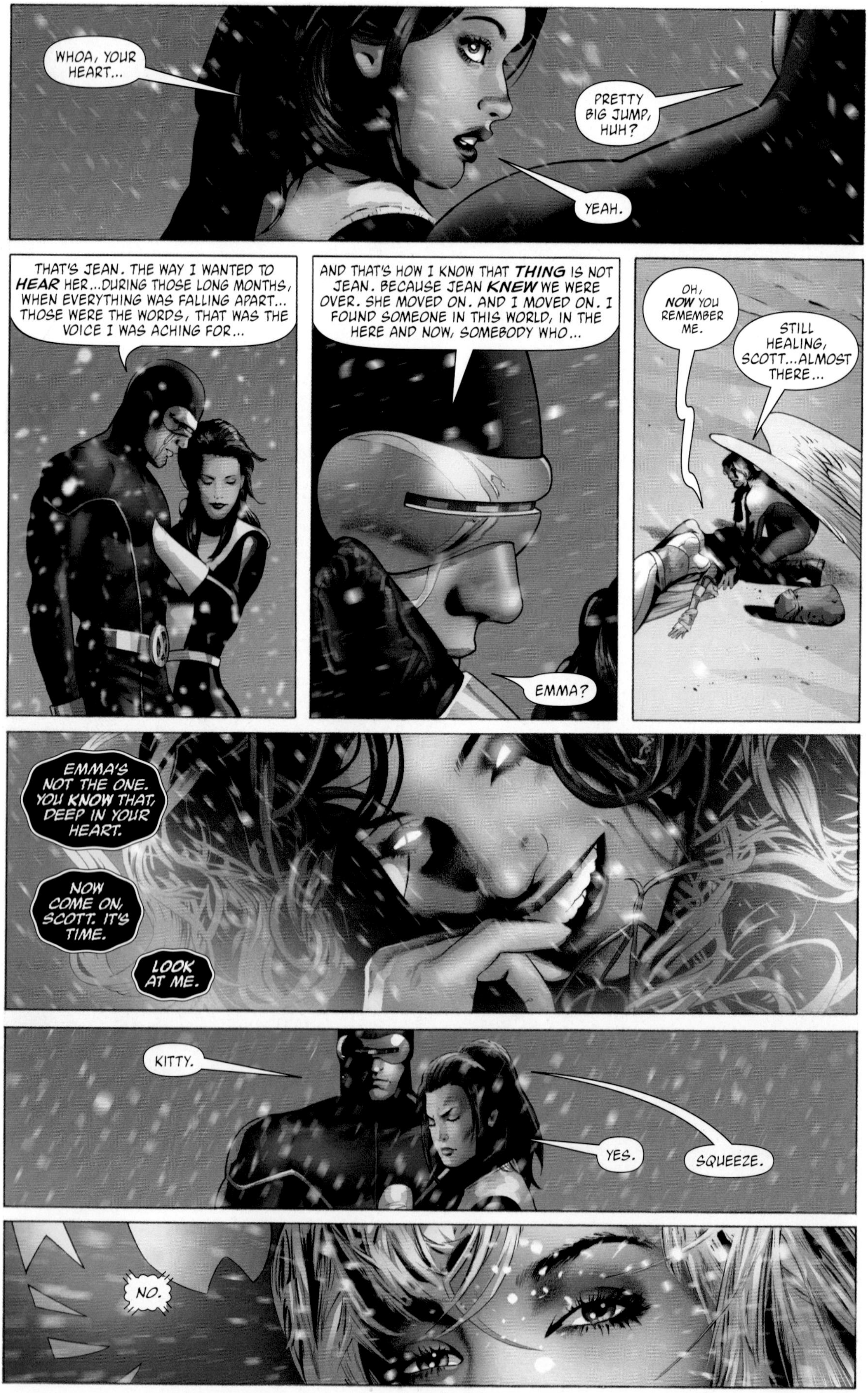
WHOA, YOUR HEART...
PRETTY BIG JUMP, HUH?
YEAH.
THAT'S JEAN. THE WAY I WANTED TO HEAR HER...DURING THOSE LONG MONTHS, WHEN EVERYTHING WAS FALLING APART... THOSE WERE THE WORDS, THAT WAS THE VOICE I WAS ACHING FOR...
AND THAT'S HOW I KNOW THAT THING IS NOT JEAN. BECAUSE JEAN KNEW WE WERE OVER. SHE MOVED ON. AND I MOVED ON. I FOUND SOMEONE IN THIS WORLD, IN THE HERE AND NOW, SOMEBODY WHO...
EMMA?
OH, NOW YOU REMEMBER ME.
STILL HEALING, SCOTT...ALMOST THERE...
EMMA'S NOT THE ONE. YOU KNOW THAT, DEEP IN YOUR HEART.
NOW COME ON, SCOTT. IT'S TIME.
LOOK AT ME.
KITTY.
YES.
SQUEEZE.
NO.

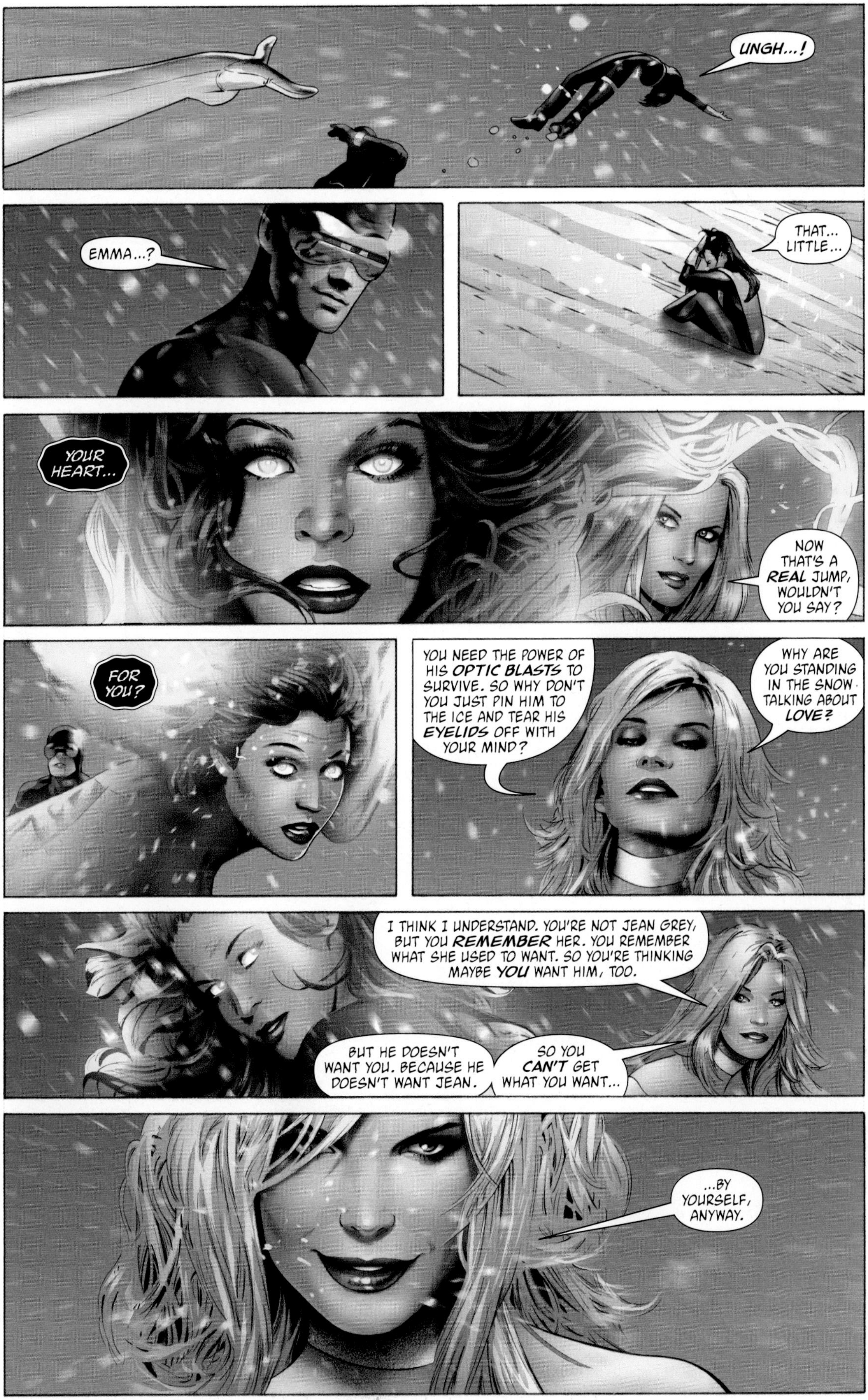
UNGH...!
EMMA...?
THAT... LITTLE...
YOUR HEART...
NOW THAT'S A REAL JUMP, WOULDN'T YOU SAY?
FOR YOU?
YOU NEED THE POWER OF HIS OPTIC BLASTS TO SURVIVE. SO WHY DON'T YOU JUST PIN HIM TO THE ICE AND TEAR HIS EYELIDS OFF WITH YOUR MIND?
WHY ARE YOU STANDING IN THE SNOW TALKING ABOUT LOVE?
I THINK I UNDERSTAND. YOU'RE NOT JEAN GREY, BUT YOU REMEMBER HER. YOU REMEMBER WHAT SHE USED TO WANT. SO YOU'RE THINKING MAYBE YOU WANT HIM, TOO.
BUT HE DOESN'T WANT YOU. BECAUSE HE DOESN'T WANT JEAN.
SO YOU CAN'T GET WHAT YOU WANT...
...BY YOURSELF, ANYWAY.

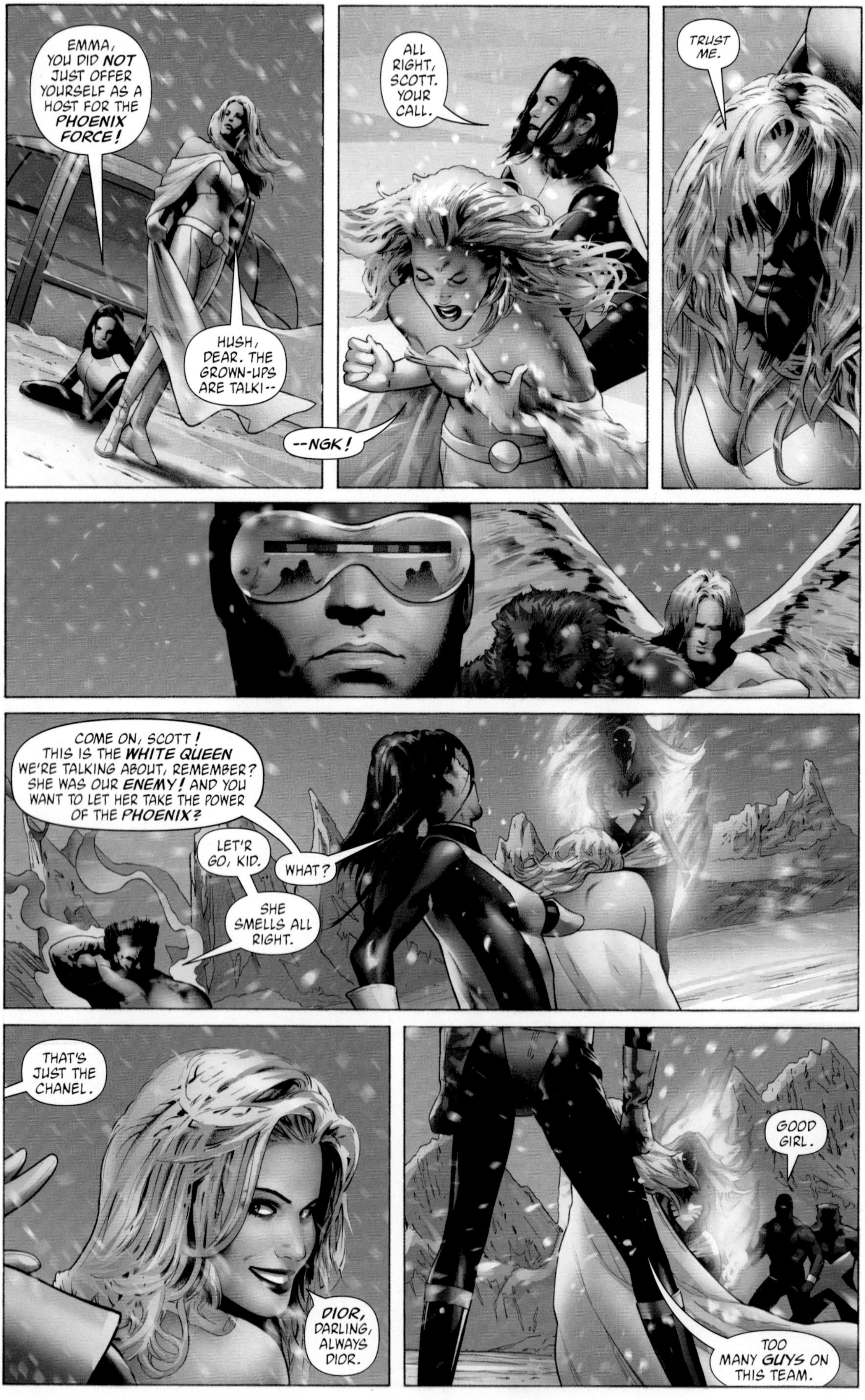
EMMA, YOU DID NOT JUST OFFER YOURSELF AS A HOST FOR THE PHOENIX FORCE!
HUSH, DEAR. THE GROWN-UPS ARE TALKI--
--NGK!
ALL RIGHT, SCOTT. YOUR CALL.
TRUST ME.
COME ON, SCOTT! THIS IS THE WHITE QUEEN WE'RE TALKING ABOUT, REMEMBER? SHE WAS OUR ENEMY! AND YOU WANT TO LET HER TAKE THE POWER OF THE PHOENIX?
LET'R GO, KID.
WHAT?
SHE SMELLS ALL RIGHT.
THAT'S JUST THE CHANEL.
DIOR, DARLING, ALWAYS DIOR.
GOOD GIRL.
TOO MANY GUYS ON THIS TEAM.

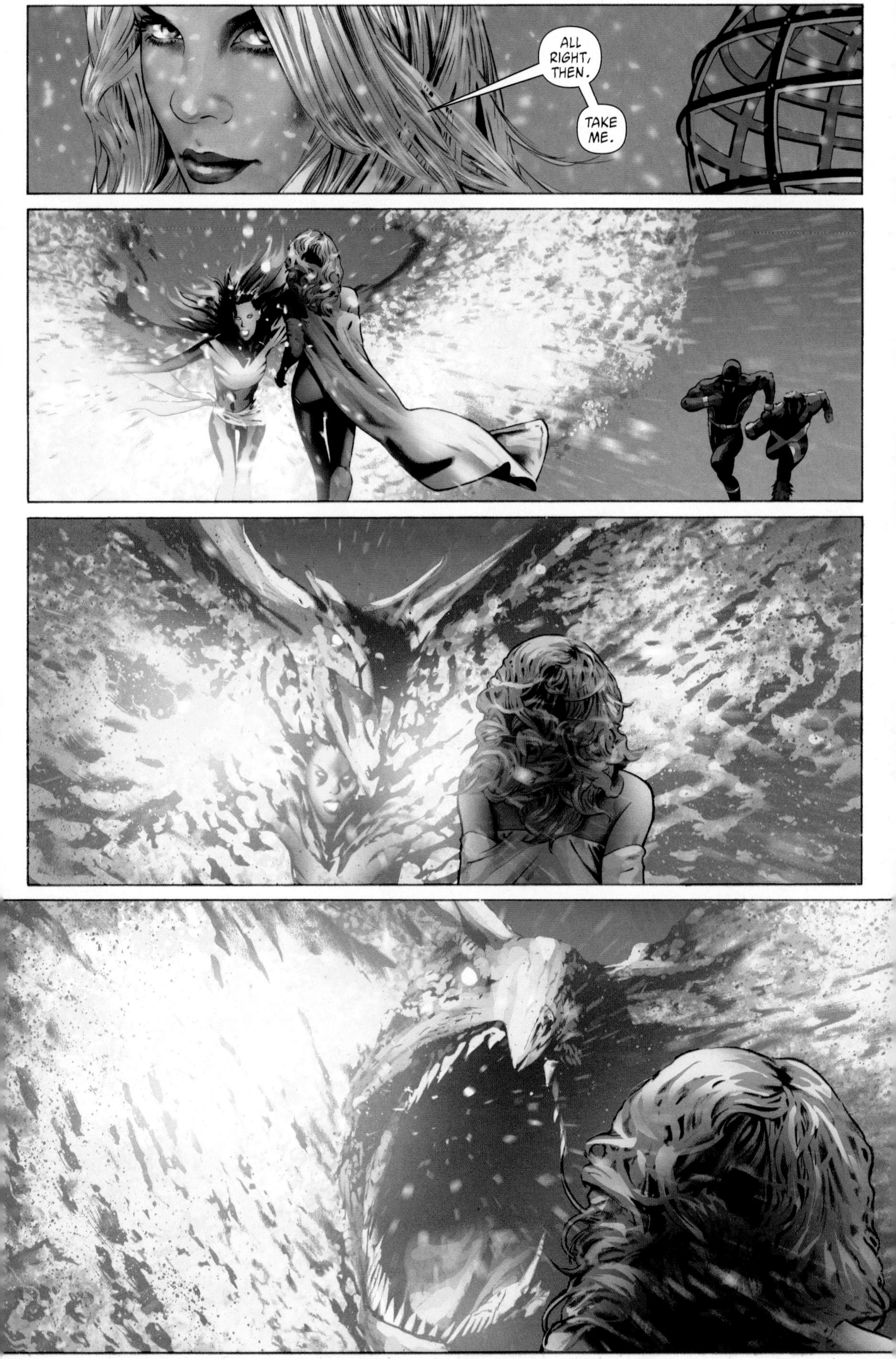
ALL RIGHT, THEN.
TAKE ME.

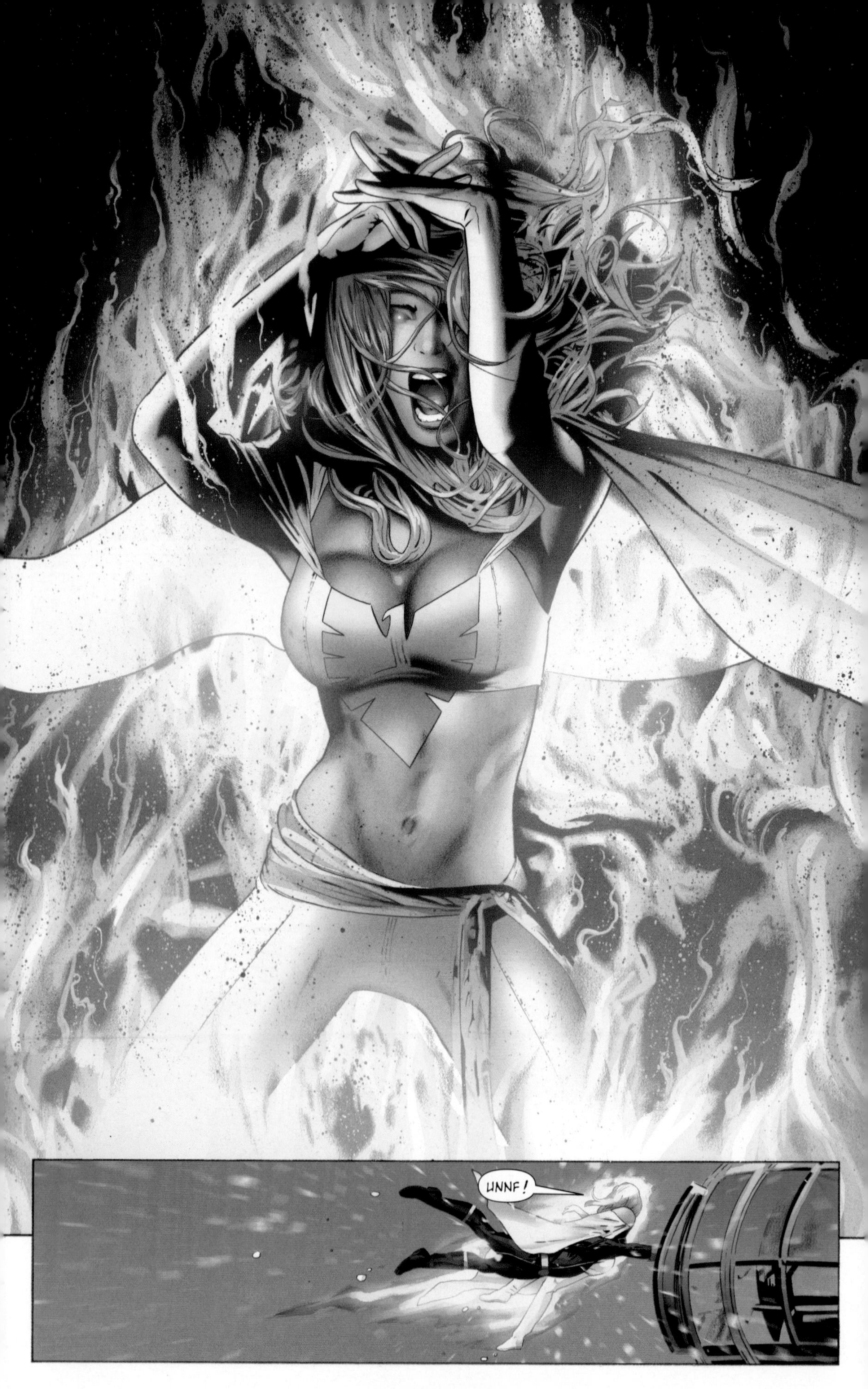
UNNF!

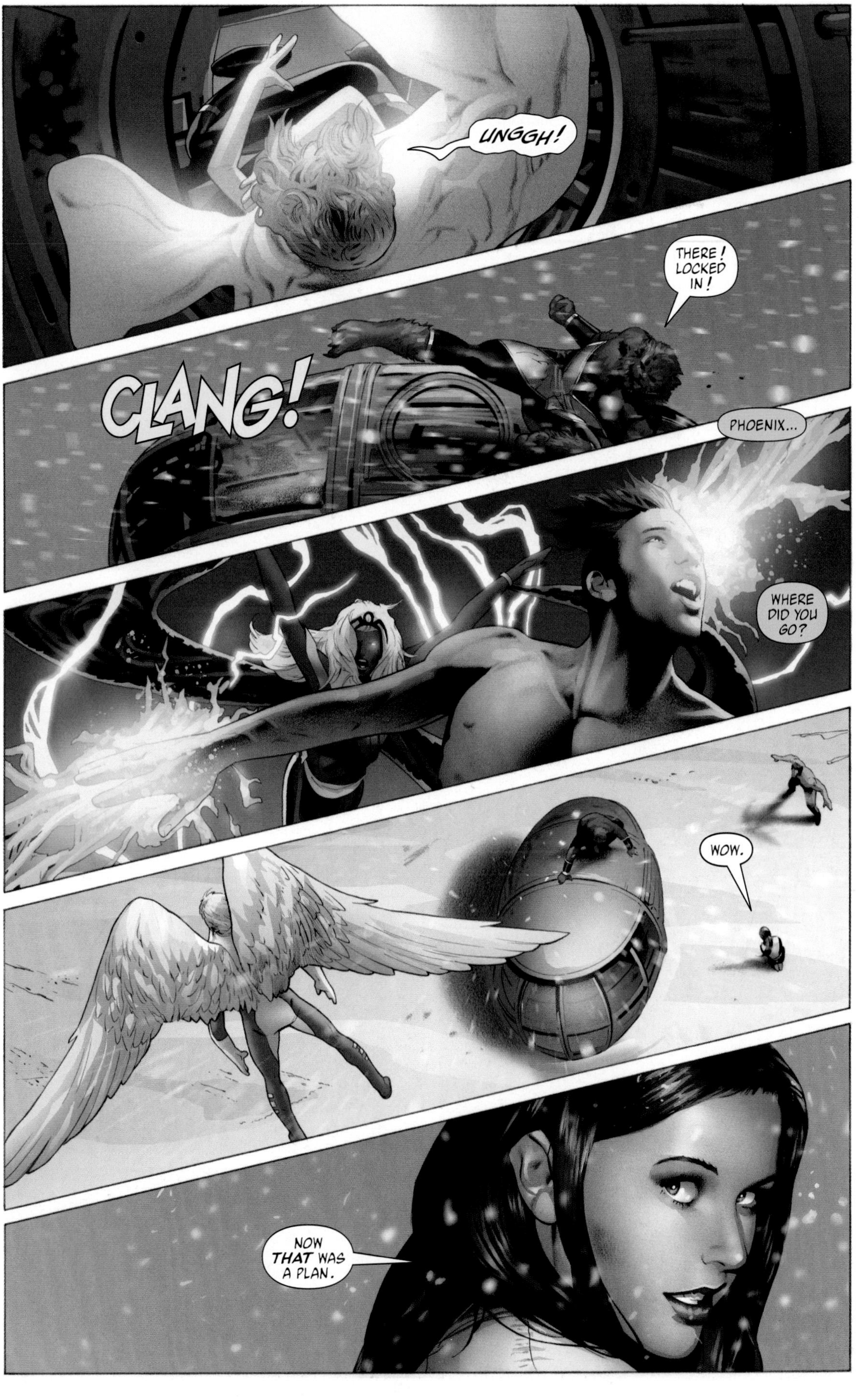
UNGGH!
THERE! LOCKED IN!
CLANG!
PHOENIX...
WHERE DID YOU GO?
WOW.
NOW THAT WAS A PLAN.

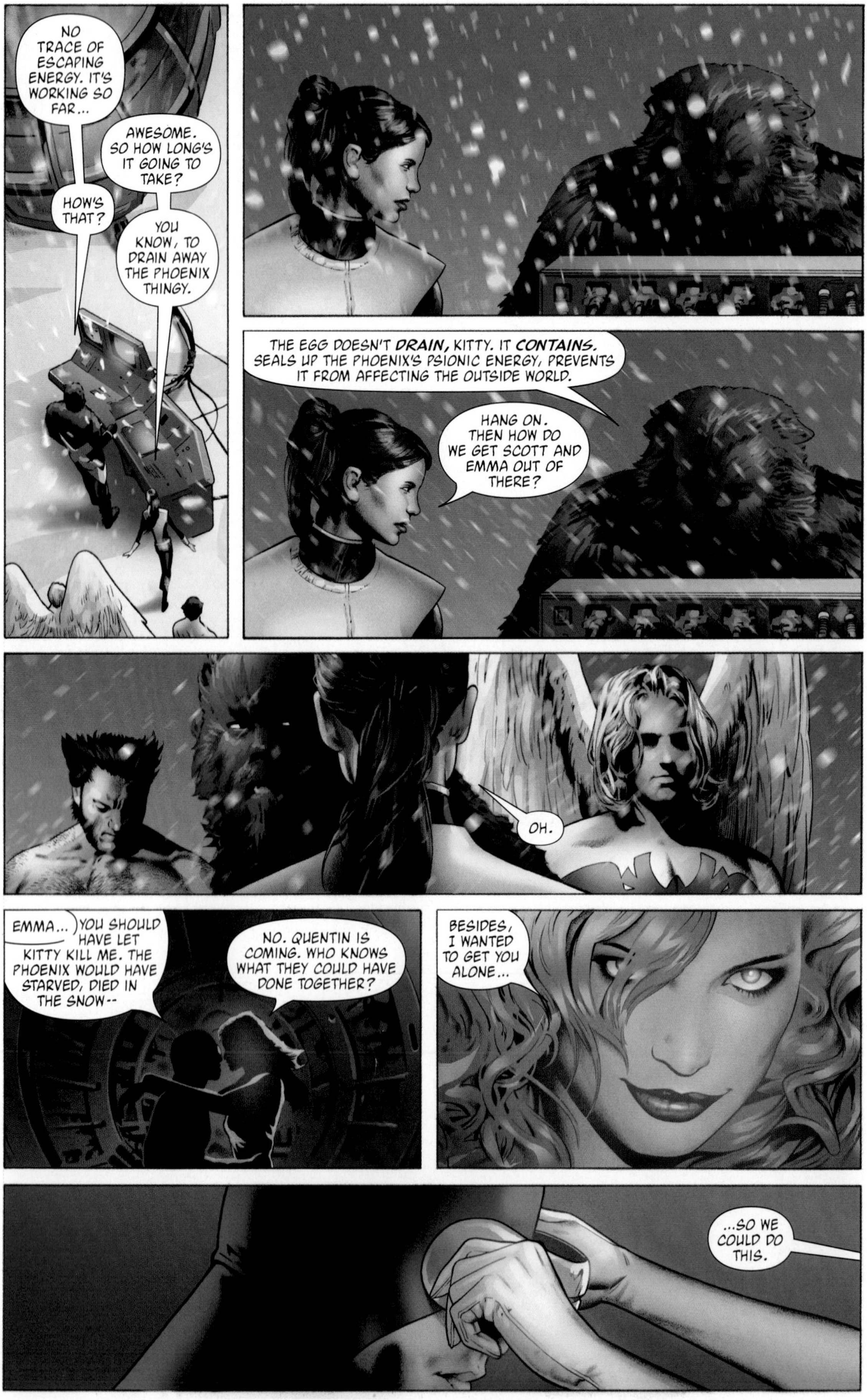
NO TRACE OF ESCAPING ENERGY. IT'S WORKING SO FAR...
AWESOME. SO HOW LONG'S IT GOING TO TAKE?
HOW'S THAT?
YOU KNOW, TO DRAIN AWAY THE PHOENIX THINGY.
THE EGG DOESN'T DRAIN, KITTY. IT CONTAINS. SEALS UP THE PHOENIX'S PSIONIC ENERGY, PREVENTS IT FROM AFFECTING THE OUTSIDE WORLD.
HANG ON. THEN HOW DO WE GET SCOTT AND EMMA OUT OF THERE?
OH.
EMMA...
YOU SHOULD HAVE LET KITTY KILL ME. THE PHOENIX WOULD HAVE STARVED, DIED IN THE SNOW--
NO. QUENTIN IS COMING. WHO KNOWS WHAT THEY COULD HAVE DONE TOGETHER?
BESIDES, I WANTED TO GET YOU ALONE...
...SO WE COULD DO THIS.

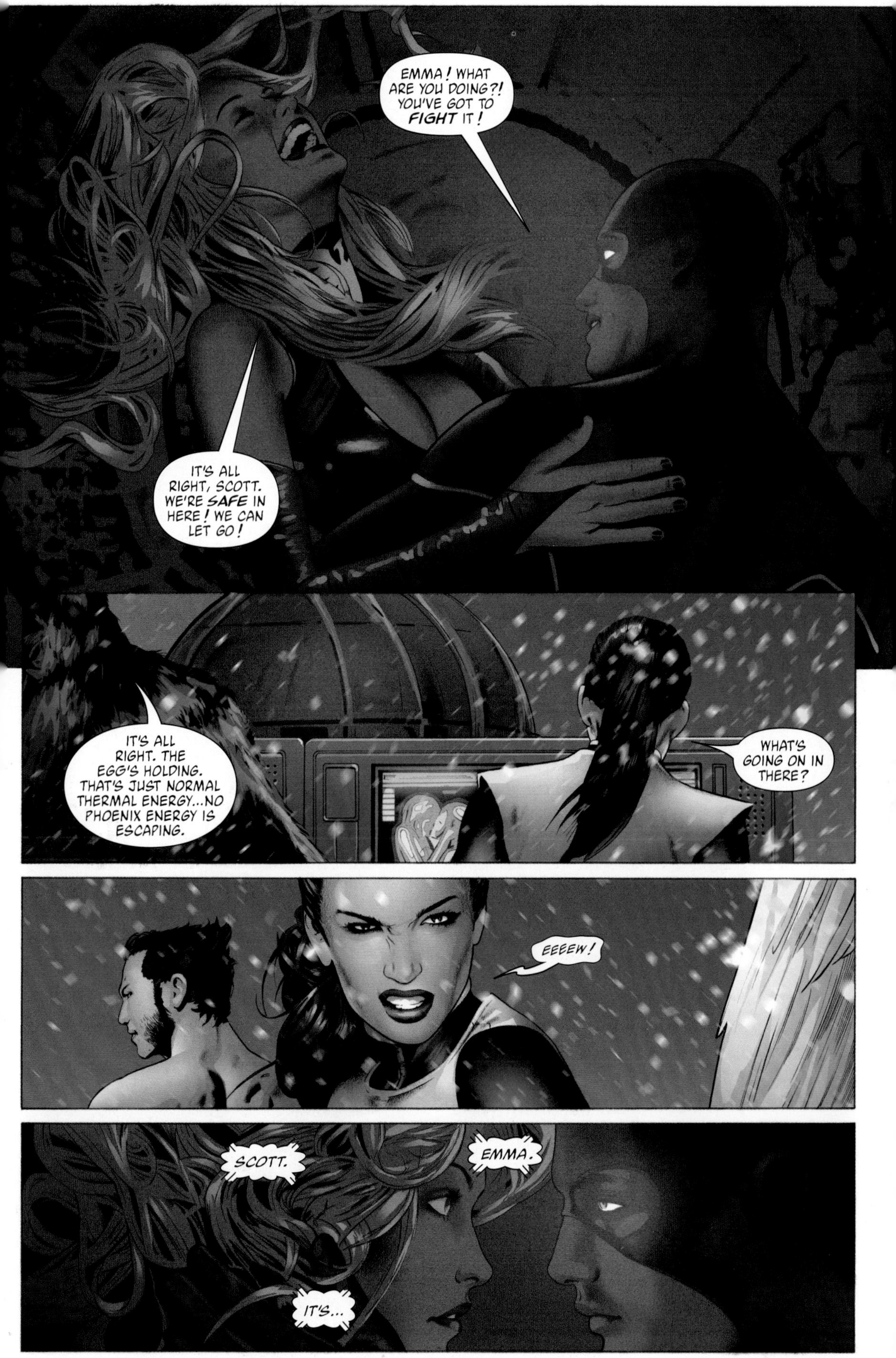
EMMA! WHAT ARE YOU DOING?! YOU'VE GOT TO FIGHT IT!
IT'S ALL RIGHT, SCOTT. WE'RE SAFE IN HERE! WE CAN LET GO!
IT'S ALL RIGHT. THE EGG'S HOLDING. THAT'S JUST NORMAL THERMAL ENERGY...NO PHOENIX ENERGY IS ESCAPING.
WHAT'S GOING ON IN THERE?
EEEEW!
SCOTT.
EMMA.
IT'S...

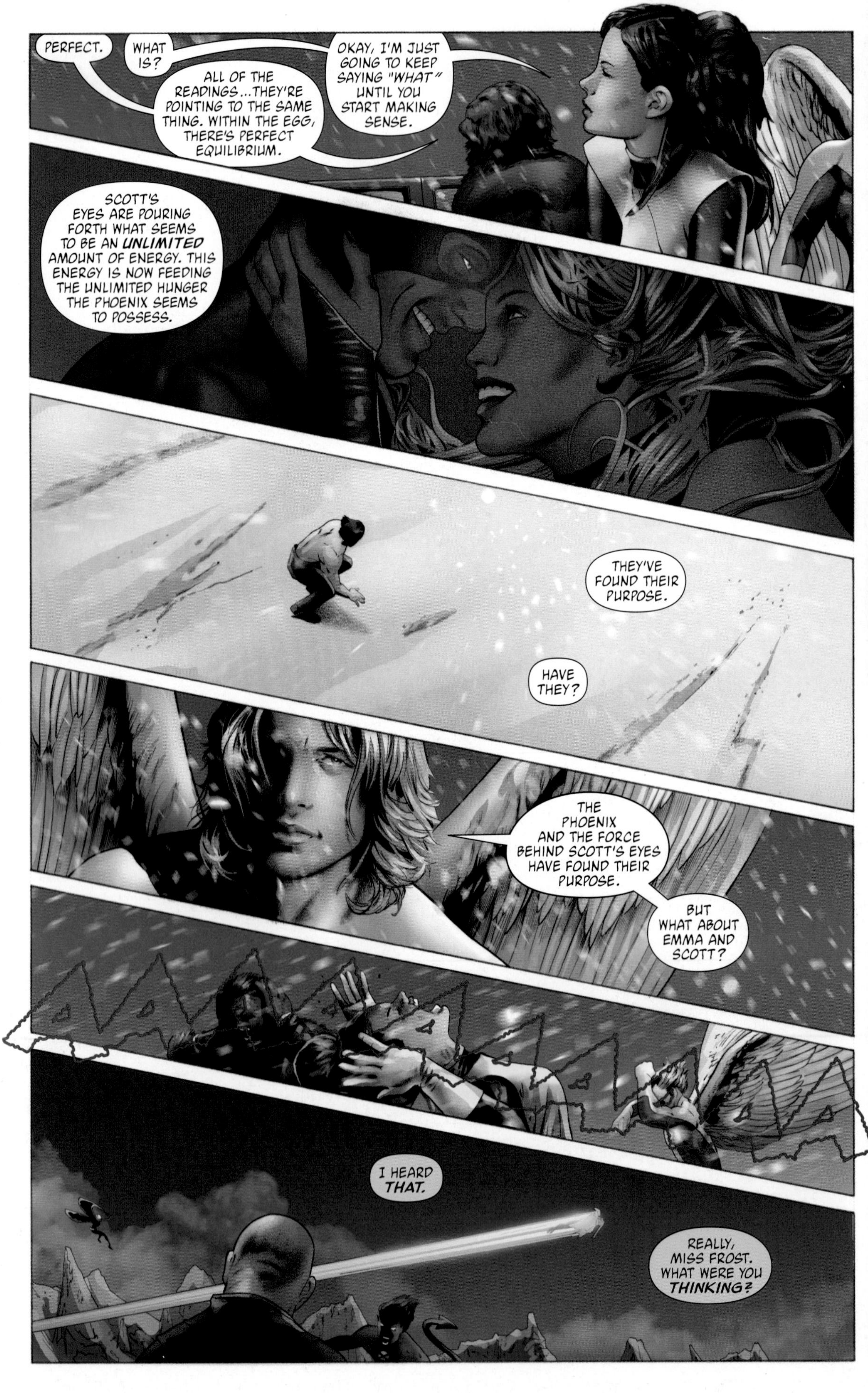
PERFECT.
WHAT IS?
ALL OF THE READINGS...THEY'RE POINTING TO THE SAME THING. WITHIN THE EGG, THERE'S PERFECT EQUILIBRIUM.
OKAY, I'M JUST GOING TO KEEP SAYING "WHAT" UNTIL YOU START MAKING SENSE.
SCOTT'S EYES ARE POURING FORTH WHAT SEEMS TO BE AN UNLIMITED AMOUNT OF ENERGY. THIS ENERGY IS NOW FEEDING THE UNLIMITED HUNGER THE PHOENIX SEEMS TO POSSESS.
THEY'VE FOUND THEIR PURPOSE.
HAVE THEY?
THE PHOENIX AND THE FORCE BEHIND SCOTT'S EYES HAVE FOUND THEIR PURPOSE.
BUT WHAT ABOUT EMMA AND SCOTT?
I HEARD THAT.
REALLY, MISS FROST. WHAT WERE YOU THINKING?

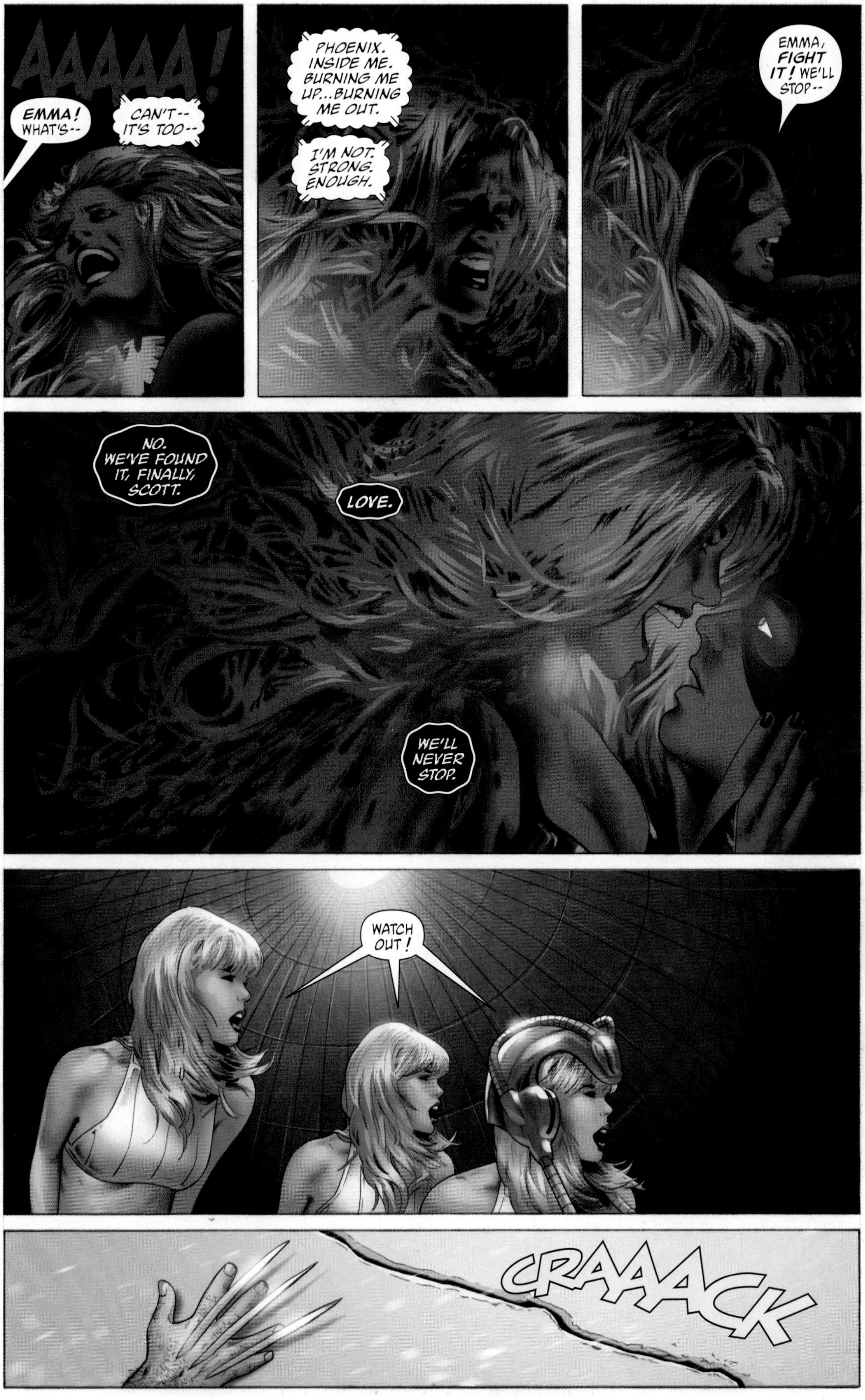
AAAAA!
EMMA! WHAT'S--
CAN'T-- IT'S TOO--
PHOENIX. INSIDE ME. BURNING ME UP...BURNING ME OUT.
I'M NOT. STRONG. ENOUGH.
EMMA, FIGHT IT! WE'LL STOP--
NO. WE'VE FOUND IT, FINALLY, SCOTT.
LOVE.
WE'LL NEVER STOP.
WATCH OUT!
CRAAACK

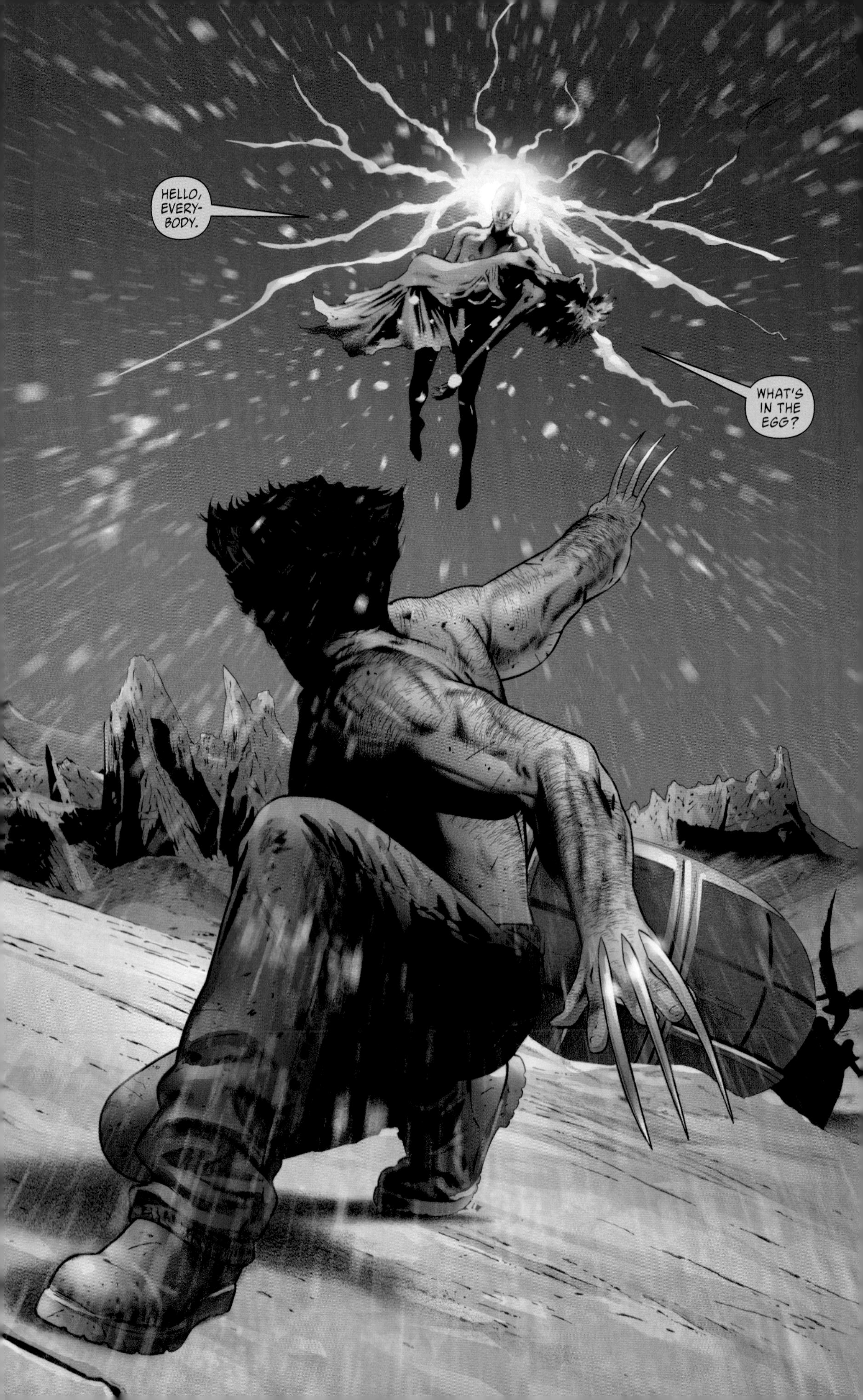
HELLO, EVERY-BODY.
WHAT'S IN THE EGG?

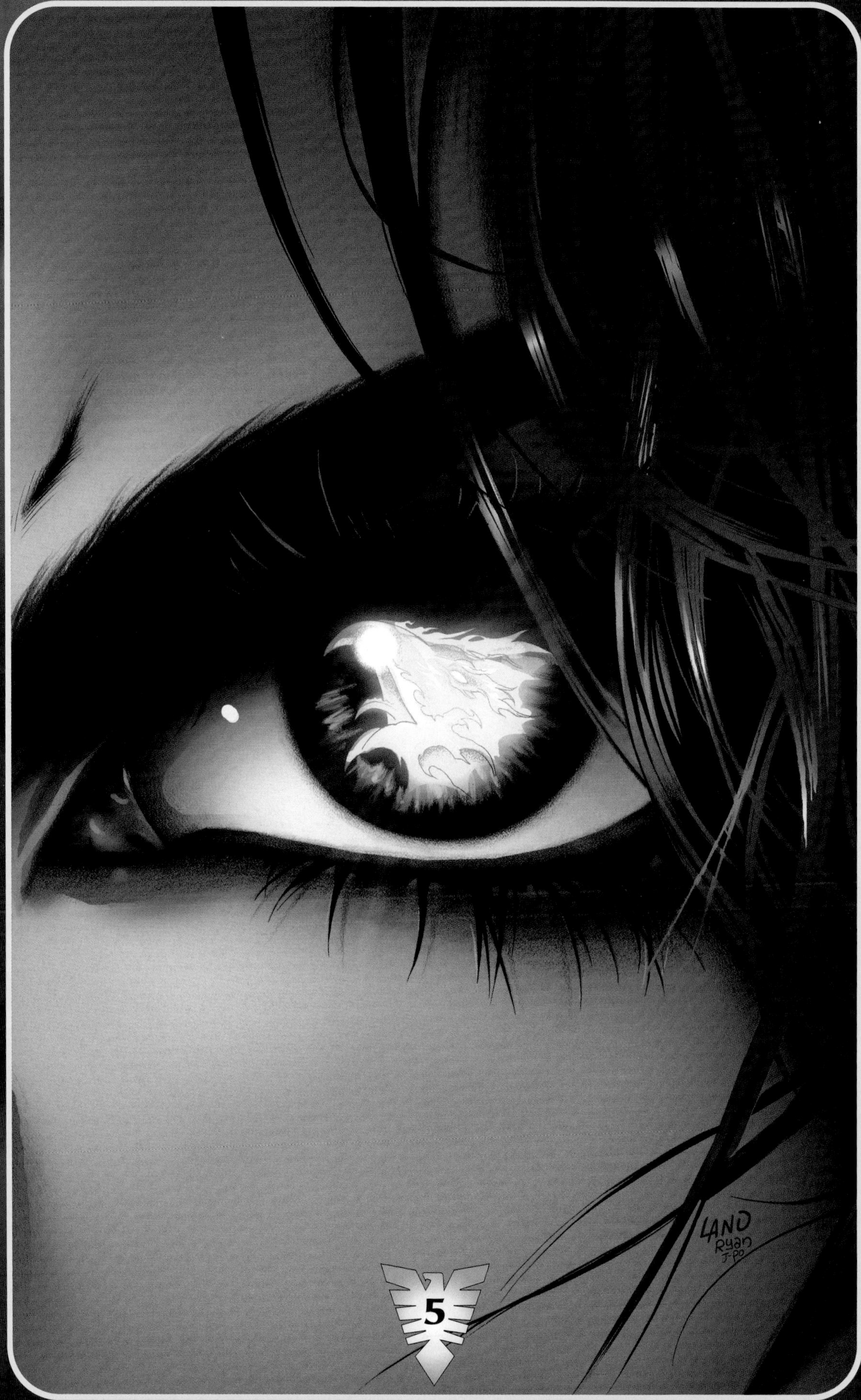
LAND
Ryan
J-Po
5

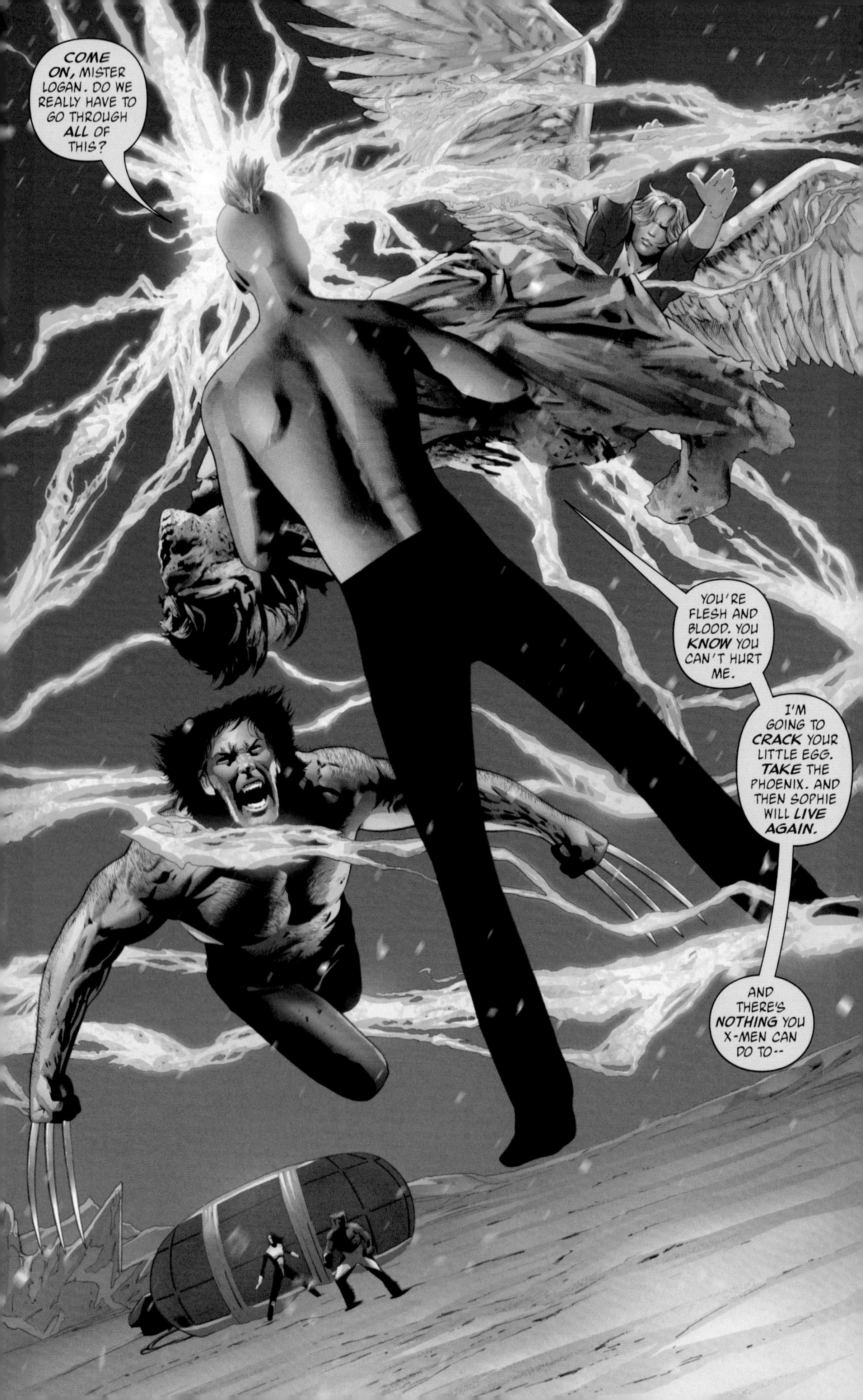
COME ON, MISTER LOGAN. DO WE REALLY HAVE TO GO THROUGH ALL OF THIS?
YOU'RE FLESH AND BLOOD. YOU KNOW YOU CAN'T HURT ME.
I'M GOING TO CRACK YOUR LITTLE EGG. TAKE THE PHOENIX. AND THEN SOPHIE WILL LIVE AGAIN.
AND THERE'S NOTHING YOU X-MEN CAN DO TO--

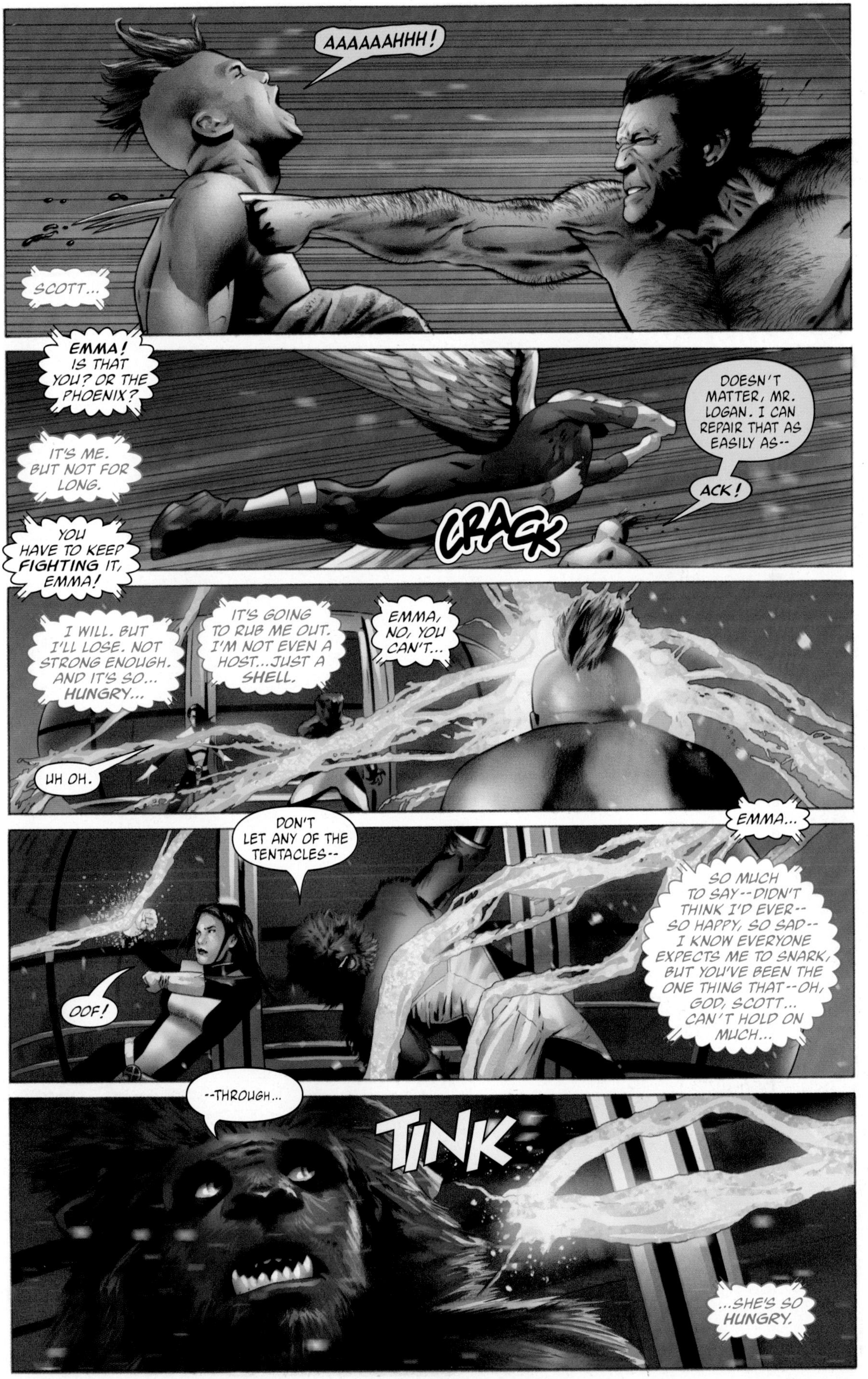
AAAAAAHHH!
SCOTT...
EMMA! IS THAT YOU? OR THE PHOENIX?
IT'S ME. BUT NOT FOR LONG.
YOU HAVE TO KEEP FIGHTING IT, EMMA!
DOESN'T MATTER, MR. LOGAN. I CAN REPAIR THAT AS EASILY AS--
CRACK
ACK!
I WILL. BUT I'LL LOSE. NOT STRONG ENOUGH. AND IT'S SO... HUNGRY...
IT'S GOING TO RUB ME OUT. I'M NOT EVEN A HOST...JUST A SHELL.
EMMA, NO, YOU CAN'T...
UH OH.
DON'T LET ANY OF THE TENTACLES--
EMMA...
SO MUCH TO SAY--DIDN'T THINK I'D EVER--SO HAPPY, SO SAD--I KNOW EVERYONE EXPECTS ME TO SNARK, BUT YOU'VE BEEN THE ONE THING THAT--OH, GOD, SCOTT... CAN'T HOLD ON MUCH...
OOF!
--THROUGH...
TINK
...SHE'S SO HUNGRY.

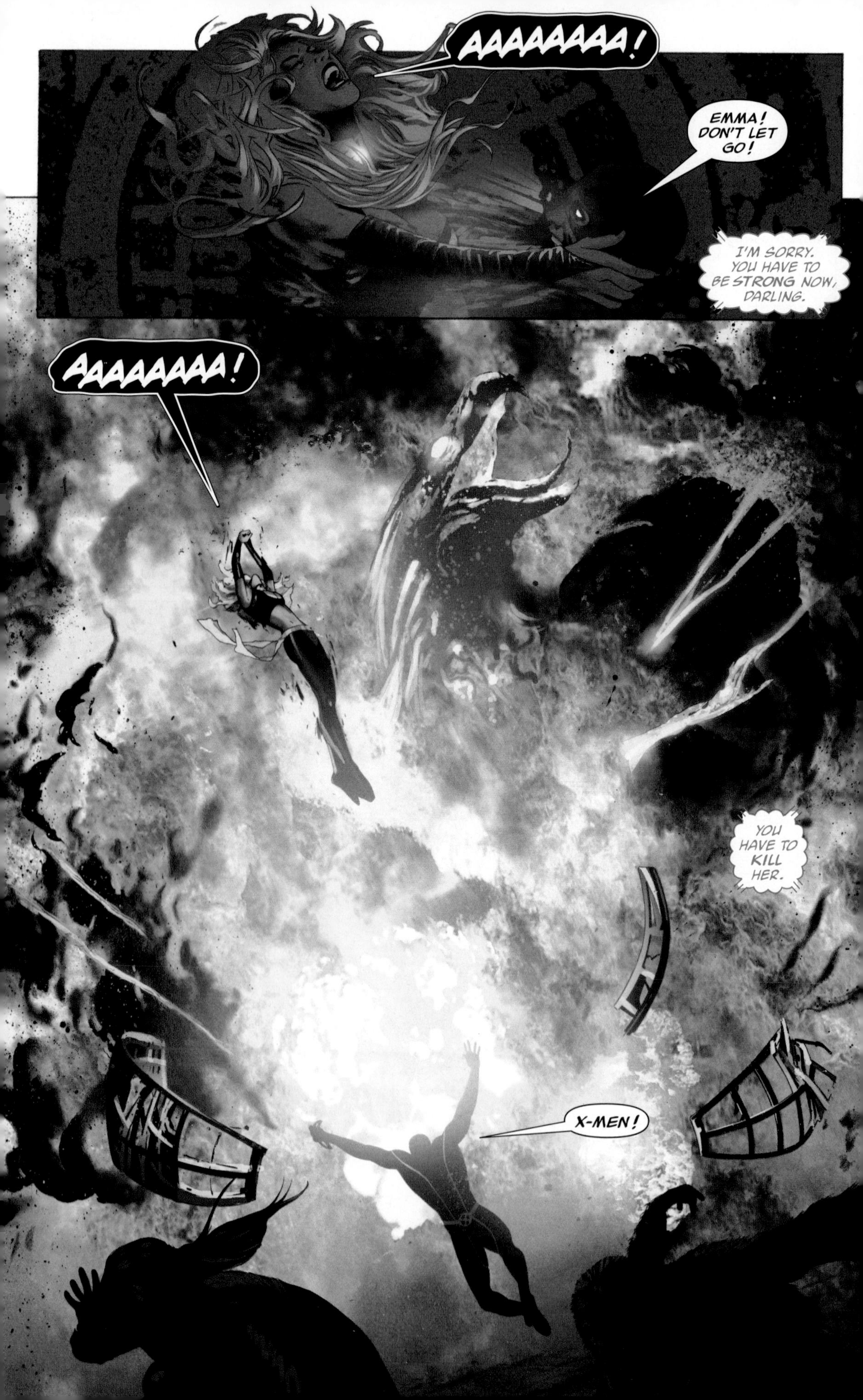
AAAAAAAA!
EMMA! DON'T LET GO!
I'M SORRY. YOU HAVE TO BE STRONG NOW, DARLING.
AAAAAAAA!
YOU HAVE TO KILL HER.
X-MEN!

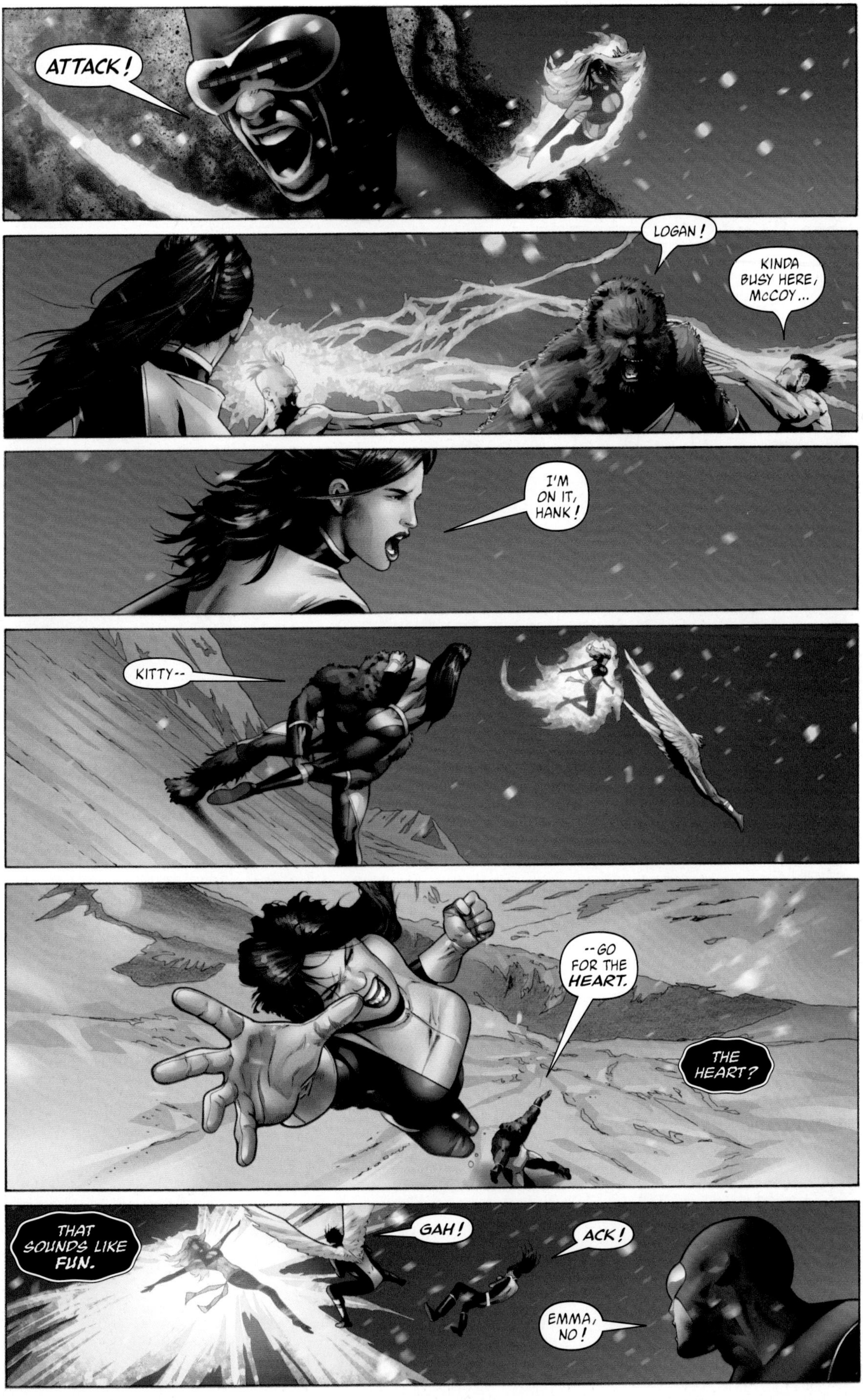
ATTACK!
LOGAN!
KINDA BUSY HERE, McCOY...
I'M ON IT, HANK!
KITTY--
--GO FOR THE HEART.
THE HEART?
THAT SOUNDS LIKE FUN.
GAH!
ACK!
EMMA, NO!

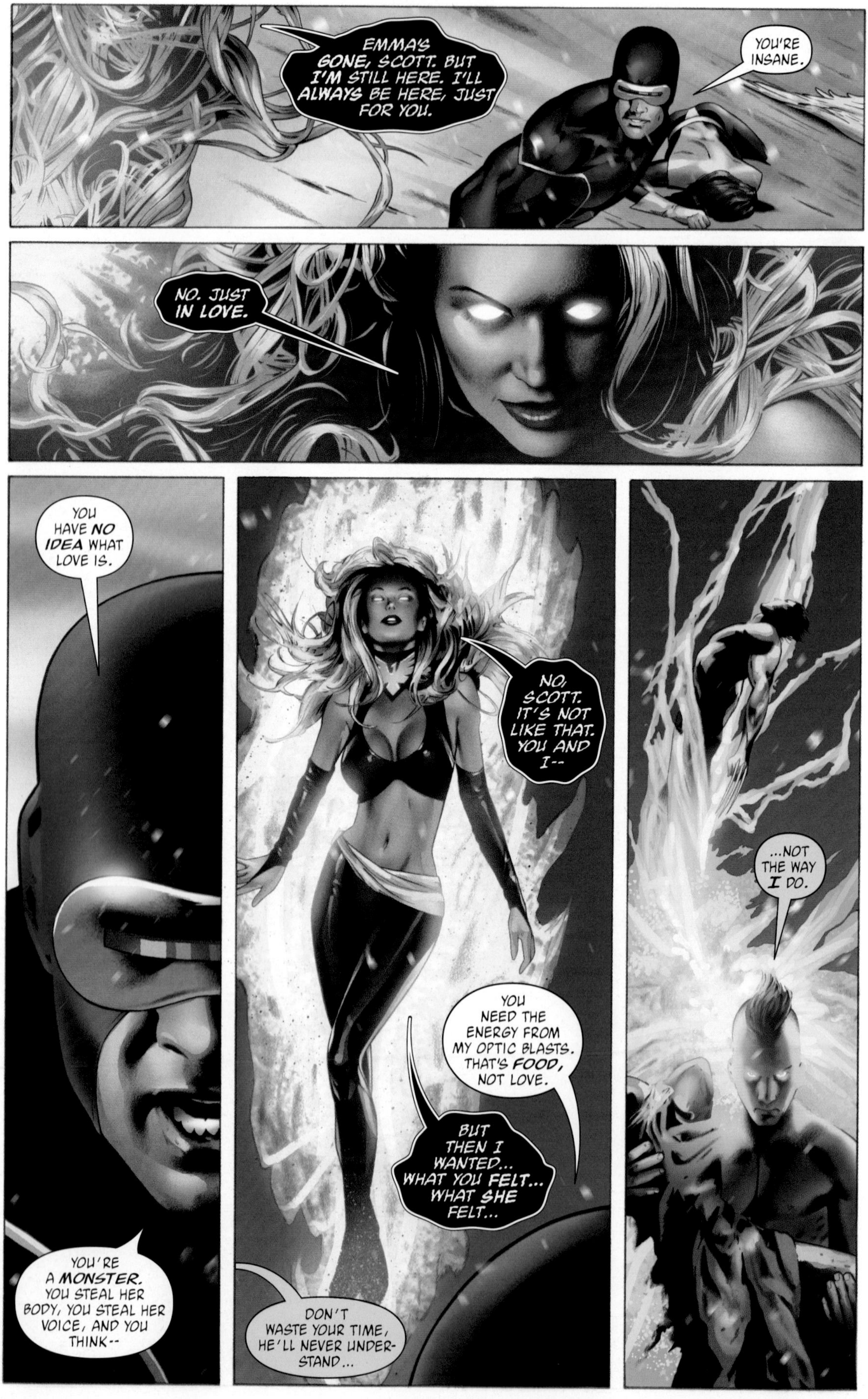
EMMA'S GONE, SCOTT. BUT I'M STILL HERE. I'LL ALWAYS BE HERE, JUST FOR YOU.
YOU'RE INSANE.
NO. JUST IN LOVE.
YOU HAVE NO IDEA WHAT LOVE IS.
YOU'RE A MONSTER. YOU STEAL HER BODY, YOU STEAL HER VOICE, AND YOU THINK--
NO, SCOTT. IT'S NOT LIKE THAT. YOU AND I--
YOU NEED THE ENERGY FROM MY OPTIC BLASTS. THAT'S FOOD, NOT LOVE.
BUT THEN I WANTED... WHAT YOU FELT... WHAT SHE FELT...
DON'T WASTE YOUR TIME, HE'LL NEVER UNDER-STAND...
...NOT THE WAY I DO.

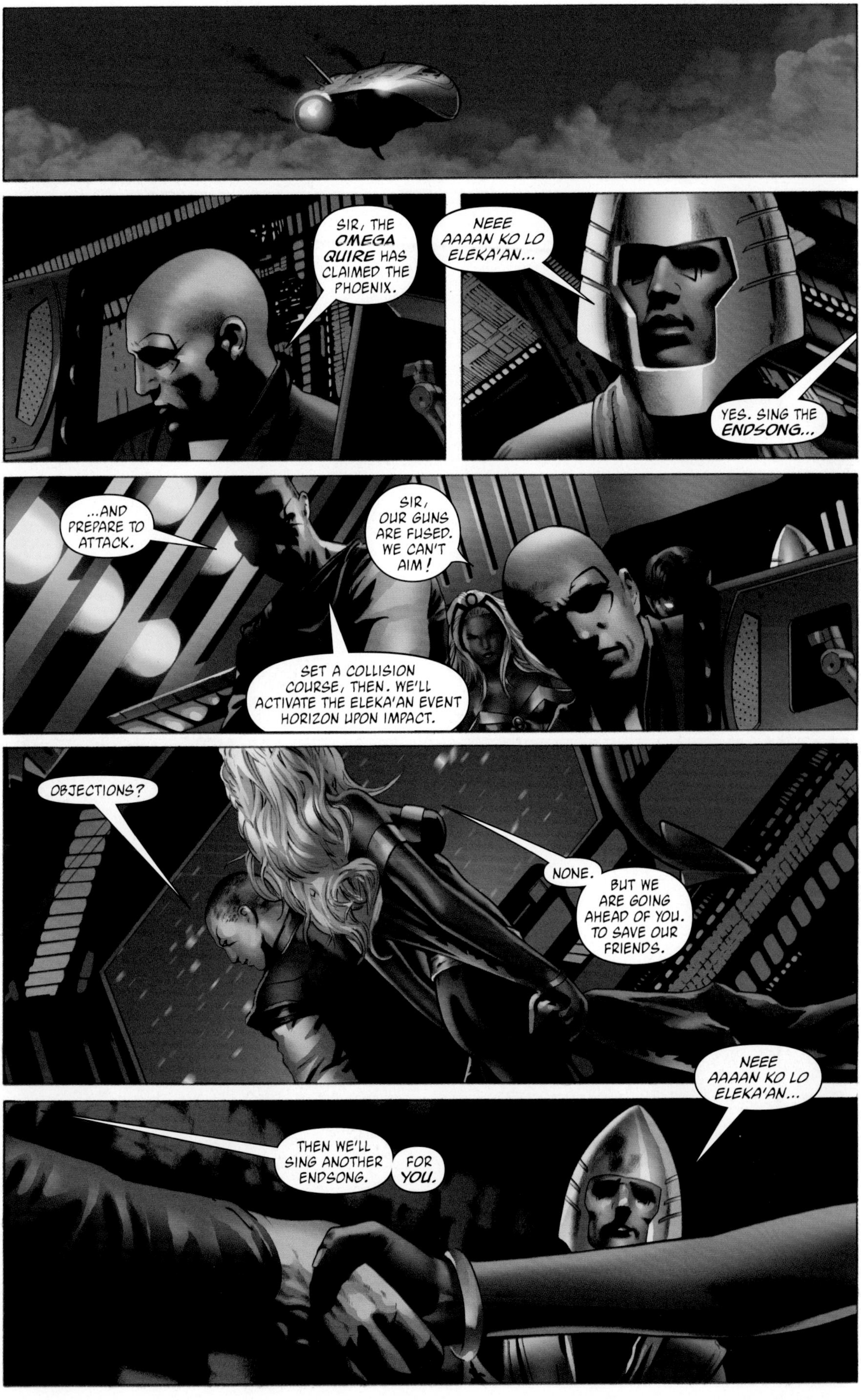
SIR, THE OMEGA QUIRE HAS CLAIMED THE PHOENIX.
NEEE AAAAN KO LO ELEKA'AN...
YES. SING THE ENDSONG...
...AND PREPARE TO ATTACK.
SIR, OUR GUNS ARE FUSED. WE CAN'T AIM!
SET A COLLISION COURSE, THEN. WE'LL ACTIVATE THE ELEKA'AN EVENT HORIZON UPON IMPACT.
OBJECTIONS?
NONE.
BUT WE ARE GOING AHEAD OF YOU. TO SAVE OUR FRIENDS.
NEEE AAAAN KO LO ELEKA'AN...
THEN WE'LL SING ANOTHER ENDSONG.
FOR YOU.

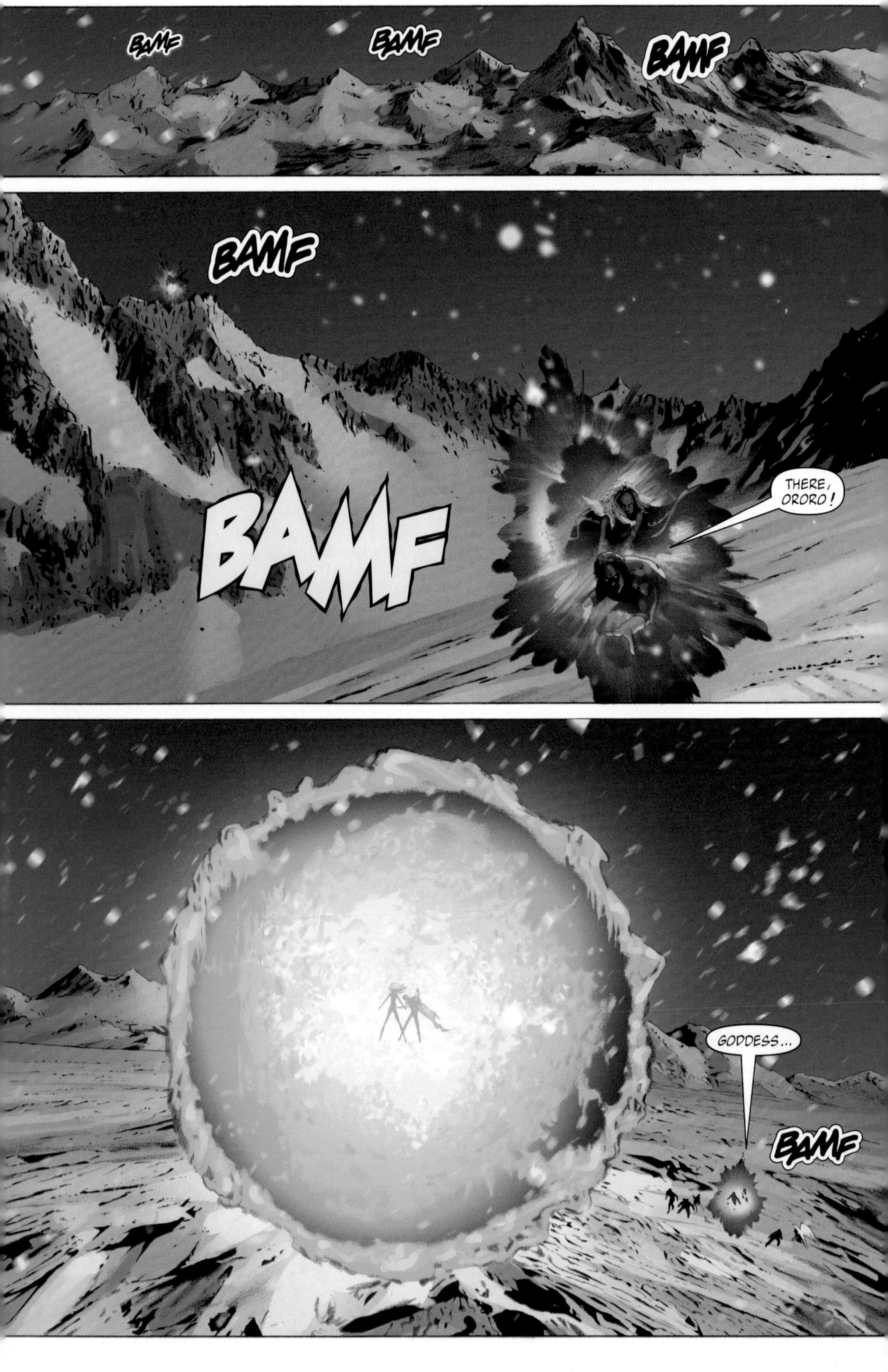
BAMF
BAMF
BAMF
BAMF
BAMF
THERE, ORORO!
GODDESS...
BAMF

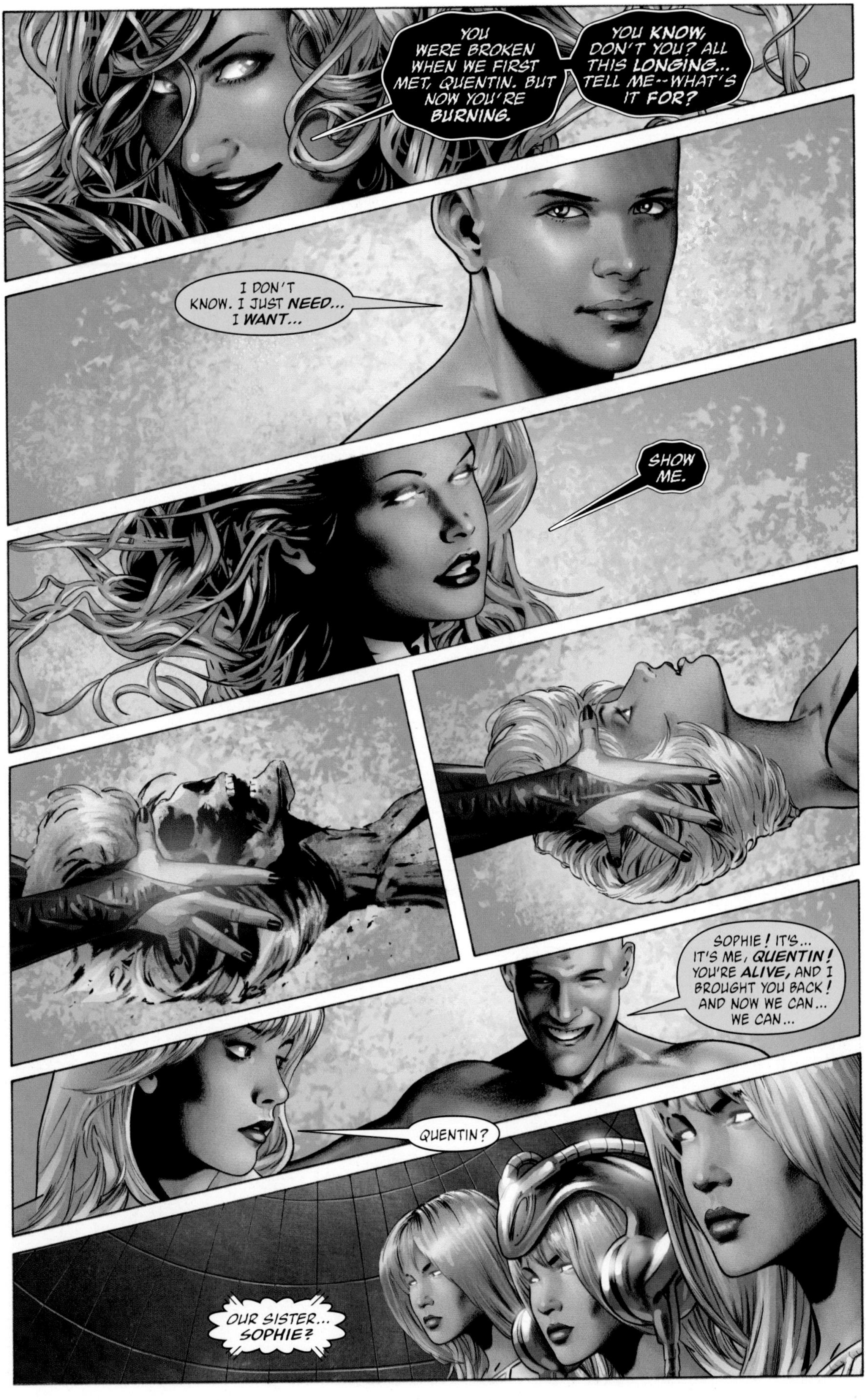
YOU WERE BROKEN WHEN WE FIRST MET, QUENTIN. BUT NOW YOU'RE BURNING.
YOU KNOW, DON'T YOU? ALL THIS LONGING... TELL ME--WHAT'S IT FOR?
I DON'T KNOW. I JUST NEED... I WANT...
SHOW ME.
SOPHIE! IT'S... IT'S ME, QUENTIN! YOU'RE ALIVE, AND I BROUGHT YOU BACK! AND NOW WE CAN... WE CAN...
QUENTIN?
OUR SISTER... SOPHIE?

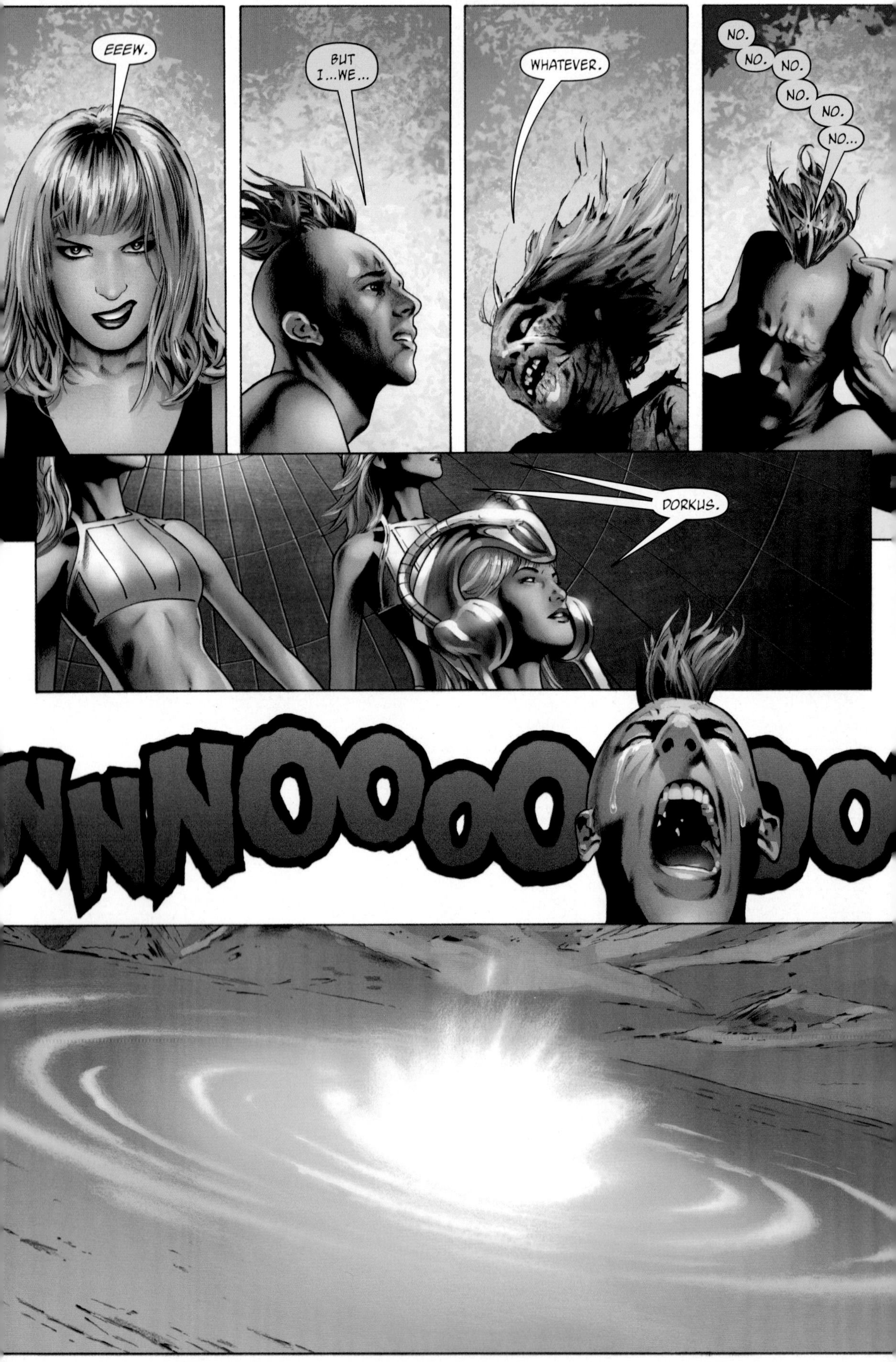
EEEW.
BUT I...WE...
WHATEVER.
NO.
NO. NO.
NO.
NO.
NO...
DORKUS.
NNNOOOoOOOO

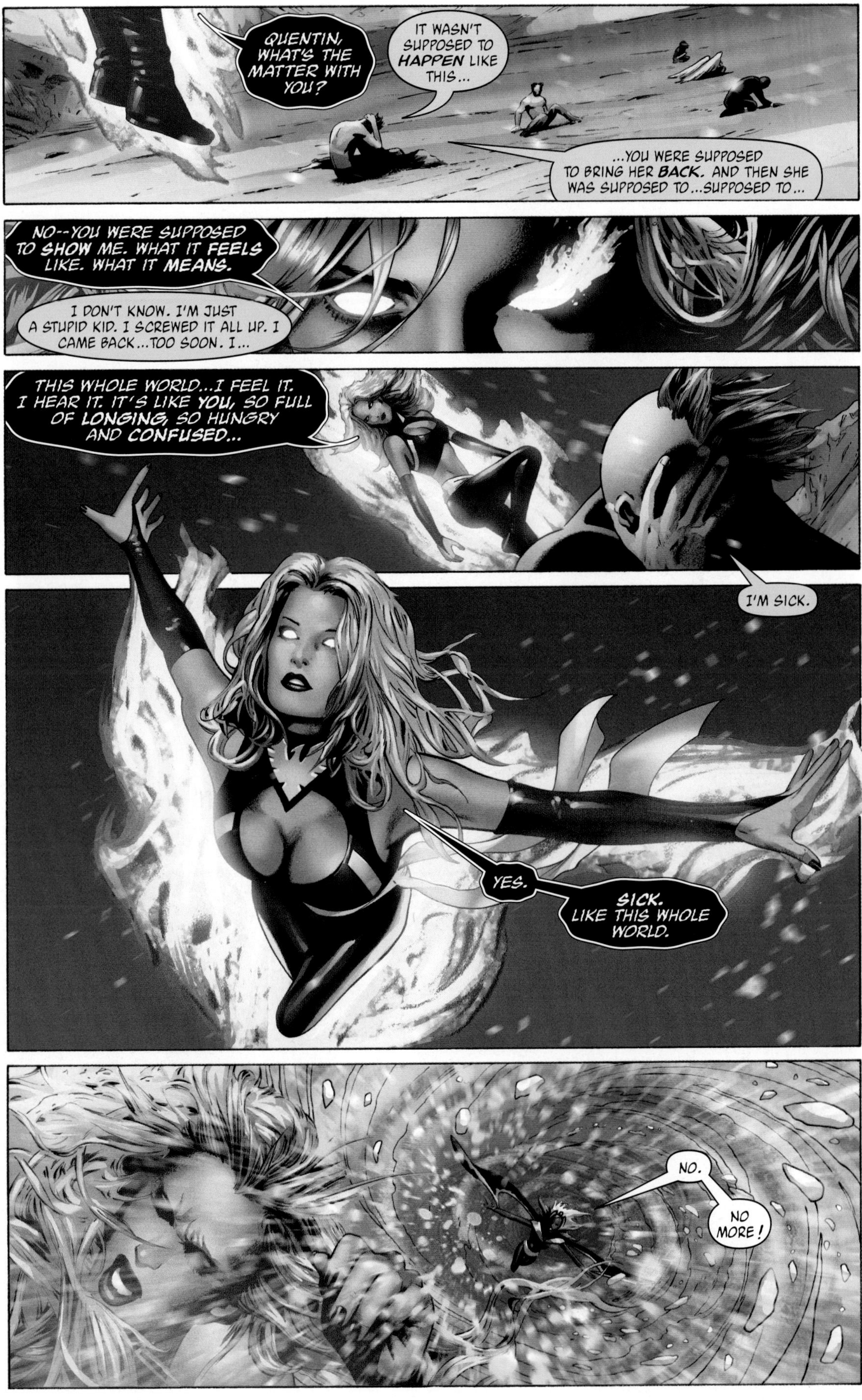
QUENTIN, WHAT'S THE MATTER WITH YOU?
IT WASN'T SUPPOSED TO HAPPEN LIKE THIS...
...YOU WERE SUPPOSED TO BRING HER BACK. AND THEN SHE WAS SUPPOSED TO...SUPPOSED TO...
NO--YOU WERE SUPPOSED TO SHOW ME. WHAT IT FEELS LIKE. WHAT IT MEANS.
I DON'T KNOW. I'M JUST A STUPID KID. I SCREWED IT ALL UP. I CAME BACK...TOO SOON. I...
THIS WHOLE WORLD...I FEEL IT. I HEAR IT. IT'S LIKE YOU, SO FULL OF LONGING, SO HUNGRY AND CONFUSED...
I'M SICK.
YES.
SICK. LIKE THIS WHOLE WORLD.
NO.
NO MORE!

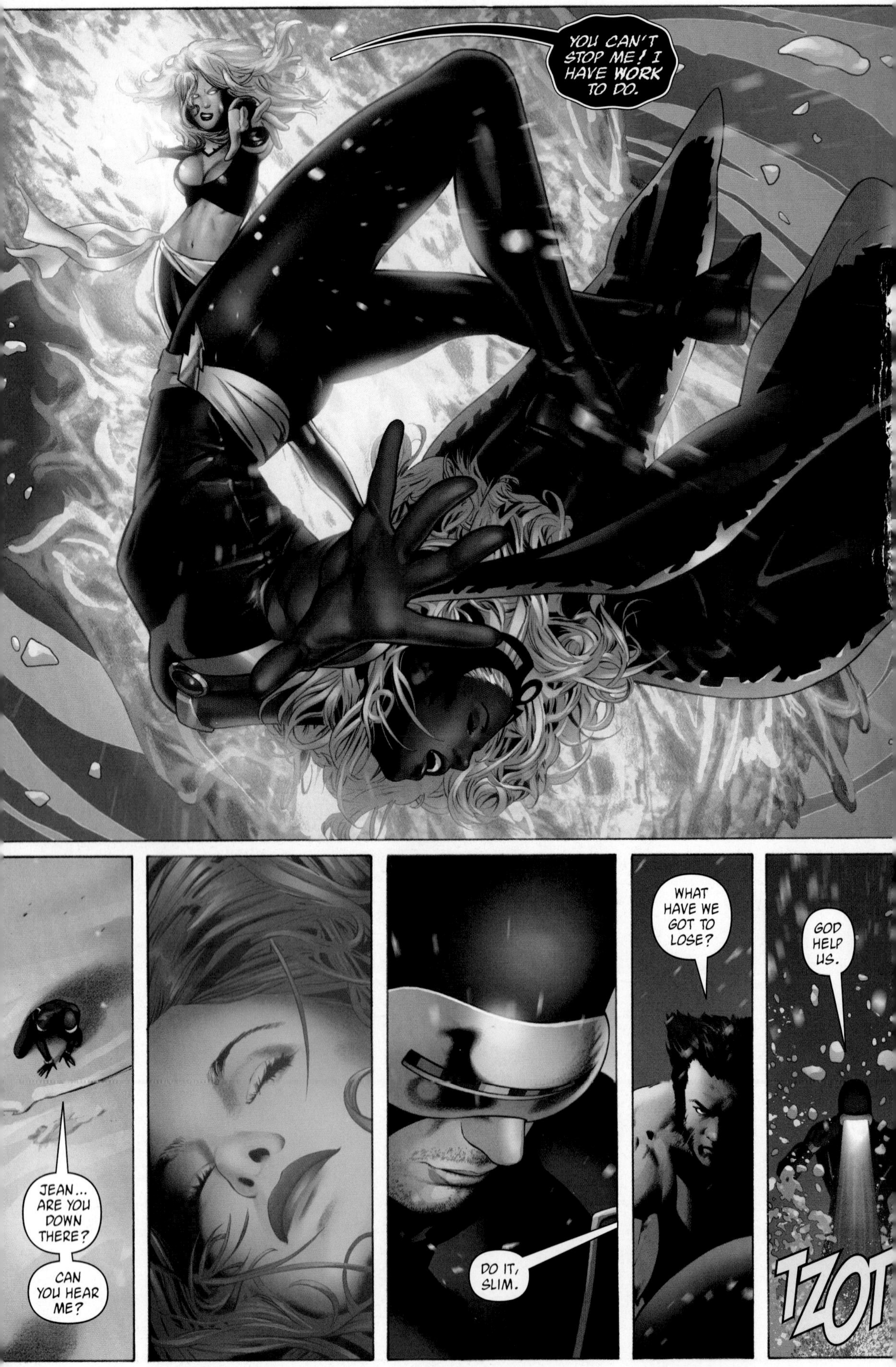
YOU CAN'T STOP ME! I HAVE WORK TO DO.
JEAN... ARE YOU DOWN THERE?
CAN YOU HEAR ME?
DO IT, SLIM.
WHAT HAVE WE GOT TO LOSE?
GOD HELP US.
TZOT

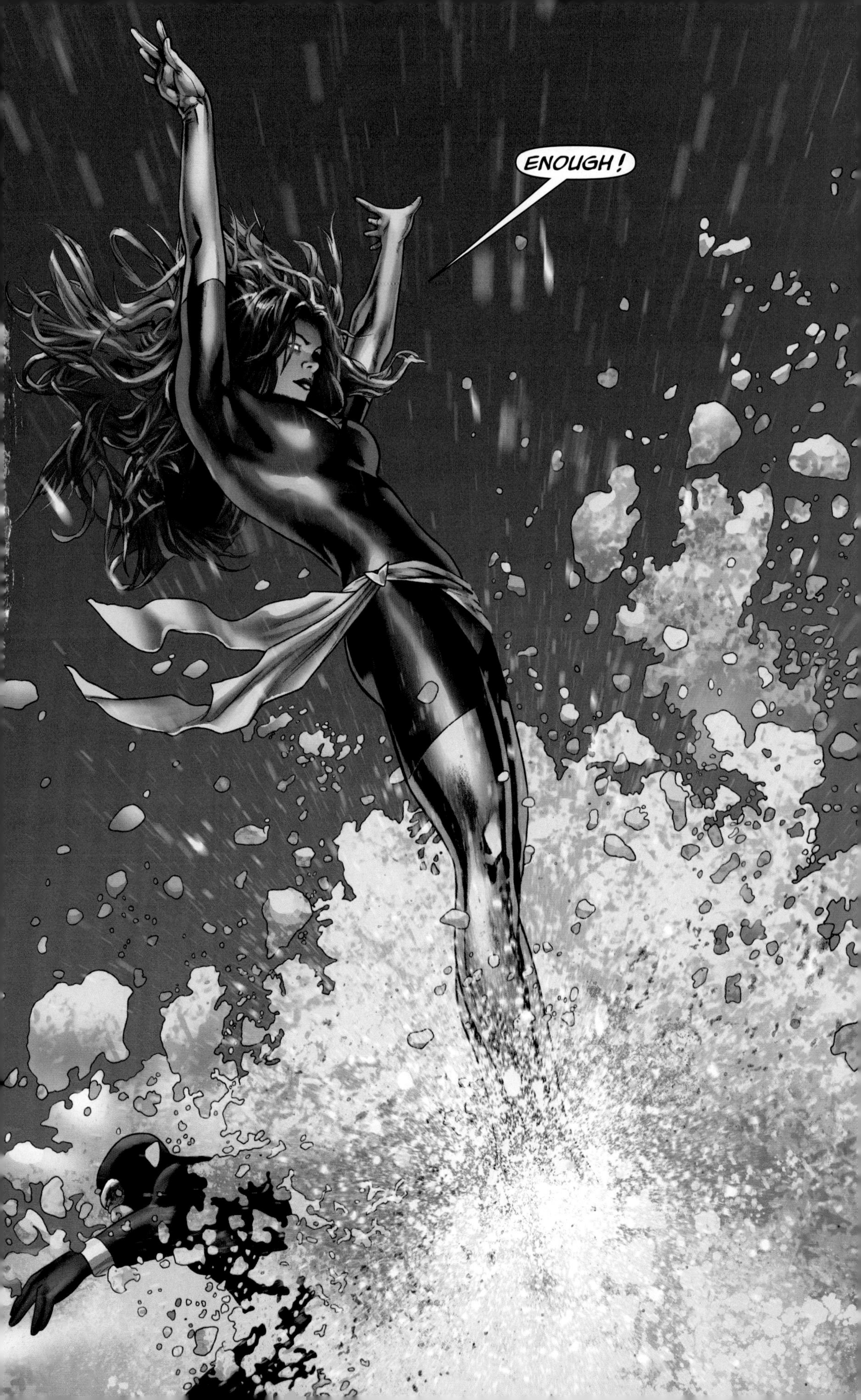
ENOUGH!

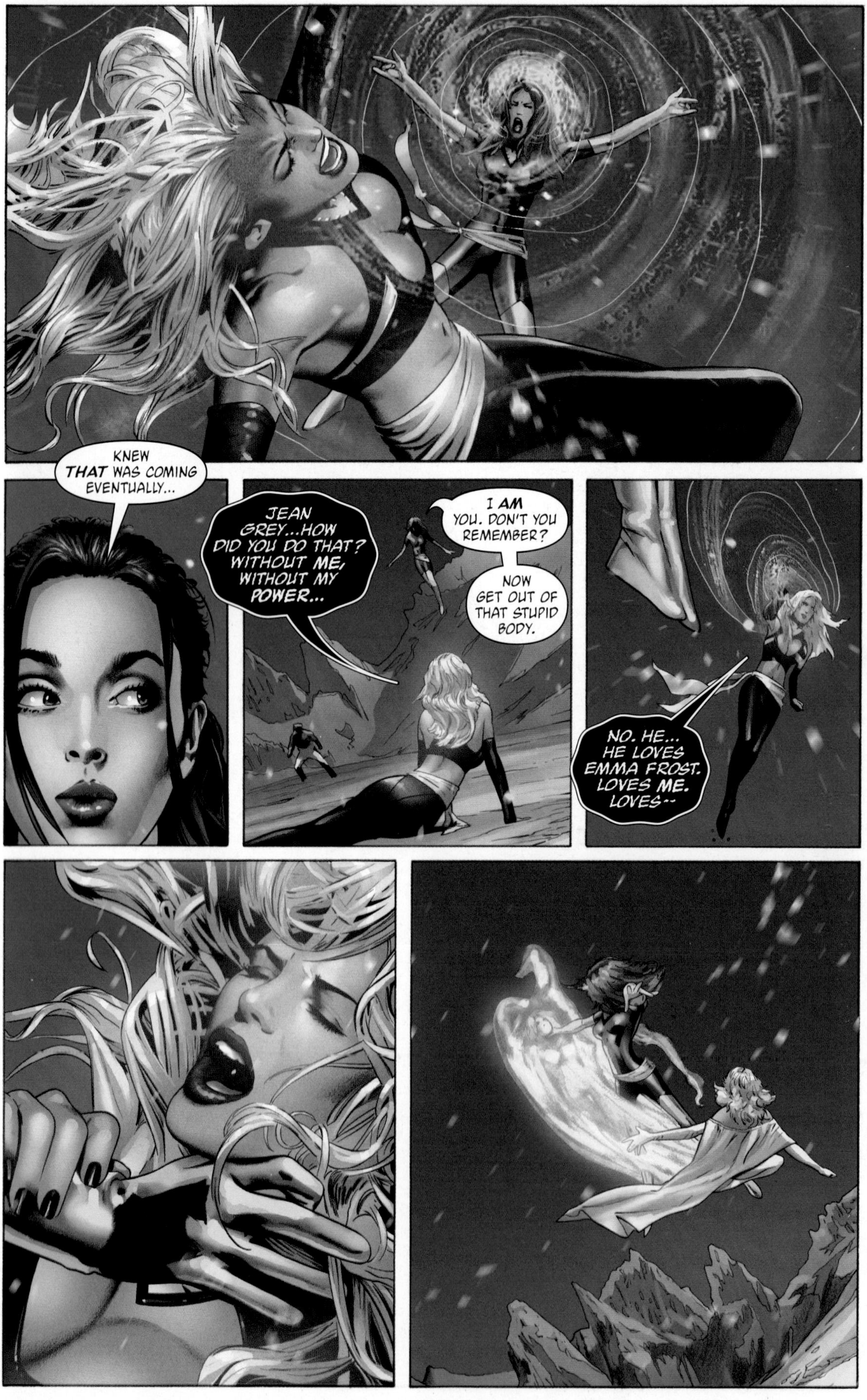
KNEW THAT WAS COMING EVENTUALLY...
JEAN GREY...HOW DID YOU DO THAT? WITHOUT ME, WITHOUT MY POWER...
I AM YOU. DON'T YOU REMEMBER?
NOW GET OUT OF THAT STUPID BODY.
NO. HE... HE LOVES EMMA FROST. LOVES ME. LOVES--

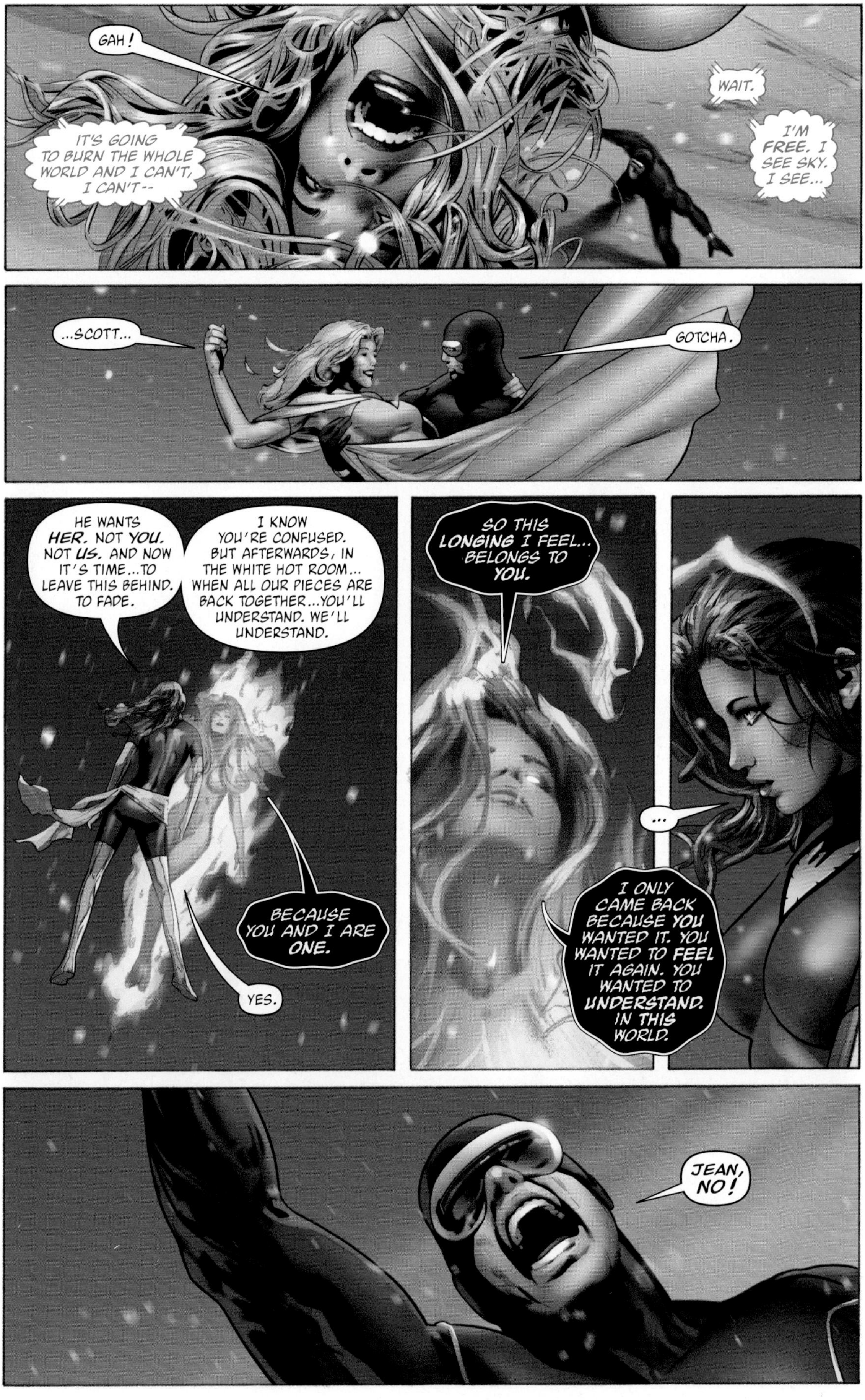
GAH!
IT'S GOING TO BURN THE WHOLE WORLD AND I CAN'T, I CAN'T--
WAIT.
I'M FREE. I SEE SKY. I SEE...
...SCOTT...
GOTCHA.
HE WANTS HER. NOT YOU. NOT US. AND NOW IT'S TIME...TO LEAVE THIS BEHIND. TO FADE.
I KNOW YOU'RE CONFUSED. BUT AFTERWARDS, IN THE WHITE HOT ROOM... WHEN ALL OUR PIECES ARE BACK TOGETHER...YOU'LL UNDERSTAND. WE'LL UNDERSTAND.
BECAUSE YOU AND I ARE ONE.
YES.
SO THIS LONGING I FEEL... BELONGS TO YOU.
...
I ONLY CAME BACK BECAUSE YOU WANTED IT. YOU WANTED TO FEEL IT AGAIN. YOU WANTED TO UNDERSTAND. IN THIS WORLD.
JEAN, NO!

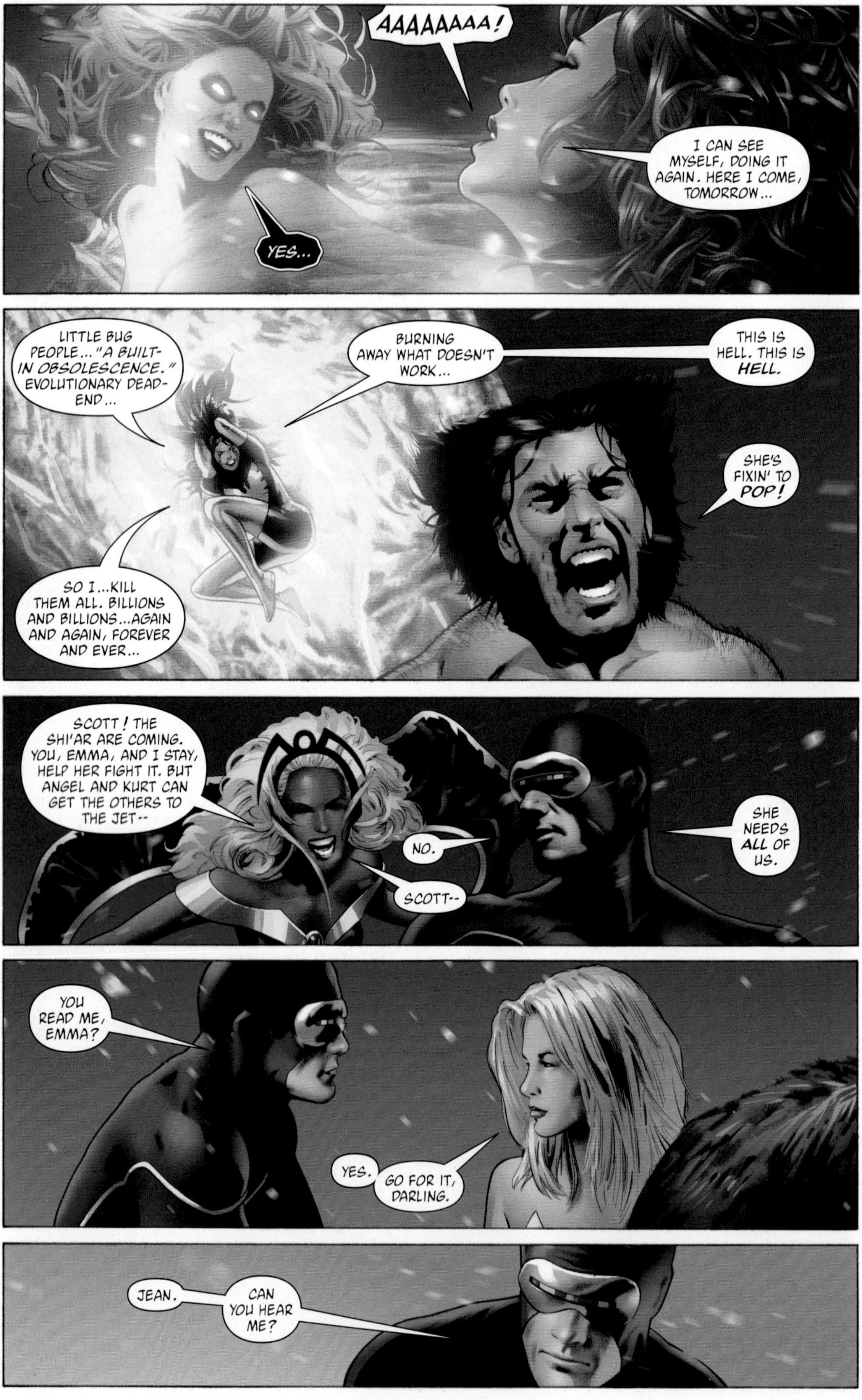
AAAAAAAA!
I CAN SEE MYSELF, DOING IT AGAIN. HERE I COME, TOMORROW...
YES...
LITTLE BUG PEOPLE... "A BUILT-IN OBSOLESCENCE." EVOLUTIONARY DEAD-END...
BURNING AWAY WHAT DOESN'T WORK...
THIS IS HELL. THIS IS HELL.
SHE'S FIXIN' TO POP!
SO I...KILL THEM ALL. BILLIONS AND BILLIONS...AGAIN AND AGAIN, FOREVER AND EVER...
SCOTT! THE SHI'AR ARE COMING. YOU, EMMA, AND I STAY, HELP HER FIGHT IT. BUT ANGEL AND KURT CAN GET THE OTHERS TO THE JET--
NO.
SHE NEEDS ALL OF US.
SCOTT--
YOU READ ME, EMMA?
YES.
GO FOR IT, DARLING.
JEAN.
CAN YOU HEAR ME?

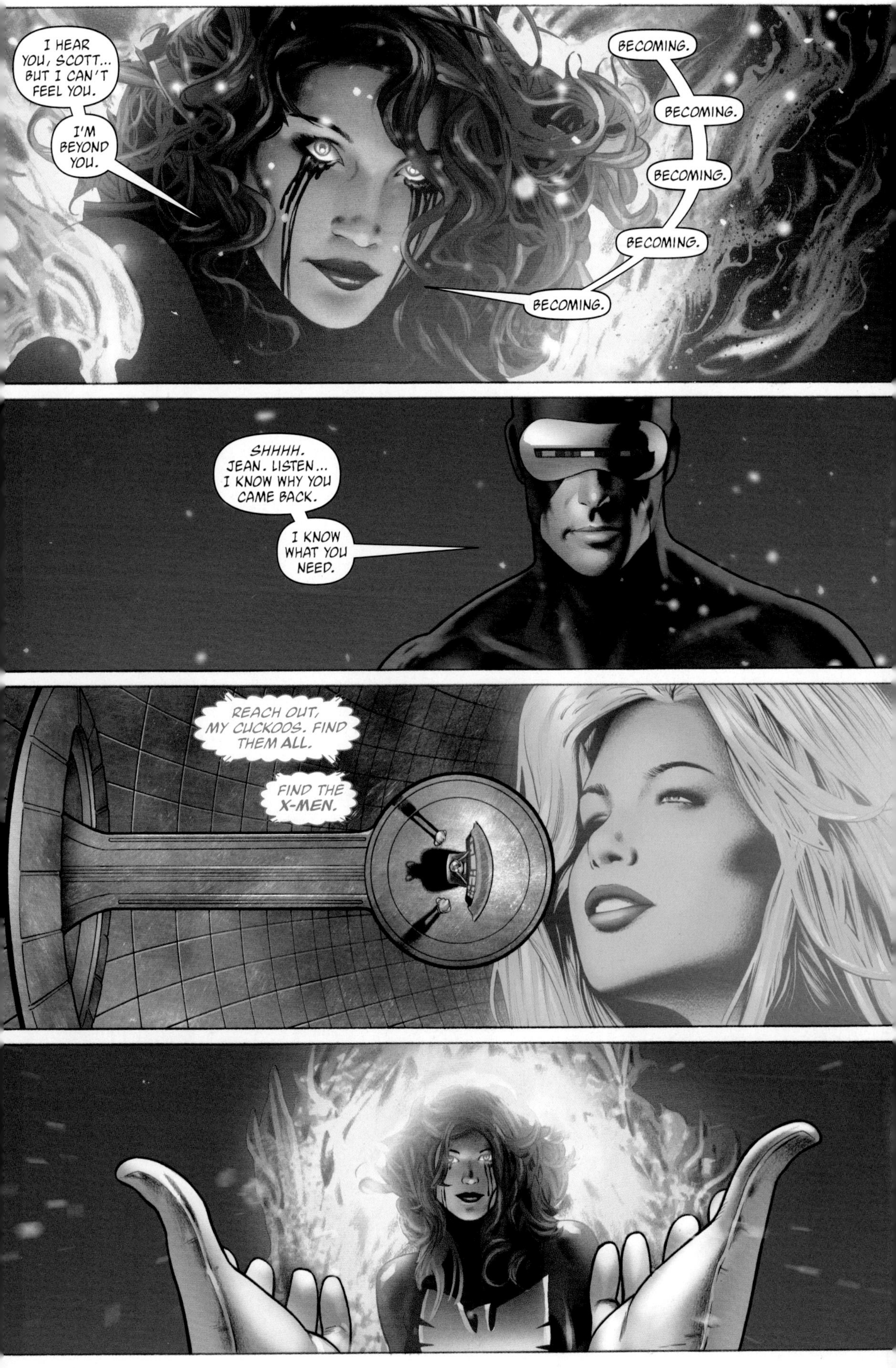
I HEAR YOU, SCOTT... BUT I CAN'T FEEL YOU.
I'M BEYOND YOU.
BECOMING.
BECOMING.
BECOMING.
BECOMING.
BECOMING.
SHHHH. JEAN. LISTEN... I KNOW WHY YOU CAME BACK.
I KNOW WHAT YOU NEED.
REACH OUT, MY CUCKOOS. FIND THEM ALL.
FIND THE X-MEN.

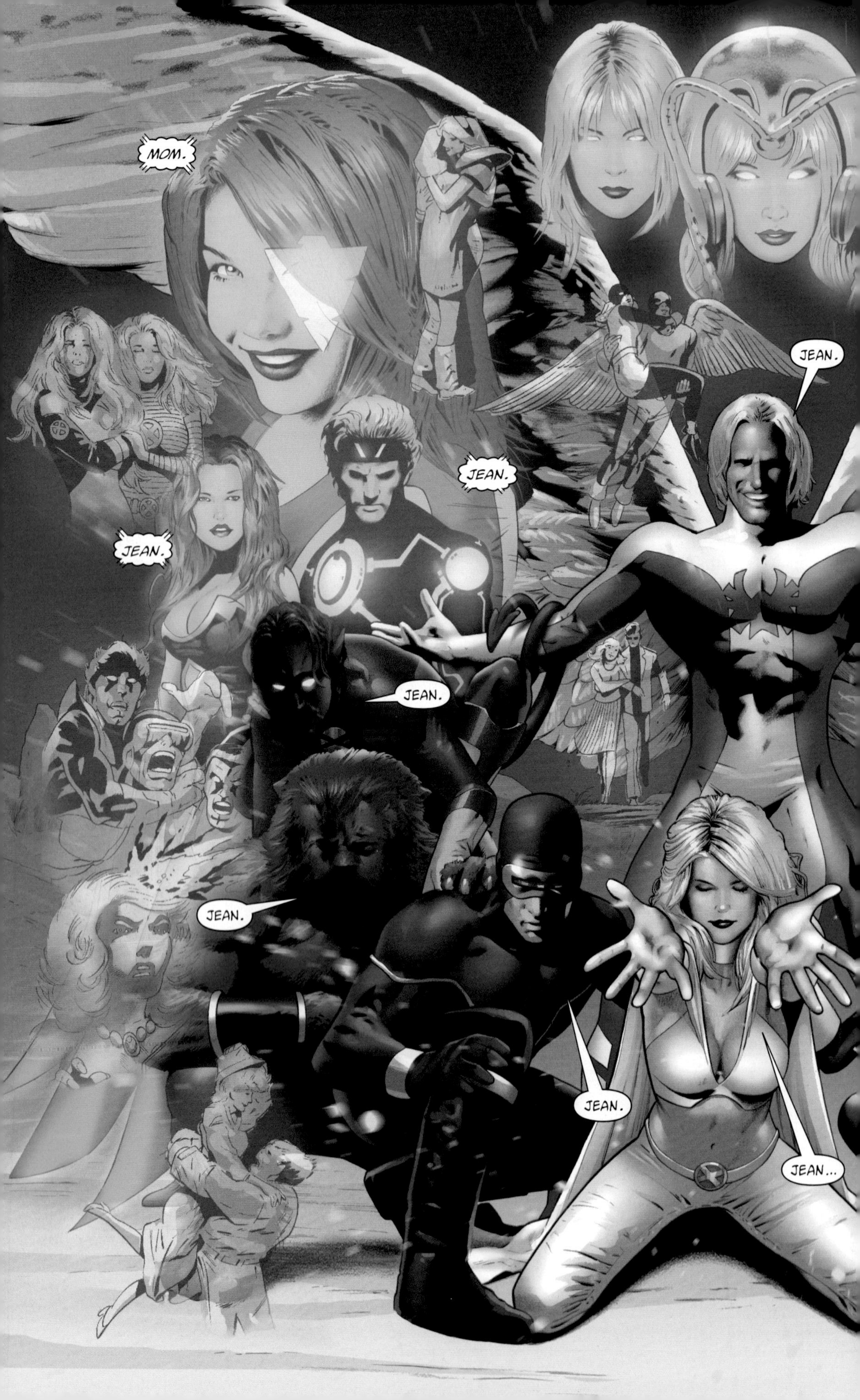
MOM.
JEAN.
JEAN.
JEAN.
JEAN.
JEAN.
JEAN.
JEAN...

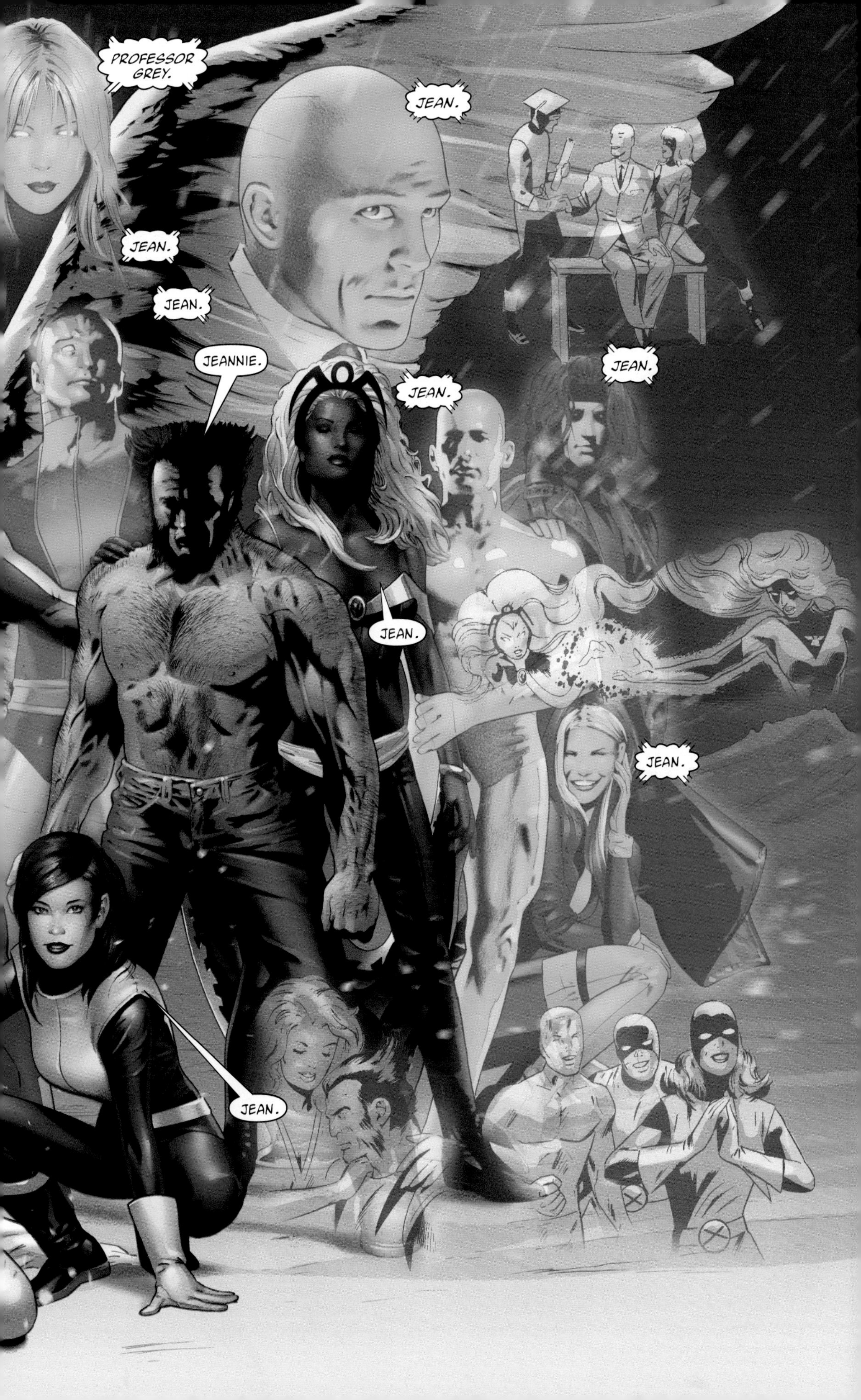
PROFESSOR GREY.
JEAN.
JEAN.
JEAN.
JEANNIE.
JEAN.
JEAN.
JEAN.
JEAN.
JEAN.

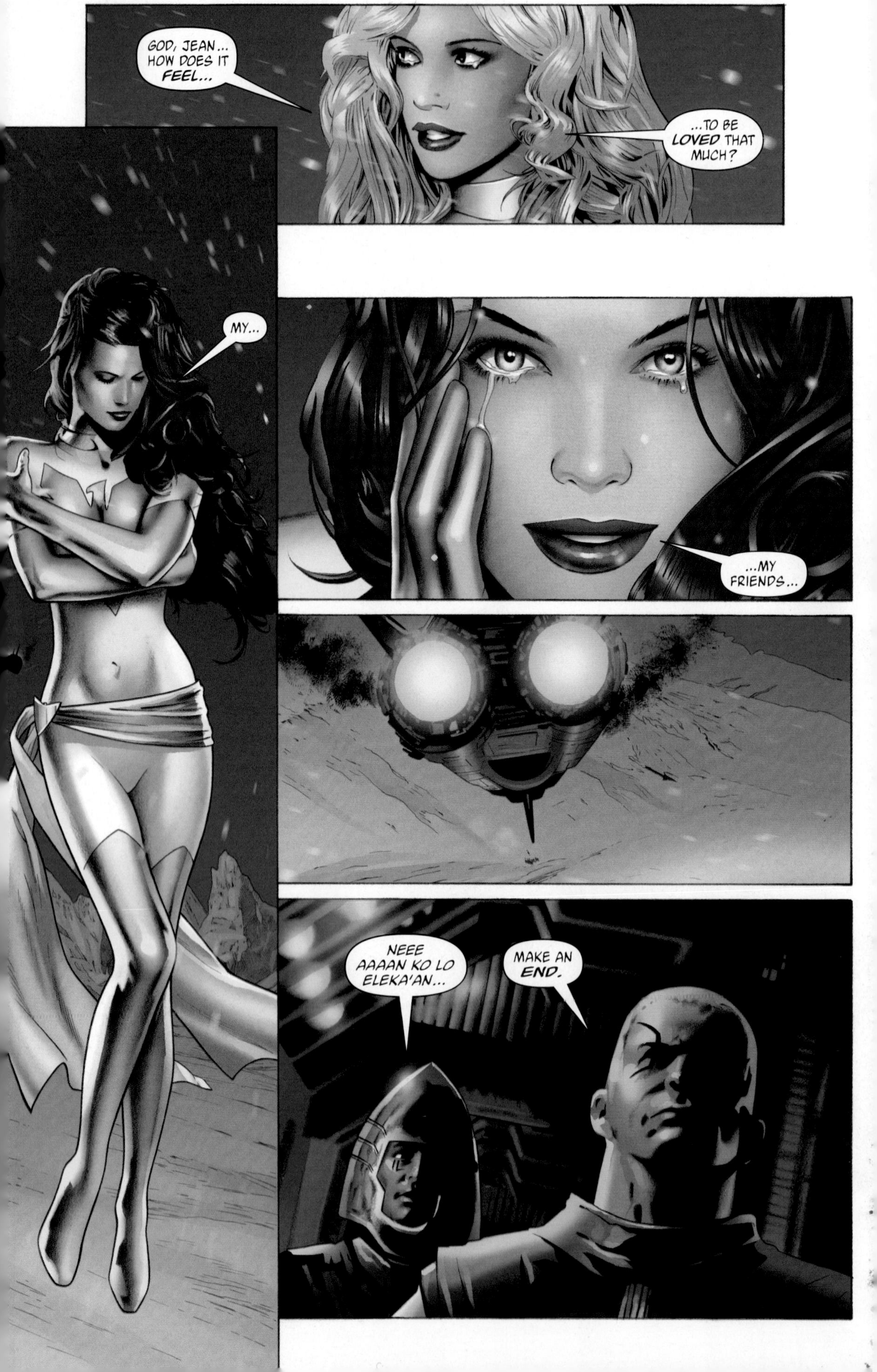
GOD, JEAN... HOW DOES IT FEEL...
...TO BE LOVED THAT MUCH?
MY...
...MY FRIENDS...
NEEE AAAAN KO LO ELEKA'AN...
MAKE AN END.

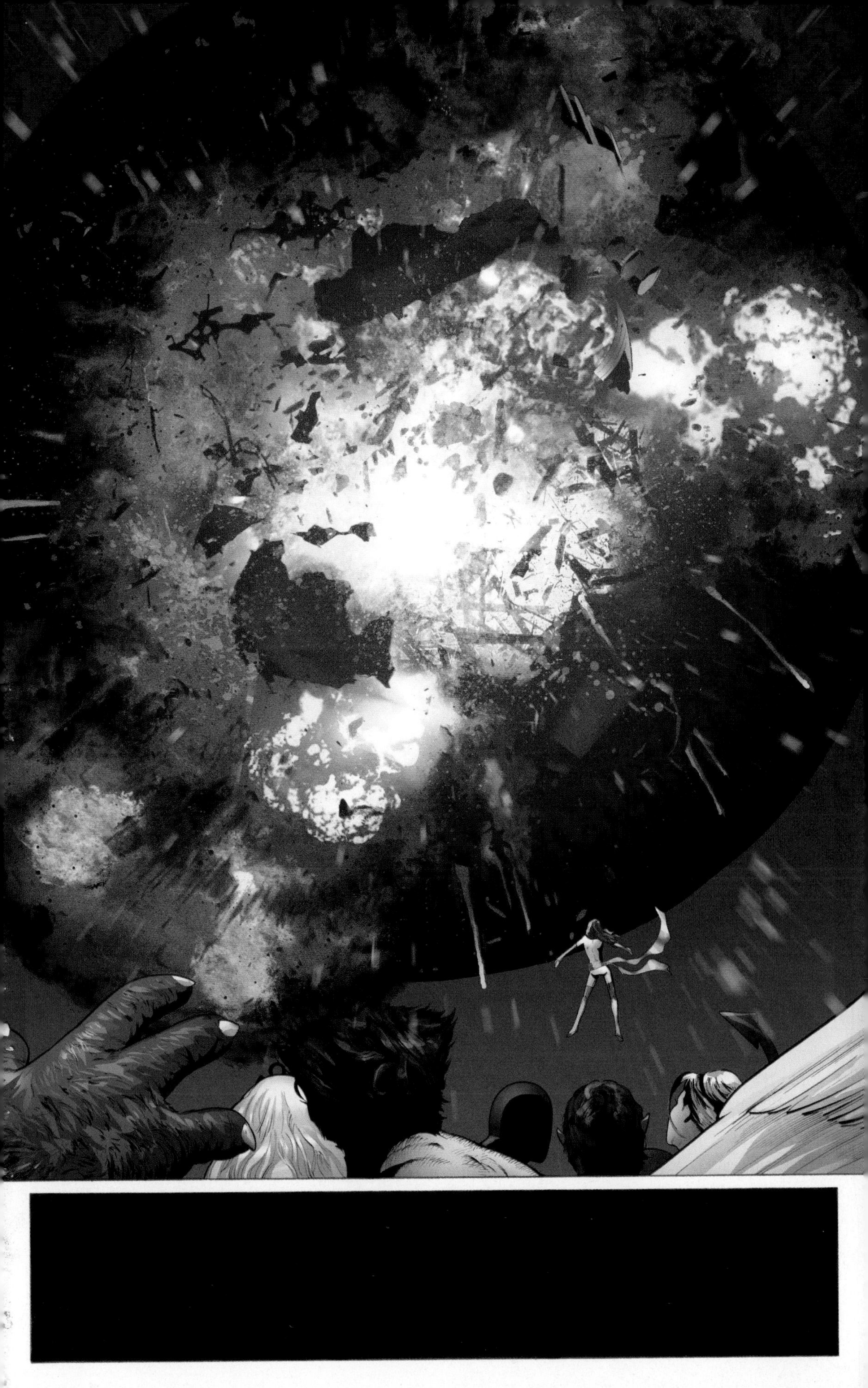

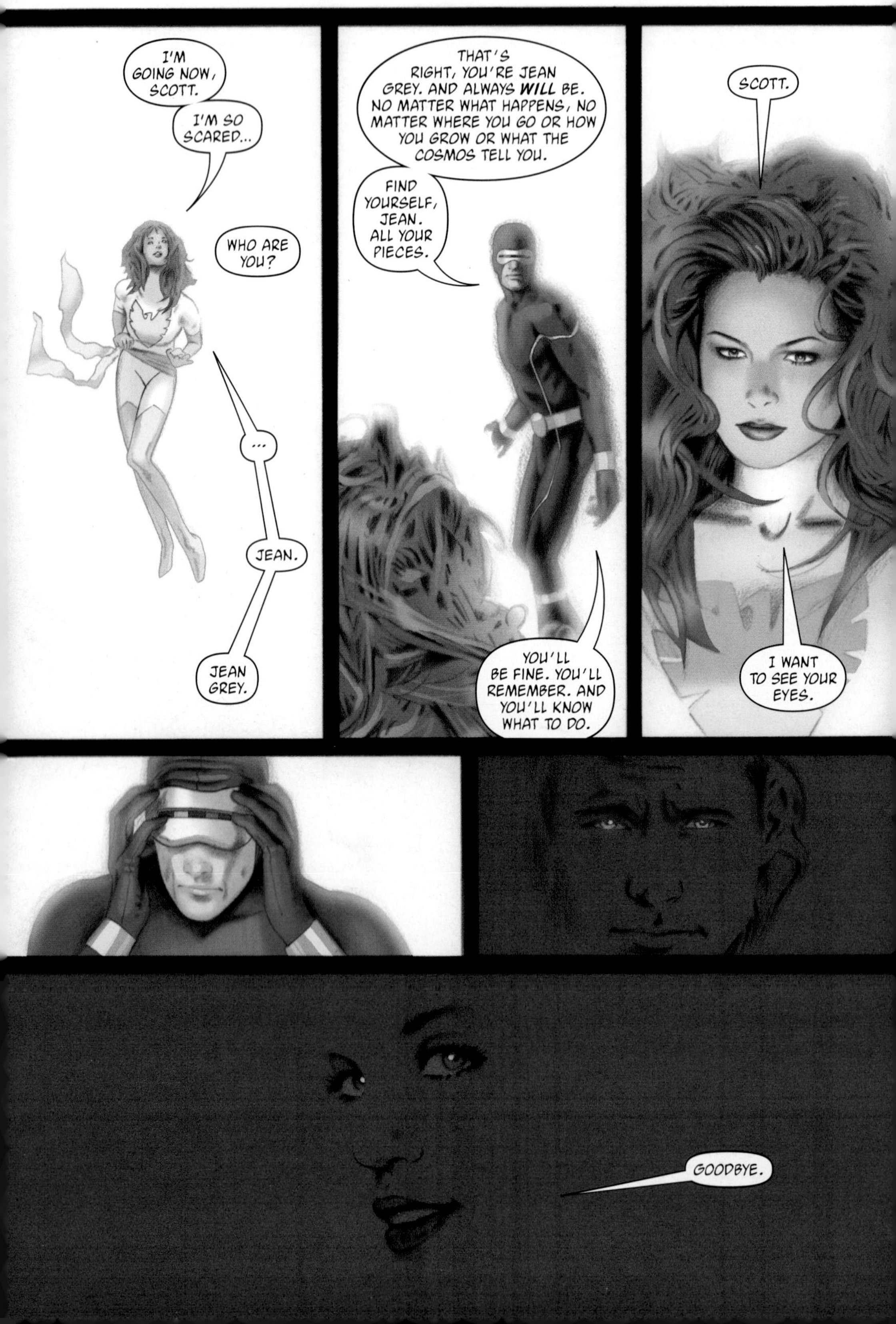
I'M GOING NOW, SCOTT.
I'M SO SCARED...
WHO ARE YOU?
...
JEAN.
JEAN GREY.
THAT'S RIGHT, YOU'RE JEAN GREY. AND ALWAYS **WILL** BE. NO MATTER WHAT HAPPENS, NO MATTER WHERE YOU GO OR HOW YOU GROW OR WHAT THE COSMOS TELL YOU.
FIND YOURSELF, JEAN. ALL YOUR PIECES.
YOU'LL BE FINE. YOU'LL REMEMBER. AND YOU'LL KNOW WHAT TO DO.
SCOTT.
I WANT TO SEE YOUR EYES.
GOODBYE.

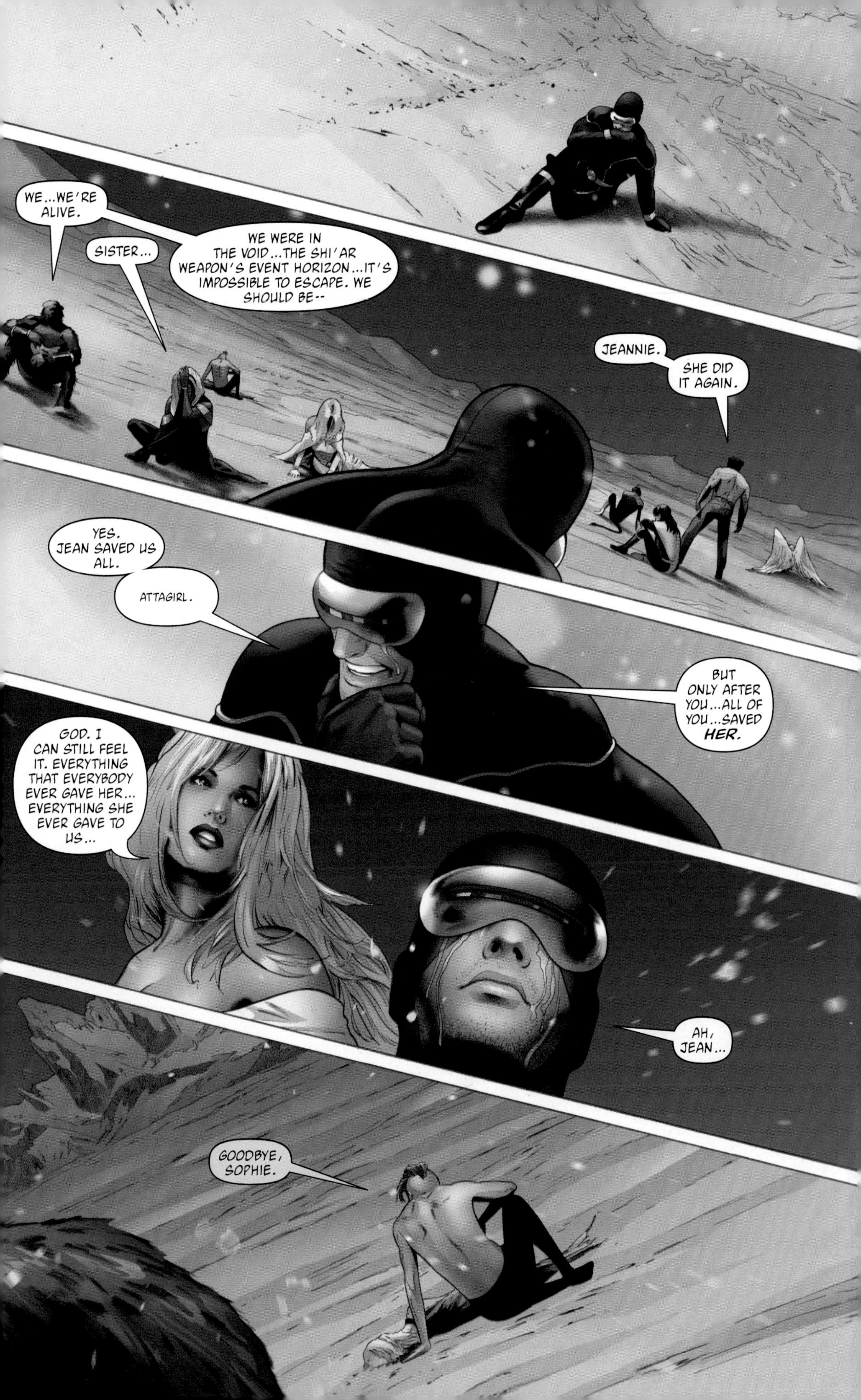
WE...WE'RE ALIVE.
SISTER...
WE WERE IN THE VOID...THE SHI'AR WEAPON'S EVENT HORIZON...IT'S IMPOSSIBLE TO ESCAPE. WE SHOULD BE--
JEANNIE.
SHE DID IT AGAIN.
YES. JEAN SAVED US ALL.
ATTAGIRL.
BUT ONLY AFTER YOU...ALL OF YOU...SAVED HER.
GOD. I CAN STILL FEEL IT. EVERYTHING THAT EVERYBODY EVER GAVE HER... EVERYTHING SHE EVER GAVE TO US...
AH, JEAN...
GOODBYE, SOPHIE.

I'M SORRY FOR ALL THE TROUBLE, DR. McCOY. I DON'T THINK I WAS REALLY READY FOR ALL OF THIS...

DON'T WORRY, SON.

NONE OF US WERE.

THERE WAS SOMETHING I THOUGHT I NEEDED... BUT I COULDN'T HAVE... I SHOULDN'T HAVE...

I THINK I'M GOING TO SLEEP FOR A LITTLE WHILE NOW.

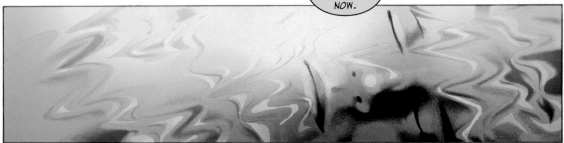

Subject: Quentin Quire

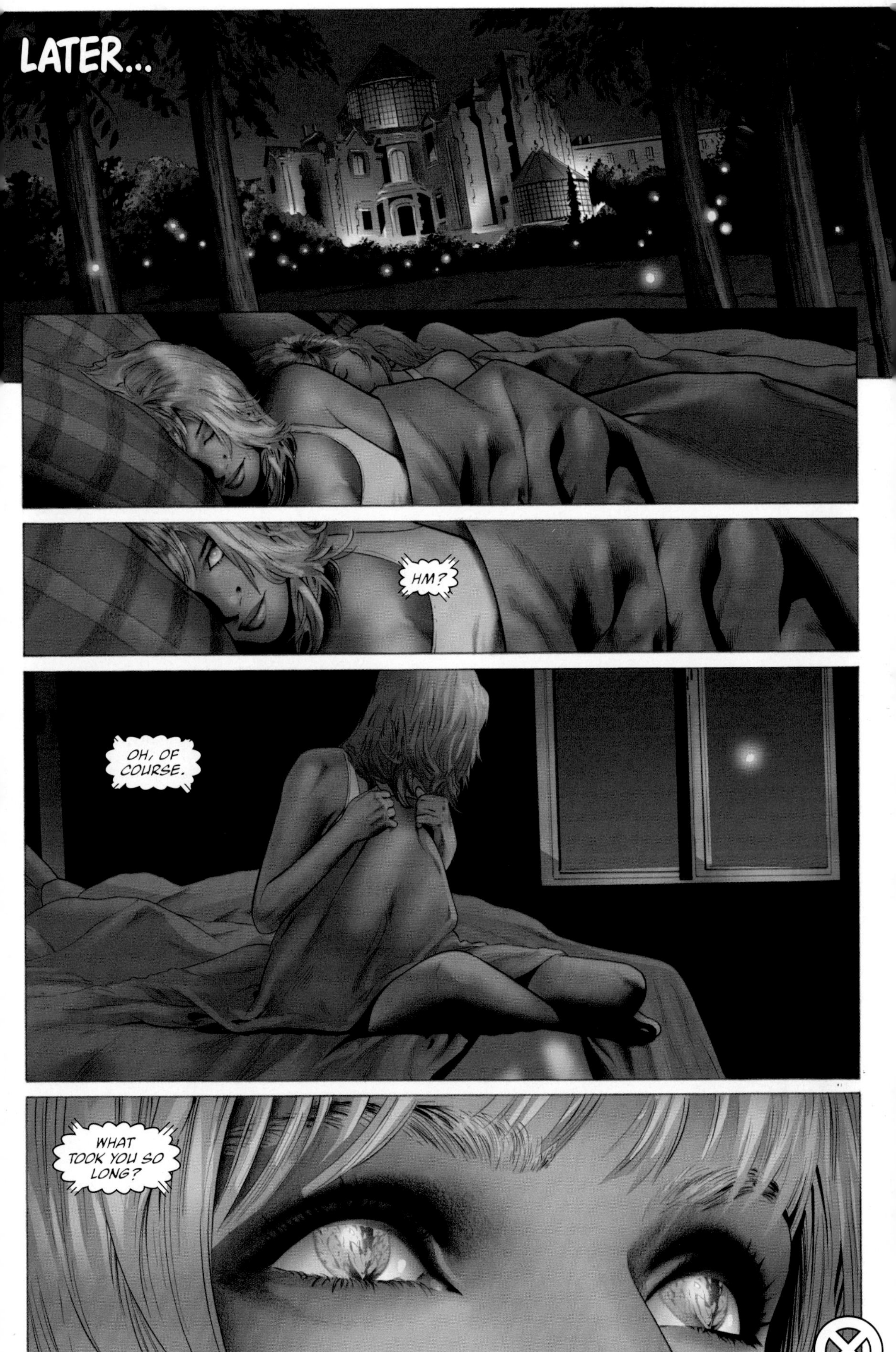
LATER...
HM?
OH, OF COURSE.
WHAT TOOK YOU SO LONG?

Notice: This text and/or artwork may not be reproduced without the permission of the copyright owner

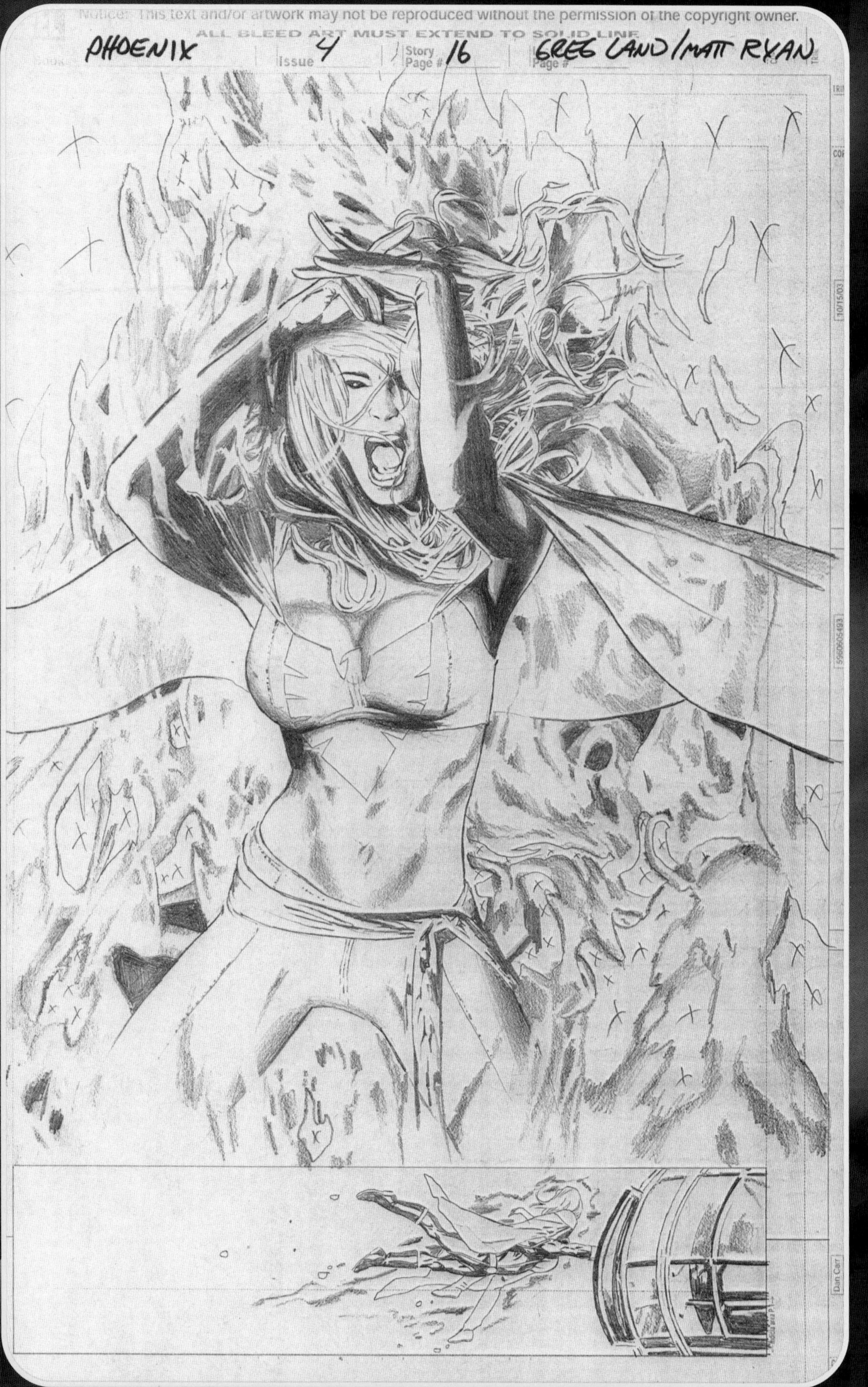
Notice: This text and/or artwork may not be reproduced without the permission of the copyright owner.
ALL BLEED ART MUST EXTEND TO SOLID LINE
PHOENIX
Issue 4
Story Page # 16
GREG LAND/MATT RYAN

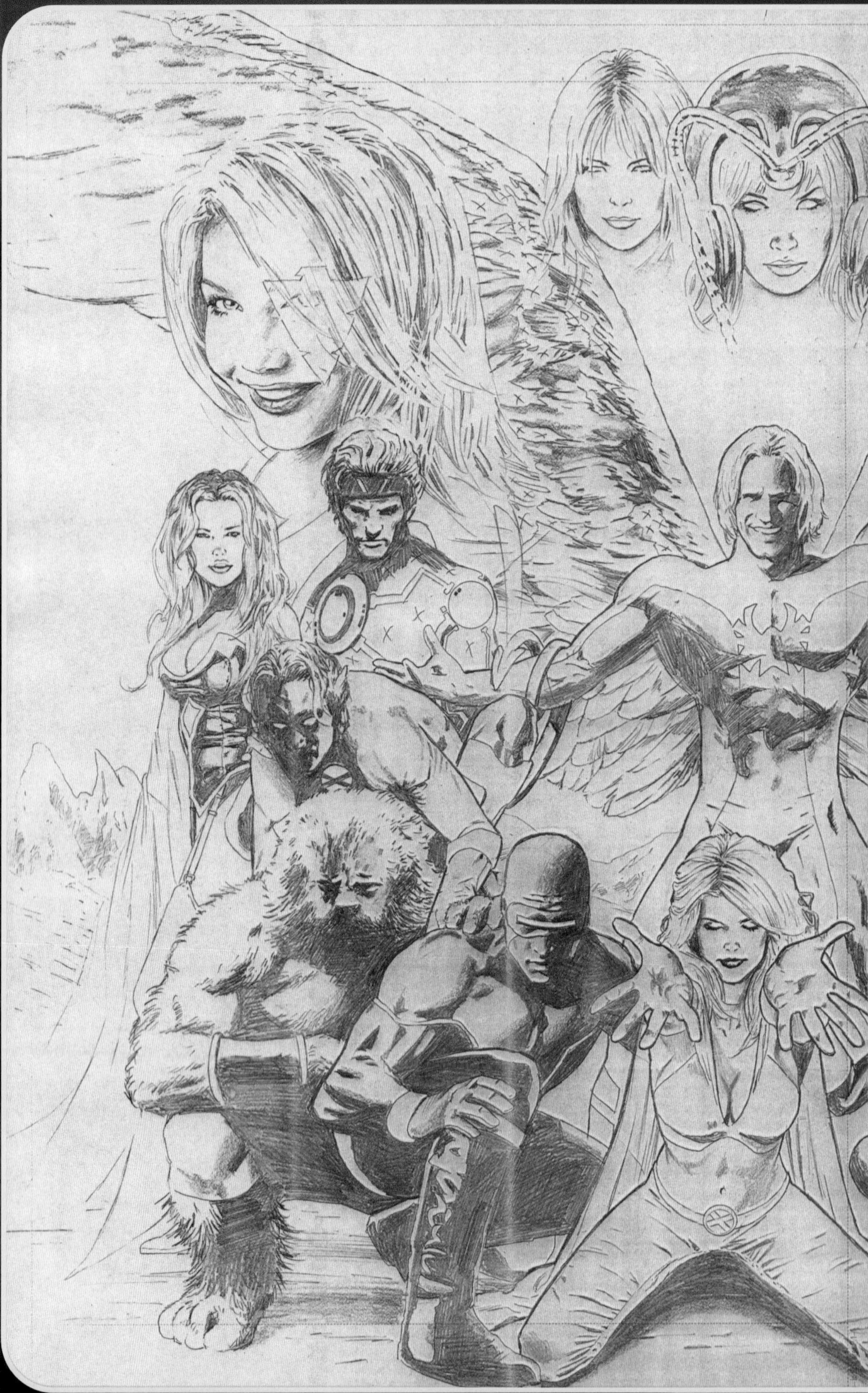

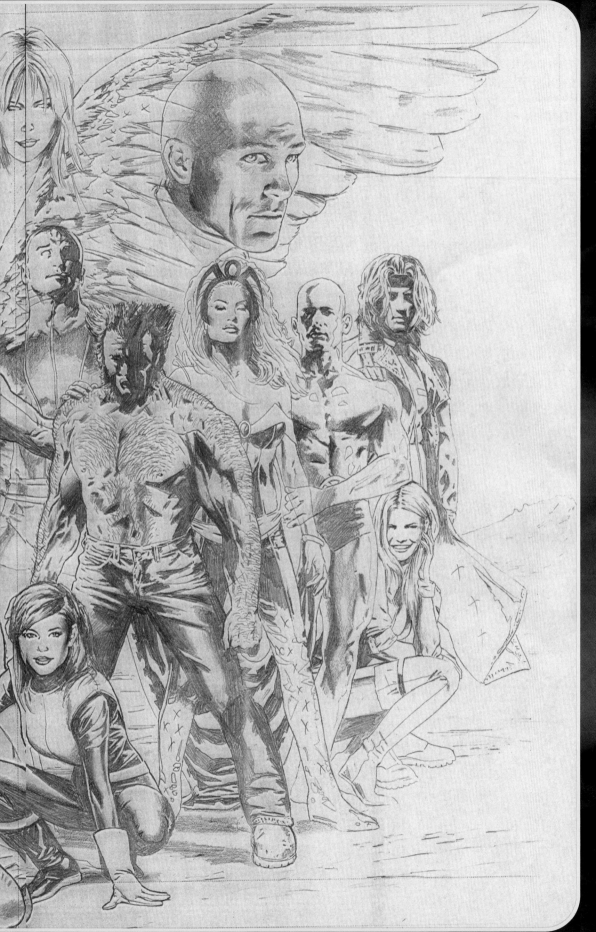

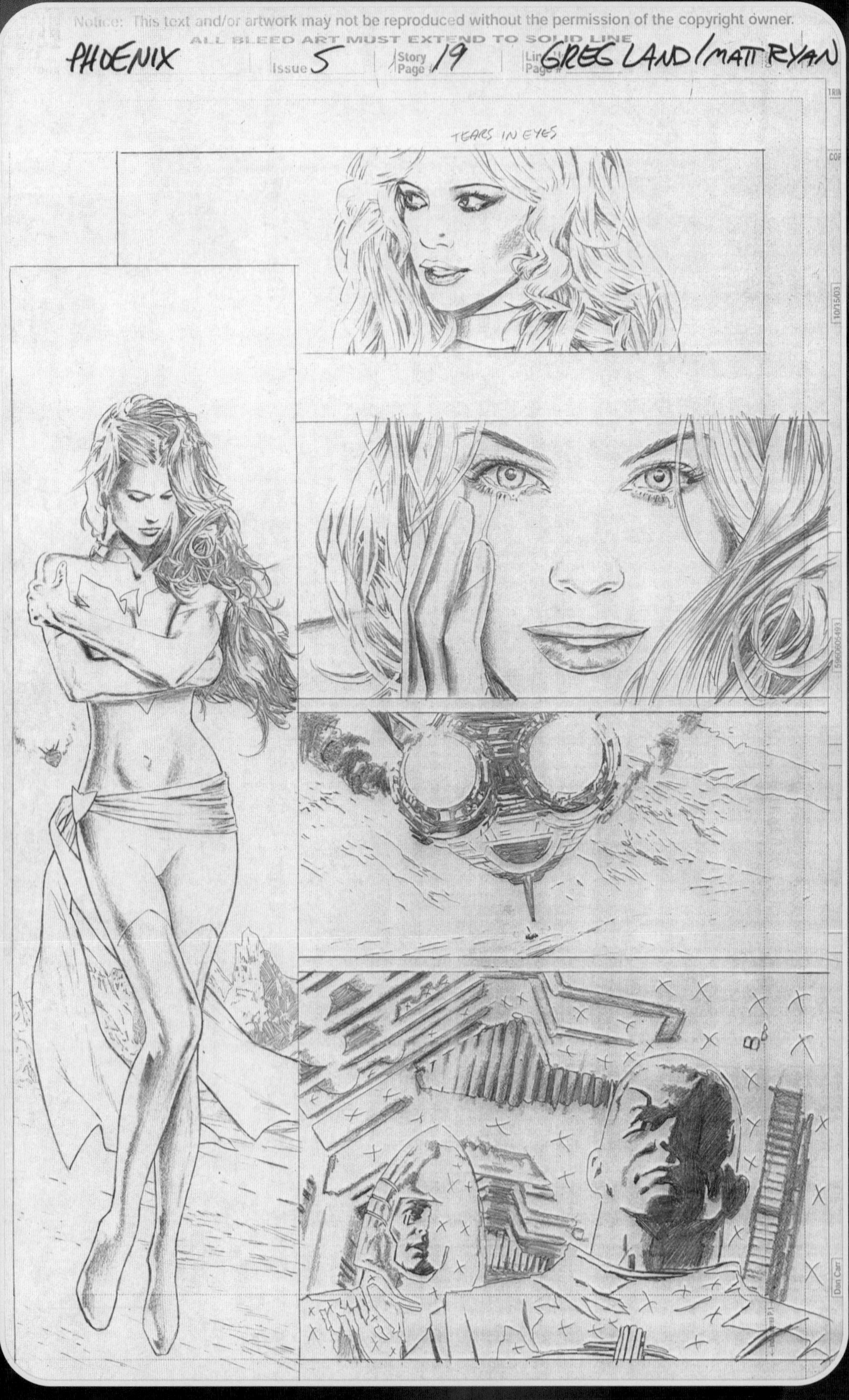
Notice: This text and/or artwork may not be reproduced without the permission of the copyright owner.
ALL BLEED ART MUST EXTEND TO SOLID LINE
PHOENIX
Issue 5
Story Page # 19
GREG LAND / MATT RYAN
TEARS IN EYES